ON ACTIVE SERVICE
IN PEACE AND WAR

VOLUME II

ON
ACTIVE SERVICE
IN PEACE AND WAR

BY

HENRY L. STIMSON

Secretary of War 1911-13, Secretary of State 1929-33
Secretary of War 1940-45

AND

McGEORGE BUNDY

Junior Fellow, Society of Fellows
Harvard University

VOLUME II

HARPER & BROTHERS, NEW YORK

About one fifth of the material in this book was
published serially under the title of *Time of Peril*

TABLE OF CONTENTS

VOLUME II

PART THREE
TIME OF PERIL

CHAPTER XIII

Call to Arms

---

1. BACK TO WASHINGTON

IN HIS New York office, on June 19, 1940, Stimson received a telephone call from the White House. "I was called up by the President who offered me the position of Secretary of War. He told me that Knox had already agreed to accept the position of Secretary of the Navy. The President said he was very anxious to have me accept because everybody was running around at loose ends in Washington and he thought I would be a stabilizing factor in whom both the Army and the public would have confidence." To say that Stimson was surprised would be putting it mildly. He had known that Mr. Roosevelt was considering the appointment of one or two Republicans and that Frank Knox was among those being considered. Like everyone else, he knew that the Secretary of War, Woodring, was at odds with both the President and large parts of the Army. He did not suspect, however, that these troubles might affect him. Some weeks before, he had heard from Grenville Clark that his name had been suggested for the job. Clark had coupled it with that of Judge Robert P. Patterson as Assistant Secretary. He knew too that this suggestion had reached the President. But that the President should have listened to it, and acted on it, was astonishing. His first reaction was to point out that he was approaching his seventy-third birthday. The President said he already knew that, and added that Stimson would be free to appoint his own Assistant Secretary. Patterson's name was mentioned and approved by both men. Stimson then asked for a few hours in which to consult his wife and his professional associates.

"I then discussed it with Bronson Winthrop, George Roberts [two of his partners] and Mabel. They all advised me to accept. About seven P.M. I telephoned the President and asked him three questions: (1) Whether he had seen my radio speech and whether it would be embarrassing to him. He replied that he had already read it and was in full accord with it. (2) I asked him whether he knew that I was in favor of general compulsory military service, and he said he did and gave me to understand that he was in sympathy with me. (3) I asked him whether Knox had accepted and he said he had.

"I then accepted." (Diary, June 25, 1940)

Stimson was inclined later to think this diary entry a trifle laconic; conversation with Franklin Roosevelt was seldom so stern and simple. It nevertheless contained the meat of what was said on both sides. Neither man mentioned any political aspect of the appointment. The only bargain struck on either side was an agreement that Stimson would be free to appoint Patterson as his own principal assistant. It was understood on both sides, then and later, that politics was not relevant; it was equally understood that Stimson was to be the undisputed head of his own Department. These understandings remained unbroken to the end.

The appointment of Stimson and Knox was announced on June 20, and Stimson speedily learned that he was a highly controversial figure. The chairman of the Republican National Committee read him out of the party, and Republican pique was general. The Republicans were about to begin their convention, and their minds were so firmly fixed on politics that they insisted on describing the President's maneuver as a political dodge. This was probably true, in part; Stimson was not inclined to deny that Franklin Roosevelt was a talented politician. But it did not seem to him that the Republican outburst was a skillful riposte. There was little political advantage in the repudiation of two stanch Republicans merely because in a time of crisis they had been willing to take office. In effect, the Republican outcry was a kindness to the President; it turned over to him what credit there might be in rising above party prejudice. To Stimson personally it mattered very little; few of the present spokesmen of the party were his friends, and from those Republicans who were close to him he had many letters of approval and congratulation. Should this outburst mean that his party intended in the crisis to take a generally obstructionist position, it would be a grave disappointment, but his familiarity with the atmosphere of conventions led him to postpone any such gloomy conclusion. His party had been caught off balance, and some unfortunate statements had been made; perhaps there was nothing more to it—perhaps the sentiment of the Republican rank and file was more accurately represented by young Harold Stassen, the Republican keynoter, who rejected efforts to make him denounce Knox and Stimson, choosing instead to argue that the President in his hour of need was forced to turn to the Grand Old Party for help.

The immediate problem now was in the Senate, where his nomination must be confirmed. On July 2 Stimson appeared before the Committee on Military Affairs, to which his name had been referred. This was a new experience. Four times before his name had been submitted to the Senate, and by four different presidents. In none of these earlier cases had his fitness been seriously questioned. This seemed an odd time to begin. His first reaction was one of annoyance; his second was more pugnacious—if these people wanted to heckle him, he would find it pleasant to hit back. His third thought, and the controlling one, was that he must so conduct himself as not to embarrass his new chief, while at the same time clearly stating his understanding of the responsibility for which he had been named.

So in his opening statement to the committee he reviewed his position. "The purpose of our military policy is . . . to protect from attack the territory and rights of the United States. . . . No one wishes to send American troops beyond our borders unless the protection of the United States makes such action absolutely necessary. On the other hand I do not believe that the United States can be safely protected by a purely passive or defensive defense. I do not believe that we shall be safe from invasion if we sit down and wait for the enemy to attack our shores."

This last point he developed in detail. He related it to the

Monroe Doctrine, and pointed out how modern warfare had forced an extension of our line of defense "far out into the Atlantic Ocean." This ocean and the bases controlling it were now gravely menaced. The menace came from potential enemies of a character unique in history. Not only were they engaged in systematic aggression, but once successful they need fear no rebellion. "Genghis Khan and Attila the Hun did not possess tanks, airplanes, or modern guns, nor could they enforce their rules on their victims by a carefully organized secret police like the Gestapo. . . . The modern conqueror, when once he gets into power, will last for a long time. . . . I feel that we are faced with an unprecedented peril."

The existence of this peril was no pleasure to Stimson; he had not conjured it up as a source of excitement for his declining years. Yet some such idea seemed to be in the minds of those who were calling him a warmonger, so he continued on a more personal note. "I am one of those many people who after the great war labored earnestly for disarmament and for the establishment among the nations of a system which should be based upon a reign of law rather than of force, and I regard it as a world tragedy that all such efforts should have resulted in failure; but the facts have to be faced today."

As a beginning in facing the facts, the President had recommended and the Congress had authorized great appropriations for increased military strength. This was a good start, but only a start. Other things than money were needed. Stimson emphasized two—time and spirit. Time could be gained only if the British fleet were sustained. Spirit could best be developed by "establishing a system of selective compulsory training and service." Such a system was in any case essential, because recruiting had already failed; but what Stimson emphasized was its value to the morale of the nation. A country in peril must be united in knowing its danger and working for its safety.

As for the New Haven speech, it had been made by a private citizen. "When you are a private citizen you can speak upon matters which are of concern to the whole Government. When you are the Secretary of War your duty is to confine yourself to preparing the national defense of the United States so that it will be ready to be used when the President and the Congress . . . say the word, and that is the extent of your duty." He was not a stranger to public office; he understood its responsibilities, and the importance of "prudence and care." Still there was nothing to be taken back in the New Haven speech; it might not fit precisely with the requirements of the moment as seen from an official position, but "everything that I have said or advocated has been said in the interest of the defense of the United States, and that alone. I have had no other motive for what I have been talking about, and it is the same one I will represent here if I am confirmed by you gentlemen as Secretary of War—the defense of the United States."

This statement of his position did not satisfy all the members of the committee. For nearly two hours they questioned him, with the extensive assistance of two Senators not members of the committee, Vandenberg and Taft. The majority of the committee were sympathetic; their few questions were simple and friendly. But a few were less gentle. Fortunately the crowd at the hearing was mainly friendly, and for Stimson it was warm work but not unpleasant.

Was he a member of Winthrop, Stimson, Putnam & Roberts? No. Well, he was listed as counsel. "That is a euphemistic term for a gentleman who sits in an office without sharing the profits." (Laughter.) Did this firm have any clients with international investments? He didn't think so, but he didn't know, because he wasn't a partner. Did he have any such clients himself? "I do not." Had he been present at a secret meeting of eighteen prominent bankers to organize the Committee to Defend America by Aiding the Allies? He had, but it was not a secret meeting; it had been held openly in one of the largest clubs in New York; not all of those present had been bankers, and the purpose of the meeting had been to meet Mr. William Allen White.

This was foolishness, but some of the questions were more serious. Stimson refused to be drawn into a discussion of his predecessor Woodring; he refused to say that he would never approve the transfer of American arms to other nations; he firmly denied that this position was the same as approval of "stripping our own defenses for the sake of trying to stop Hitler 3,000 miles away."

As for his relations to the President, of course they had had differences on domestic issues. No, this did not mean that they could not co-operate for national defense. He explained to the committee exactly how he had been appointed; the whole thing had no relation to politics. He was out of politics now. He retained his convictions, but he had a right to subordinate their expression to the paramount duty he had accepted from the President; his position was the same as that of any officer of the United States Army.

In the same way he refused to be drawn into discussion of matters that were properly the business of the President or the Secretary of State. He was unwilling to discuss the detailed present application of policies he had advocated in 1939. The more he was quoted the better his prophecies seemed, but he must repeat that the Secretary of War does not make policy in foreign affairs. "Policy is determined by other branches of the Government, and it is his duty to prepare for the troubles that may be brought about by their determinations." (Laughter.)

Senator Vandenberg was courteous and his questions were fair. Would the policies advocated in the New Haven speech amount to acts of war? Stimson refused a direct answer; he preferred to call them legitimate acts of self-defense in an emergency in which traditional concepts of neutrality no longer applied. He further pointed out that as Secretary of War these would not be his problems to decide. The Vandenberg questions were the most interesting and sensible that he was asked by any opposition Senator, however, and on his return to New York after the hearing he sent a written statement to the committee and to Senator Vandenberg pointing out that many close students of international law felt that the whole theory of neutrality vis-à-vis an aggressor had disappeared with the Kellogg-Briand Pact, so that any of the acts advocated in his New Haven speech would be fully legal under international law.

After Vandenberg came Taft; only the day before, both these gentlemen had seen their ambitions thwarted by the nomination of a dark horse to be Republican candidate for President, and Stimson allowed himself the small satisfaction of asking the chairman if he also had Wendell Willkie around. But to Taft this was no laughing matter. Neither was it to Stimson; he sought no conflict with the son of his old friend and chief, and the only regret he carried away from the hearing was that the questions put to him by Robert Taft should have been so pointedly unfriendly. Here was no effort to find out what he really thought; it was a debater's attempt to make him say things he did not mean, and it was not worthy of a son of William Taft. And the worst of it was that Senator Taft, driven by his own bitter convictions, could see no unfairness in what he was doing.

First Taft remarked that Stimson had presented a novel view of the functions of a Cabinet officer. How could he argue that his general views were not relevant to his work as Secretary of War? His views and advice, as given to the President, would be just as important as the administration of the War Department. How could he immunize his views? Taft here made a fair point; Stimson's opening statement was too strong in its insistence that a Secretary of War should confine himself to preparing the national defense. Although he would not have the responsibility for foreign affairs, he would certainly be an adviser. Stimson acknowledged his error, admitting that he could not immunize himself; it was for that reason, he said, that he had been so frank with the committee.

The discussion then turned back to the New Haven speech. Stimson remarked that since making the speech he had learned that the time for providing bases to the British fleet had probably not come; Great Britain's position was not quite as desperate as he had thought, and she could still use her own bases. "Then," said Senator Taft, "as I understand you, you are in favor of joining in the war just as soon as you figure that the British have no longer a chance."

"That is not quite a fair way of putting it. So long as there is a chance of preserving their fleet and so long as it is evident that without our doing that [providing bases] . . . , they would not be preserved, then I think that we ought to do it."

And then Taft tried to force other conclusions. Would Stimson favor giving credits to the British if they ran out of money? Would he go to war to prevent the defeat of England? It was not the questions but the manner of their asking that was offensive. Each time Taft tried to frame a conclusion and put it in Stimson's mouth. And each time Stimson refused to eat; Taft had so framed the question as to leave out an essential condition. The question of credits to the British would depend on the circumstances at the time, and so, much more, would the question of war. The essential element every time would be what were the best interests of the United States, and you could not tell in advance how events might affect those interests. "Until you put in all of those conditions, you have got to refrain from asking dogmatic questions and I have to refrain from answering such questions."

This was not Stimson's first brush with the isolationist mind, nor was it to be his last; this time he was especially hampered by the necessity of confining his remarks to lines which would not embarrass President Roosevelt and Secretary Hull, and of course it was just that embarrassment which Taft was eager to produce. That the Senator should try to gain his end by a cross-examination so narrow and mistrusting deeply disappointed Stimson. He was not personally damaged; he felt afterward that he had more than held his own. But this readiness, in a great national emergency, to seize every opportunity of embarrassing the administration seemed to him a fantastic distortion of partisan duty. He had been questioned for two hours, and not a word had been said about his competence to direct the Army; the whole discussion had turned on other subjects. This was to be the attitude of the isolationists for the next eighteen months whenever he went to the Capitol. In the Congress were some of the ablest and most farsighted men in the country, and with their help the essential measures were passed, but the hearings and debates also became a sounding board for the hopelessly twisted views of a small group of men who, in the name of peace, would have kept America from acting to delay or block the greatest aggression in history.

From the hearing Stimson went back to New York to complete the windup of his personal affairs. On July 8 he returned to Washington, moving into Woodley. It was good to be back in the house which, next only to Highhold, was his home.

That same day he had a long talk with General Marshall, the

second since his nomination had been announced. George C. Marshall was an officer Stimson had known for over twenty years. His name had appeared on lists of especially qualified officers collected by Stimson for Theodore Roosevelt in 1916 when the latter had hoped to raise a division. When Stimson was himself a soldier in 1918, he had met Marshall at the Staff College in Langres and had been so much impressed that ten years later he had tried unsuccessfully to persuade Marshall to go as his aide to the Philippines. Now he began to know and appreciate still better the quality of the Chief of Staff. He soon understood that the greatest problem a Secretary of War can have would never face him while Marshall was alive and well. He would not have to search the Army for a good top soldier. The right man was already there. Only once in the next five years did it occur to Stimson that he might need a new man, and that was when he was urging the appointment of General Marshall to what he then considered a still more difficult and critical position.

It was only too clear that there was much to be done in the War Department: an enormous program of rearmament was only at its beginning; an equally great expansion of the Army's numbers was but sketchily charted; no trusted staff of civilian assistants was at hand; and meanwhile the last bastion of freedom in Europe was in deadly danger. But when Stimson's nomination was confirmed on July 9, by a vote of fifty-six to twenty-eight, he already felt that there were better days ahead. He was at work again, under a chief whom he was able to admire and like as a man, even as he respected him for his office. He was in charge of the United States Army, which for thirty years he had known and loved and trusted. And he had a good Chief of Staff. No man, he later said, could have asked more of fortune in a time of national peril.

2. THE NEWCOMER

When he was sworn in at the White House on July 10, 1940, Stimson entered an administration which had been in undisputed control of the national government for over seven years. At first he felt some of the sensations of a college freshman, and the kindness and co-operation which he found among his new colleagues were heartening. It was immediately clear that there was no division in Franklin Roosevelt's Cabinet on the central issue—the whole administration knew that the nation was in danger. Stimson had been appointed to take charge of the Army, and he was welcome. With Secretary Hull he had right at the start "the longest, most intimate and confidential talk I have ever had with him," and it was perhaps indicative of their new relationship that "for the first time he went into domestic politics as well as foreign affairs." (Diary, July 16, 1940) Stimson had his differences of opinion with Cordell Hull, then and later, but from his side at least there was never any lack of trust and affection for a man whose position in the government was a good deal more difficult than his own.

A more surprising but equally gratifying cordiality was shown to Stimson on his arrival by Secretary Morgenthau. The Secretary of the Treasury had been closely concerned with many of the problems now entrusted to Stimson; his Department had been drawn into military matters as a result of Mr. Roosevelt's lack of confidence in Stimson's predecessor. To Stimson now Morgenthau gave friendly and tactful help in learning the ropes. Much later, when Stimson was forced to disagree radically with Morgenthau in certain subjects, he remembered the kindness the latter had shown him when he most needed it.

The new Secretary of the Navy, Frank Knox, was an acquaintance of nearly thirty years' standing. He had come to Stimson's office in the War Department at the end of 1911 bearing the best possible introduction, a short note from T.R. at Sagamore Hill with the familiar and compelling recommendation, "He is just our type!" The record which Knox later made as a liberal Republican had won Stimson's respect, and in the spring of 1940 his voice, raised from Chicago in energetic advocacy of help to Britain and an end to partisan squabbles, had been even more impressive; in May and early June the two men had begun a correspondence full of the urgency both felt. In Washington Knox at once became to Stimson a friend in all things, and a partner in most.

As the months passed Stimson gradually became a well-established and familiar member of the government. Mr. Roosevelt's was an administration whose inherently disorderly nature he never learned to love, but for its individual members he soon came to have respect, and with most of them he established relations of friendly confidence. They were certainly not the collection of dangerous and unprincipled power seekers that he had heard denounced in New York for seven years. If as a group they had a failing, it was in their constant readiness for internecine strife, but for this they were perhaps less to blame than their chief, who not infrequently placed his bets on two subordinates at once. To Stimson the whole notion of such conflict was abhorrent, and he found that if he earnestly avoided battle he could generally disarm the advancing enemy. Much of the trouble grew out of the clashes of subordinates whose loyalty was not to the administration as a whole but to some part of it, and in these cases it was a sound rule to smoke a pipe of peace with the rival chieftain rather than to scamper to the White House with some one-sided grievance. Thus it became his practice to keep his troubles away from the President as much as possible, and he found that with men like Hull, Morgenthau, Knox, Ickes, and Jackson he could usually reach a friendly answer to the questions noisily raised by subordinates. There were cases, later on, when no such answer could be found, and more than once Stimson found himself fully engaged in the unpleasant task of winning Presidential support for his position against that of a colleague, but such battles were never of his own choosing.

Although he thus established effective working relations with its leaders, Stimson never became one of the special intimates of the administration, and he occasionally felt that the President listened too much to men who were not his direct constitutional advisers. Fortunately, the principal adviser of this kind was Harry Hopkins, a man for whom Stimson quickly developed the greatest respect, and with whom he established a relation of such close mutual confidence that he was often able to present the position of the War Department more effectively through Hopkins than he could in direct conversation with the President. Hopkins was an extraordinary figure; he possessed a mind of unusual quickness and flexibility, and a sure judgment of both men and affairs; his special value to the President lay in his combination of complete loyalty and a sensitive understanding of Mr. Roosevelt's complex nature. During Stimson's years in Washington, the great influence of Hopkins was time and again exerted on behalf of the War Department. "The more I think of it, the more I think it is a godsend that he should be at the White House." (Diary, March 5, 1941)

Another White House "godsend" was Major General Edwin M. Watson, called "Pa" by half official Washington. Watson's extraordinary personal friendliness and conviviality covered a discerning mind and a strong heart and, like Hopkins, Watson loved his chief too well to withhold frank advice and counsel. To Stimson he was invariably a sympathetic and knowing helper.

No discussion of Stimson's relationship to the administration would be complete without one further name, that of Mr. Justice Frankfurter. Without the least deviation from his fastidious devotion to the high traditions of the Supreme Court, Felix Frankfurter made himself a continual source of comfort and help to Stimson. Although he never heard a word of it from Frankfurter, Stimson believed that his own presence in Washington was in some degree the result of Frankfurter's close relationship to the President. In any event, he found Frankfurter always the most devoted of friends and the most zealous of private helpers, and the Justice's long and intimate knowledge of the Roosevelt administration was placed entirely at his disposal. Time after time, when critical issues developed, Stimson turned to Frankfurter; sometimes he heard from Frankfurter even before he had turned. It is not fitting that the activities of a Justice still serving on the Court should be discussed in detail, and Mr. Justice Frankfurter will not be mentioned again; there was in his relationship with Stimson nothing, of course, that even remotely touched upon his duties as a Justice, while there was much that added to the country's debt to a distinguished American.

And as time passed, Stimson fully clarified his purpose and his position in the eyes of the professional politicians and

Congress. After the first loud objections to his appointment, on the ground that it was the product of a devious political mind, there was not much noise until just after the election, when there were rumors that now the superannuated Republican stopgap would resign, his function fulfilled. "Of course it is not a pleasant matter and troubled . . . me . . . a good deal, so I decided to take it up with the President after the Cabinet meeting. I did so and he was very nice about it and I found out from him then that he had already this morning taken the matter up at his press conference. The question had been asked him on the subject and he had stigmatized it 'off the record' as a lie, and 'on the record' that it was only imaginary." (Diary, November 8, 1940) Stimson never knew whether the President had originally intended that he should stay indefinitely as Secretary of War, but this interview in November was typical of the response he met from the White House on the two or three later occasions when he was concerned about his usefulness to his chief. On the whole it seemed likely that the President thought about the matter as little as Stimson himself. The latter had believed in the beginning that he would be in Washington perhaps a year or eighteen months, until the War Department was fully abreast of its duties and the work had become routine. No such time ever developed, and by the spring of 1941 he no longer thought of any early end to his labors. He and Knox had established themselves as permanent members of the administration.

As doubts about his permanence died down, he found himself in an unusual position, politically. He owed nothing to anybody except the President who had appointed him, and the President demanded absolutely none of the usual political support and assistance. This independence Stimson demonstrated in the campaign of 1940 by maintaining a silence so complete that, as he remarked to a friend, 'no one but my Maker knows how I am going to vote.' The diary entry of October 27 explains this decision. "I shall not take any part in the campaign. I think that is more in accord with the job that I have taken and the way in which it was offered me and the way in which I have accepted it. I think it would probably be better for the President as well as myself if I remain as I have been—a Republican doing nonpartisan work for a Democratic President because it related to international affairs in which I agreed and sympathized with his policies. To go actively into the campaign would arouse great antagonism from a great many people on immaterial issues and would prevent me from doing the service that I want to do for the country and for the cause of national defense. Having made that decision I felt better and enjoyed my ride. . . ." As a matter of fact Stimson voted for Roosevelt; it was a natural decision, and perhaps many men guessed Stimson's mind, but he spoke no public word whatever, and his reasons for his vote, like his reasons for silence, were confided only to the diary: "Roosevelt has won another sweeping victory. . . . It is a tremendous relief to have this thing over and I think that from the standpoint of immediate events in the war, particularly during the coming spring and summer, the election will be very salutary to the cause of stopping Hitler." (Diary, November 6, 1940)

This decision to remain completely out of politics Stimson considered one of the wisest he ever made. By it he and his Department avoided any responsibility for any part of the President's record except as it concerned the national defense; he also avoided antagonism from the Republican side which would have been inevitable if he had thrown his weight publicly against the Republican candidate. He was thus able to maintain his position before Republicans in Congress as counsel for the situation. "Jim Wadsworth [Congressman James W. Wadsworth of New York, Stimson's old friend] came in to see me and I had a long talk with him. . . . He was very much impressed with the seriousness of the [international] situation and told me so. His advice was that I should get in touch with the Republicans so far as I could of the Congress. . . . He said ——— was an honest man and that he trusted me, which I was very much surprised at and I told Wadsworth so. Wadsworth repeated it as being true of practically all of the Republicans." (Diary, January 24, 1941)

At the same time, taking their cue from the President, the Democrats maintained a continuously friendly attitude toward Stimson, accepting with good will his insistence that the War Department could not permit political considerations to control its decisions. He, for his part, maintained cordial relations with the Democratic leaders and, as always in his political life, found that once the central issue of partisan opposition is removed, there are few roses so sweet as those that grow over the party wall. The following diary entry is typical; just before the 1940 election he learned that "a mistake had been uncovered in the Adjutant General's Department in regard to Senator Pat Harrison's request for establishing a C.C.C. camp distribution system at McComb, Mississippi, instead of across the river in Louisiana. The Department had reported that it couldn't be done as cheaply in Mississippi as Louisiana. I was rather distressed at this because we have been obliged to refuse already one or two other requests of Harrison's who has always been a faithful and loyal helper in military matters. This seemed to me a request that we ought to be able to grant. It now appeared by telephone . . . that the Adjutant General was mistaken and that it could be granted more cheaply for McComb than for Louisiana, and I told Brooks at once to telegraph Harrison and his committee who were coming up to see me about it, that they needn't come and the request was granted. When I arrived back in Washington . . . I found a very grateful telegram from him." (Diary, November 2, 1940)

Only once in this period did Stimson have a painful reminder of the baneful influence of politics. The diary entry speaks for itself. "Bob Patterson has been making a number of appointments in the Procurement Branch of the office—this time of young lawyers to help out. All his appointments are good, chosen purely from a professional standpoint and men of high character. But among them he selected Henry Parkman, Jr., of Massachusetts, to be one of the attorneys of the Department and Parkman was the Republican candidate in Massachusetts last fall for Senator against Senator Walsh. Consequently when I got back to the Department yesterday I was met with a terrific telegram from Walsh, professing to be astounded at such an appointment; claiming that Parkman had conducted a very low campaign against him; stating that he was personally obnoxious to himself (Walsh) and demanding that I reconsider the appointment. This made a tough situation, for Walsh is quite capable of doing much harm to the Department's work up on the Hill and undoubtedly may try to do so. I had a talk with Patterson . . . and of course he was pretty stiff about not yielding, but unfortunately he has not got as much experience as I have had with the difficulties of such a situation with a hostile Senator. I talked with Parkman whom I had not met before but who was a very fine-looking fellow and evidently a good man and he was considerate enough to suggest that he had better withdraw. I told him not to do so for a while—that I felt very badly about it and that I would talk with Walsh and see first what could be done. Unfortunately Walsh was not in Washington, so . . . I called him on the long-distance telephone at Clinton, Massachusetts, and he nearly blew me off the end of the telephone, he was so angry and bitter. He is evidently making it a party matter, as the Democratic chairman has also written to Roosevelt about it. Of course it was not a party matter, but the trouble is no one will believe it. No one will believe that we did not both know that he was a Republican candidate for Senator, although as a matter of fact I had never heard of him. . . . It is pretty hard to have such a thing happen, making the possibility of such a critical mess to the Department. It brings out the delicacy of the situation in which I am, in a Democratic Cabinet, and the good luck I have had thus far in avoiding trouble all through the political campaign. I am very anxious not to spoil all matters now by this kind of a row which may spread in all directions. On the other hand, it is very hard to sacrifice Parkman, although he was very nice about it, and his withdrawal will not really be commensurate with the harm that may be done to the Department." (Diary, December 11, 1940)

The core of the difficulty here was in the fact that Walsh, a vindictive man, was no friend to the President; he was also an isolationist. As a veteran Democrat quite prepared to cause maximum embarrassment to the administration in its policy toward the world crisis, he was extremely dangerous. Stimson reached his decision that same night. "I spent considerable time in my bed last night thinking the thing out and finally came to the conclusion that it was my duty toward the job and toward the President not to allow this row with Walsh to come up in the Department, particularly because I did not want to have him raise the issue that he surely would raise of the President's conduct of the war, now, prematurely, before the President has chosen his own ground." Stimson asked a close friend who also knew Parkman to explain the situation to the latter, and "Parkman came back and positively refused to run the risk of embarrassing us and declined to take the job. He behaved very finely about it. I felt very badly and told him so." (Diary, December 12, 1940) This surrender to Walsh was a bitter decision; Stimson took great satisfaction in Henry Parkman's later distinguished service as an officer who rose to the grade of brigadier general, and he was delighted when Walsh was finally retired from public life by another soldier in 1946.

In a sense, of course, it was politically unwise for Patterson to have appointed Parkman in the first place, but it was this kind of political unwisdom that Stimson loved in Patterson; his rugged integrity was in the end an asset that far outweighed the occasional difficulties it caused. The real significance of the Parkman case was that it stood almost alone. In only one other case throughout the war did Stimson have to withdraw an intended appointment to his Department, and in this instance the veto came from the President, probably as a result of misinformation given him by others. Stimson, however, did not go out of his way to appoint the avowed enemies of powerful Senators, and in all important cases he cleared his appointments with the White House.

It was Walsh's isolationism that made him dangerous, and throughout the war Stimson was to find his principal political difficulties with those in both parties whose objective was to discredit the administration's foreign policy. Thus his real opponents were the President's opponents, too, and his position in this respect was like that of any ordinary Cabinet member. With these opponents there could be no real peace or mutual trust, but it was important to fight them only on the central front.

The success with which the War Department kept itself
aloof from politics was strikingly demonstrated much later,
in 1944, when the Congress entrusted the supervision of voting
in the armed forces to a three-man commission consisting of
the Secretary of War, the Secretary of the Navy, and the
chairman of the Maritime Commission, Admiral Land. Stimson observed with some amusement that two members of the
original commission were Republicans, while the third was
a professional sailor. There was a mild flurry at the White
House over the composition of the staff which Stimson established in the War Department to manage his share of the
soldier voting; the officer in charge of the work was Colonel
Robert Cutler, and although he had been politically active
only as corporation counsel to a Democratic mayor of Boston,
he was a registered Republican. But Mr. Roosevelt was less
disturbed than his professional Democratic advisers, and
Cutler remained on the job, with a Democrat added to his
staff in order to disarm criticism. Both in the War Ballot
Commission and in the Army, soldier voting was so smoothly
and fairly handled that Stimson felt a deep personal debt to
Cutler. No job entrusted to his supervision during the entire
war had held more explosive possibilities, and none was accomplished with less friction.

3. THE BEST STAFF HE EVER HAD

It is a sound rule for a newcomer in any organization to
learn his own particular job before he makes much noise.
Stimson's attention, in the early summer of 1940, was directed
mainly at his own Department. There was much to be done.
The first task, and perhaps the most important, was to restore
the unity and morale of the Department. The civilian chiefs
of the service departments, Stimson once remarked, may not
be able to do very much good, but they certainly have it in
their power to do a vast deal of harm. They necessarily out-
rank any and all military men, and when their power is mis-
used, or when they are at odds with one another, the results
within the service are distressing. Some such situation seemed
to have arisen in the months before Stimson's arrival, and his

first job was to re-establish a proper mutual confidence between the Secretary, the Assistant Secretary, and the Army.

As for his own relationship to the Army, Stimson could only say that the problem never came up. He had the very great—and unusual—advantage of extensive experience with military men, and from his first day in office he found no cause to complain of any lack of loyal support. In his first message to the Army, on July 19, he remarked on the "good spirit of co-operation" he had already found, and this was not wishful thinking. If the Cabinet had shown him the cordiality of sympathetic strangers, the Army seemed to meet him as an old friend. To those who disliked soldiers, this friendship might give the appearance that one more civilian had been captured and tamed by the ferocious militarists. To Stimson it was encouraging assurance that an essential condition of his effectiveness had been fulfilled.

Just as important as his own relationship with the Army was the development of a staff of assistants who would work in the same spirit. The most important single accomplishment of Stimson's first year in office was his success in assembling a team of civilian associates which he later believed to be the best he ever had, in any office. Even if it had been possible to make the War Department a one-man show, Stimson's whole experience of administration was against such a course. At the same time he was not temperamentally fitted for service as a figurehead. He therefore required as his principal assistants men who could combine intelligence and initiative with flawless loyalty to him as chief, and such men are more easily described than found. During his first months in Washington he was greatly helped by Arthur E. Palmer, a young lawyer from his New York firm, but Palmer was too young to be happy out of uniform, and only Patterson of all his civilian assistants was with Stimson from the beginning to the end.

In accordance with the original understanding between the President and Stimson, Patterson was appointed and confirmed as Assistant Secretary of War and was at work by the end of July. His arrival ended for good the division between the Secretary and the Assistant Secretary which had been conspicuous in the early months of 1940. He at once assumed direct responsibility for the vast Army program of procurement, and throughout the five years that followed he relieved Stimson of all but occasional labors in this great field.

Probably no man in the administration was more ruthlessly determined to fulfill his assignment than Patterson; he proposed to let nothing block him in his effort to equip the armies of the anti-Axis world. He had known war at very close range in 1918; he was at war from 1940 onward, and he had a fierce hatred of all delay and any compromise; his only test of any measure was whether it would help to win, and for any group or individual who blinked at sacrifice he had only scorn. He himself was so zealous to fight that only Stimson's personal plea prevented him from resigning his office in 1944 to take a commission as an infantry officer again. Patterson was a fighter, and although he was perhaps not always perfect in his choice of a battleground, his instinct in the choice of enemies was unerring.

The next great find was John J. McCloy, a man whose record so distinguished him that Stimson's principal difficulty was to retain his services for the War Department. He first came to Washington at Stimson's personal request to advise the War Department in its counterintelligence work; after years of work as a lawyer investigating the Black Tom case he had a wide knowledge of German subversive methods. Stimson's early high opinion of him was reinforced by every report received on his work, and in October, 1940, he was appointed as a special assistant. So varied were his labors and so catholic his interests that they defy summary. For five years McCloy was the man who handled everything that no one else happened to be handling. He became Stimson's principal adviser in the battle for the Lend-Lease Act and it was his skillful preparation that cleared the way for the War Department's successful assumption of the whole military burden of lend-lease procurement. Later he was Stimson's chief adviser on matters connected with international relations and his agent in supervising the great work of military government. He was equally good in a complicated interdepartmental negotiation or in dealing with Congress. His energy was enormous, and his optimism almost unquenchable. He became so knowing in the ways of Washington that Stimson sometimes wondered whether anyone in the administration ever acted without "having a word with McCloy"; when occasionally he was the first to give McCloy important news he would remark that his assistant must be weakening.

The third of the Secretary's principal subordinates was Robert A. Lovett, who arrived in November, 1940, to be Stimson's air assistant. For this duty he was conspicuously suited. His enthusiasm for airplanes had made him a naval pilot of distinguished skill in World War I, and in the years between wars he maintained his keen interest in the subject. In 1940 when he came to Washington he had just completed, as a private citizen, a careful survey of the whole problem of air power and aircraft production in the United States. He thus brought to his job the understanding and enthusiasm which were indispensable to a civilian dealing with the Army Air Forces, while at the same time his sensitive intelligence enabled him to maintain cordial relations with the non-fliers of the Department. Lovett possessed incisive judgment and a pertinent wit. He served Stimson in all matters affecting the Air Forces as Patterson served in procurement and supply. Both were in a high degree autonomous officers; both combined initiative with loyalty.

By April, 1941, these three men were in the jobs they were to hold throughout the war. In December, 1940, Patterson had been appointed to the newly created office of Under Secretary, and in April McCloy succeeded him as Assistant Secretary, while at the same time Lovett was appointed to the long-vacant position of Assistant Secretary for Air.

In the same month Stimson acquired a fourth assistant in Harvey H. Bundy, who had served with him before as Assistant Secretary of State from 1931 to 1933. With the title of Special Assistant to the Secretary, Bundy became "my closest personal assistant." A man of unusual tact and discretion, Bundy handled many of Stimson's troubling problems of administration and correspondence and served as his filter for all sorts of men and problems. He also became the Secretary's personal agent in dealings with scientists and educators, two groups whose importance was as great as it was unfamiliar in the great new army of machines and civilian soldiers.

These four men were the "sixty-minute players" in a team to which many others were added for special purposes at different times. Their characteristics as individuals are perhaps less important than the things they had in common. All were men in the prime of life, the forties and fifties, but all were so much younger than Stimson that none ever called him by his first name. All four had been conspicuously successful in private life, three as lawyers and one as a banker; all of them came to Washington at serious financial sacrifice. None of them had ever been politically active, and none had any consuming political ambition. All four were men of absolute integrity, and none was small-minded about credit for his labors. All but one were Republicans, but not one of them ever aroused partisan opposition. They were civilians, but they earned the unreserved confidence of the Army. All of them were wholehearted in their loyalty, but none interpreted loyalty as merely a duty to say yes, and Stimson often trusted their judgment against his own, especially when he was angry. In later chapters their names will be often mentioned, and even when they are not mentioned the reader must bear in mind that very little of what Stimson did was done without their advice and help.

And with these men Stimson established a relationship that was in many ways closer than anything he had known before in public office. These were men who knew how to laugh with him at trying events; nor were they put off or dismayed by his occasional thunderous anger. They could complain about him to Mrs. Stimson as a bad-tempered tyrant who "roared like a lion," but such complaints were registered in his presence with the teasing smile of members of the family. And as he looked back in 1947, he felt a deep and affectionate nostalgia for the days when he had shared Patterson's wrath at incompetence, laughed at the zealous omniscience of his heavenly twain McCloy and Lovett, fumed at Bundy's constant advice not to act on impulse, and lectured them all over the interoffice "squawk box" in tones they all proclaimed as unintelligible.

CHAPTER XIV

The First Year

1. MEN FOR THE NEW ARMY

DURING the months in which he was feeling his way toward full membership in the administration, and well before he had obtained the help of most of the civilian assistants upon whom he later so heavily relied, Stimson was fully engaged in the urgent immediate task of raising an army.

At New Haven in June, in his talks with the President, before his appointment, and at the Senate hearing on his confirmation, he had emphasized his conviction that a selective service bill should be enacted at once. Such a bill was pending before Congress when he took office, and his energies, through July and August of 1940, were largely devoted to the struggle for its enactment.

The principal difficulty was not in the opposition of those groups which always oppose conscription but rather in the widespread feeling among its supporters that no act so controversial could be passed in an election year. Even the Army, which of course supported the bill as essential to an effective mobilization of manpower, was at first pessimistic. The soldiers had been outcasts for so long that they were afraid to count on early acceptance of the novel principle of compulsory peacetime service. Nor could they be of any great assistance in winning support for such a measure; it was better that the "militarists" should remain in the background.

The Burke-Wadsworth Bill was thus not, in its origin, a War Department bill, though it was based in large part on joint Army-Navy staff studies. It was introduced by two farsighted members of Congress; it had been framed by a small group of well-informed private citizens in the Military Training Camps Association. Without this private initiative, and particularly without the indefatigable and intelligent work of Grenville Clark, Stimson was convinced that there would have been no Selective Service Act in 1940.[1]

Stimson's own principal labors in support of the measure were two. First, with General Marshall he determined the position of the War Department, which was essentially that any workable bill would be satisfactory to the Army. As for the necessity of such a bill, the War Department's figures spoke for themselves. The Army had in May been authorized to expand its regular strength to 375,000. The rate of recruiting indicated that by the volunteer system even this small figure could be achieved only very slowly. If Congress wanted an army large enough to defend the country, it must provide for compulsory service. This was the lesson of every previous emergency in American history. Stimson repeated to the House Committee on Military Affairs convictions which he had held for over twenty-five years. Selective Service was the only fair, efficient, and democratic way to raise an army.

His second task was that of insuring active Presidential support of the bill. Here he found himself engaged in a form of sport which had become familiar in the seven years of the New Deal. Franklin Roosevelt was firmly convinced of the need for selective service, and in the end his support was decisive in securing passage of a satisfactory act, but his watchful waiting, on this and many other later issues, was as tantalizing to Stimson as it was to many other men whose policies he in the end supported. In this case, however, 'he came down firmly on the right side every time we asked him to,' and at least once his statement preceded Stimson's request. The effect each time was immediate, and Stimson learned a lesson about the power of Mr. Roosevelt's leadership which he did not forget.

With the help of evident public approval throughout the country, the supporters of compulsory training were able to

---

[1] There might also have been no Stimson as Secretary of War in that year; it was Clark's fight for Selective Service that led him to take the initiative which resulted in the suggestion of Stimson's name to Mr. Roosevelt.

defeat all efforts at delay and all vitiating amendments, and on September 16 the President signed the Selective Service Act of 1940. In retrospect Stimson saw this act as one of the two or three most important accomplishments of the American people in the whole period before the outbreak of active war. It made possible a program of training which fully occupied the Army's resources through the next year; the invaluable months before the shooting began were thus not wasted. And as an unprecedented departure from American peacetime traditions, it demonstrated clearly the readiness of the American people to pay the cost of defense in terms more significant than dollars.

Together with the Joint Resolution of August 27, 1940, which authorized the President to call out the National Guard and the Organized Reserves, the Selective Service Act laid the necessary legislative foundation for a new army of 1,400,000 men. In view of the pressure under which the Army was forced to work, its preparations for housing and training these men seemed excellent to Stimson, and he said so firmly on October 17 when the question appeared briefly in the Presidential campaign.

A more difficult task was the organization of the Selective Service System. Here, too, the Army was prepared. The results of fourteen years of study were incorporated in the Department's plans, and with the advice of Major Lewis B. Hershey, Stimson and the President found it surprisingly easy to organize the great machine which was to serve so well for the duration. The administration of the draft, from the beginning, was a triumph of decentralization; throughout the war it maintained its reputation for fairness, and this reputation rested principally on the character and ability of the thousands of men who served on the local boards. To Stimson this was another proof of the competence of the Army; the methods of 1940 were built on the War Department's study of the magnificent achievement of General Crowder in 1917. President Roosevelt insisted on the appointment of a civilian director, and after some delay Clarence Dykstra was selected, but the success of the draft was not the work of any one man— it was the natural result of many years of careful thought in the War Department. It was a deep personal satisfaction to Stimson to watch the President learning that his fears of a militaristic administration of the draft were unfounded, and the appointment of General Hershey to replace Dykstra when the latter resigned in the middle of 1941 seemed to him a proper recognition of the trustworthiness of the military.

The beginning of the draft, for the sixteen million registrants, was the drawing of numbers on October 29. The same occasion marked for Stimson the ending of four months of arduous argument and preparation. "We had a very impressive ceremony. . . . The President first made an admirable speech on the purposes and methods and democratic nature of the draft. Then I was blindfolded and drew the first capsule. . . . This drawing took place, as will be noted, before election, although everybody was hinting around a little while ago that it would not be done until after election. It thus was a brave decision on the part of the President to let it come now, when there is a very bitter campaign being made against it. . . . In my opinion he showed good statesmanship when he accepted the issue and his technique in bringing it on in this public manner and the solemn nature of the occasion and the character of the speech which he made . . . served to change the event of the draft into a great asset in his favor." (Diary, October 29, 1940)

With manpower for the new army assured, the War Department tackled the equally important problem of leadership. It was apparent that large numbers of additional officers would be required.

Where should they be obtained? Grenville Clark, and many others who had studied the problem, strongly urged that in addition to promotion from the ranks the War Department should go straight to the civilian world, organizing training camps for citizen volunteers on the lines of those which Stimson himself had so much admired in 1916-1917. This solution also appealed to the President, who, however, left the final determination to the War Department.

General Marshall took a different view. Given a Selective Service System, he believed that for the first time in its history the Army would now be in a position to draw its officers from its own ranks. With a large pool of National Guard and Reserve officers to draw on, the Army had no immediate need for more officers; its problem was rather to insure the effective training of those it had. In March, 1941, the matter came to a head.

The issue here was a broader one than any of the participants then realized, and in retrospect Stimson believed that the solution reached was a better one than any of them anticipated. After much discussion it was agreed that there should be no separate "Plattsburg camps"; the Army would instead enlarge its already projected program for training officers from the ranks. As a concession to men not yet subject to draft who might be particularly qualified as leaders, it would offer a special arrangement later known as the Volunteer Officer Candidate program, but even this concession was later withdrawn. In the great task of finding junior officers the Army thus limited itself mainly to its own men, and from this decision grew the Officer Candidate Schools. This was the fair and democratic way to form an officer corps. It also turned out to be the efficient way.

A Secretary of War does not see much of lieutenants, however hard he may try, and Stimson was in no position to offer any final judgment on the quality of the junior leaders thus developed. The Army's insistence on finding its officers among its enlisted men was not duplicated during the war by either the Navy or the Air Forces (in the latter case for what seemed to Stimson sufficient reasons), and Stimson feared that perhaps the Army had lost many fine youngsters who were not reluctant to take the short cut to commissioned responsibility offered by other services. On the other hand, the principle established by the Army was right, and the record of the Officer Candidate Schools was a proud one. These schools were a new development in American military experience, and Stimson did not doubt that many mistakes were made, but he felt sure that the Army of the future would build its leadership on the principles thus boldly and successfully followed throughout Word War II.

Although the Officer Candidate Schools became the source

of most of the Army's new officers, there were of course many specialized skills for which the War Department had to go directly to civil life. The most obvious such cases were doctors, dentists, and chaplains. For other cases, less obvious, Stimson on October 14, 1940, laid down his policy in a "memorandum of suggestions." Commissions direct from civil life were not to be given to men otherwise liable to service under the draft; "all political or personal considerations should be rigidly excluded"; and "commissions should only be given where the individual has special qualifications for the service he is expected to perform."

At first Stimson tried to enforce this ruling by requiring his personal approval for all appointments from civil life. As the Army expanded, such personal supervision became impossible, and the job was turned over to a board of officers under General Malin Craig, who had been Marshall's predecessor as Chief of Staff. General Craig's firm but fair-minded application of Stimson's policy was a great protection to the Army. War generates many pressures, but perhaps none more insistent than that of the enormous number of men who are convinced that they can be useful only as commissioned officers.

This difficulty of course made itself felt also in lower echelons. Replying to one eager mother whose favorite private soldier had not yet been handed his marshal's baton, Stimson remarked that the only course which would satisfy everyone would be to abolish the rank of private.

Quite as important as the procurement of capable junior officers was the selection of their seniors. The policy pursued in promotion of officers was the work of General Marshall. Stimson's only concern was with promotions to general officer's rank, and even here the framing of the lists was a job for the soldiers. The Secretary was in complete sympathy with the Chief of Staff's insistence on selective advancement of the ablest men, regardless of age, and after careful study of Marshall's first list with his old friend Frank R. McCoy, "We both decided that it was an outstanding departmental paper and that the recommendations contained in it were very admirable and clear. Marshall had had the courage and breadth of view to disregard the ordinary official records of officers in certain cases where it was important to do so, and to appoint several men whom McCoy and I knew to be good war men and yet who might not have had as good a record on paper." (Diary, September 21, 1940)

Stimson approved the list, and the President signed it, unchanged; this became the almost invariable practice, although on a later list, in October, Stimson felt it necessary to reinforce Marshall's recommendation for the promotion of George S. Patton to major general, having heard that this name was doubtfully viewed in the White House.

The obverse of promotion was the unpleasant task of weeding out incompetents. At lower echelons this work was slow in development; eventually it was handled by reclassification boards. Complaints against reclassification from influential quarters forced Stimson in 1944 to make a personal investigation of the process of reclassification; he found as he had expected that the rights of officers subjected to this process were almost too carefully safeguarded and flatly refused to intervene. At higher levels he followed the same policy, pointing out to the friends of officers removed from high positions or retired from the Army that any interference from the Secretary's office would be prejudicial to good order and discipline.

This firmness was particularly necessary in the case of senior officers of the National Guard. Stimson had himself been a Guardsman, but partly for that reason he understood how little the training of the Guard had equipped many of its officers for modern field service, and he therefore fully supported General Marshall in the fairly drastic reorganization which was required in making effective fighting units of the Guard divisions.

2. SUPPLIES

The number of men in the United States Government whose central interest was preparation for war, in the summer of 1940, was not very great. Stimson and Judge Patterson were two of them, and in the uphill battle which they fought for the Army's equipment they soon learned all the good reasons why this or that part of their program must be delayed. The basic difficulty was a simple one—the country as a whole was not ready to make any serious sacrifices for national defense; nothing that was done in production before Pearl Harbor involved the same degree of sacrifice as the nation's decision to raise an army by selective service, but each man squealed as he was hurt. This was true of management and of labor, and it was true of many branches of the Government. The tensions developed during the years of the New Deal were not the perfect background for the labors of Dr. Win-the-War—especially since that doctor could not yet be called by his right name. The President himself had set the tone for this period by a remark that no one need be "discomboomerated" by the crisis.

The one thing upon which the whole country was agreed was that the services must have enough money. At no time in the whole period of the war emergency did Stimson ever have to worry about funds; the appropriations of Congress were always prompt and generous. The pinch came in getting money turned into weapons. Right at the start, Stimson found his temper sorely tried by six weeks of delay in passing a tax law under which contracts could be speedily signed. The issue was a simple one. The existing tax laws made no provision for the special circumstances of defense production, in which large plants must be built which would have almost no value after the emergency had ended. No businessman wanted to be saddled with such white elephants, and it was generally agreed that the law must be changed to permit contractors to write off such construction expenses within a five-year period. The administration insisted, however, that such relief must be accompanied by a stringent excess-profits tax. To all this Stimson agreed, in principle. He was not eager to see business making unnatural profits out of national defense. At the same time the essential thing was speed, and while he did not venture to determine who was right in the mutual recriminations between the Treasury and Congress, it seemed to him clear that neither side was sufficiently concerned with getting the bill passed. Businessmen must be prevented from making excessive profits, but they were not going to sign contracts until they had a bill protecting them against large losses, and too many men in Washington refused to face that simple fact. "The whole thing is a great clash between two big theories and interests. If you are going to try to go to war, or to prepare for war, in a capitalist country, you have got to let business make money out of the process or business won't work, and there are a great many people in Congress who think that they can tax business out of all proportion and still have business-men work diligently and quickly. That is not human nature." (Diary, August 26, 1940)

The War Department had its troubles with more than one company which was slow, or inefficient, or selfish, and Stimson himself had a stiff verbal engagement through the press with certain airplane makers who seemed to think the expansion of civil airlines more important than the growth of the Army Air Forces, but on the whole he was not inclined to blame businessmen for their reluctance to enter defense work without some protection. After World War I he had himself defended companies harried by the Harding administration for having done in wartime what the Wilson administration asked them to do. As for profits, it was obvious that if the government must guarantee against loss, it must also prevent excessive gain, and in the machinery for contract renegotiation as it finally developed Stimson was satisfied that in general this goal was achieved.

A striking example of this reluctance of businessmen to enter the uncertain field of defense production was the manufacture of powder. In the summer of 1940 powder was the most critical shortage of all, but Stimson was forced to make personal pleas to such companies as Du Pont before they would return to the work they had been so unfairly damned for doing in the previous war. One thing was absolutely clear: whoever started America toward war in 1940, it was most certainly not the munitions makers; they went about their work efficiently when called upon, but they did not push.

The most difficult problem in production, during Stimson's first year in the War Department, was inside the Government, in the organization of an effective team of leaders. The War Department itself had much to learn; the mixed atmosphere of the nation did not permit the application of its carefully deliberated plans for mobilization, and the insistent demand was for men who could throw away the book and get results in the face of unexpected handicaps and obstacles. Patterson was such a man, and so was Colonel Brehon Somervell, who in December took charge of the great task of camp construction. Stimson was further greatly assisted by Robert Proctor, a lawyer from Boston whose volunteer services expedited the signing of airplane contracts in the summer of 1940. The regular officers charged with procurement were diligent, but too few of them were men of drive and imagination. Nothing was to be gained by putting unknown hopefuls in their places, however, and Stimson and Patterson for a time did their best with what they had. For the moment the Army was not the critical point in the problem. Even unimaginative officers had more demands than industry could fill. The real confusion in the Government was in the great field of industrial mobilization. Who was to do the job that had been done under Bernard Baruch in 1918?

Franklin Roosevelt experimented with solutions to this problem for nearly four years; his first effort was the appointment of the National Defense Advisory Commission, in June, 1940. This was a committee of seven. In Stimson's view it was just six men too many, but in William S. Knudsen the President found a man who understood production; from the beginning Knudsen was "a tower of strength" in the practical matter of translating a military demand into an operating production line.

There were other problems involved in industrial mobilization, however, and it was not long before the NDAC began to show its inadequacies. Seven advisers could not make decisions. What was needed was a single head, as Stimson, Knox, Patterson, and Forrestal agreed in a long conference on December 17. After discussion with Morgenthau and Jesse Jones, and after the agreement of both William Green and Sidney Hillman had been secured, they went to the President on December 18 to suggest that Knudsen be made the one responsible director of war production. As a concession to the President's fear that such a "czar" might trespass on the legitimate functions of the War and Navy Departments, they further suggested that Stimson and Knox should serve as advisers to Knudsen. From this recommendation developed the Office of Production Management, OPM, to which the President appointed Knudsen as director, Hillman as associate director, and Stimson and Knox as members of the board. The attempt to get a single head had failed, but the new arrangement was certainly an improvement. Stimson's major contribution to its work was his personal intervention to insure the appointment of John Lord O'Brian as general counsel. O'Brian held this position in successive reorganizations throughout the war, and it would be difficult to overestimate the value of his service to his country.

3. TO BRITAIN ALONE

However urgent the work of raising and arming her own military forces, the attention of America in 1940 and early 1941 was mainly centered on Great Britain. In Stimson's office visitors from England were always welcome, and he followed with anxious care the course of the air and sea battle. On two matters his informants all agreed. The British were wholly determined to fight to the end, and to do it successfully they needed all the help they could get. It was the policy of the American Government to provide this help, but it was easier to announce such a policy than to execute it.

The main difficulty, of course, was that America simply did not have much to give; by the standards that were to become familiar in the later years of the war, she had nothing. In 1940 planes were counted one at a time, and even the very few on hand were not battle-tested. The same thing was true of all modern weapons. This brutal fact was too painful to be properly accepted, and during the next two years Stimson had many a bitter hour with Allied leaders who could not believe that the American larder was bare. The President himself was an occasional offender; in his eagerness to help an ally he sometimes gave assurances that could not be fulfilled. It was not easy for anyone to possess his soul in patience during the long months that separated vast programs from finished weapons.

In 1940 the only weapons available in the United States in any quantity were surplus stocks from the last war. Even these were not readily transferable, but in the emergency just after Dunkirk the President and General Marshall succeeded in getting to the British a very substantial number of infantry weapons; this was done by selling them to the United States Steel Export Company, which in turn resold them to the British. The subterfuge was obvious, and unconcealed, but in the emotional reaction to the situation in June, 1940, it was generally approved. And the weapons were, in fact, surplus— there remained enough of these old Enfields and outdated machine guns to equip an army twice the size of anything contemplated in 1940.

A much more complicated question was presented in early August. Ever since May the British had been asking for destroyers. The American Navy had about two hundred old four-stackers in cold storage. They were, however, a part of the Navy's wartime force, and if the United States should be drawn into the struggle they would certainly be used. To the American people, furthermore, ships of the Navy have a special sentimental value. And again, Congress had on June 28 passed a bill providing that no material belonging to the American Government should be delivered to foreign forces unless the Army's Chief of Staff or the Chief of Naval Operations certified that such material was surplus. It was not readily apparent how Admiral Stark could give any such certificates for his destroyers. Finally, there was an old statute apparently forbidding the transfer of naval vessels to a belligerent.

The famous "destroyer deal" by which this log jam was broken was the personal triumph of President Roosevelt. To Stimson this was the President at his best. The obvious answer was that the British should give some *quid pro quo*, and such a suggestion was made by the British on August 5. But it was the President himself, on August 13, in a meeting with Morgenthau, Stimson, Knox, and Welles, who drafted the essential principles of the agreement which was finally reached. In return for fifty destroyers, the British were asked to give the United States the right to fortify and defend certain British held bases in the Atlantic. Such a trade would strengthen both nations, and in the larger sense each would be further strengthened by the increased power of the other. If it was the American interest that the British should master the Nazi submarine, it was clearly the British interest that America should be strong in the Atlantic.

To the successful completion of the President's plan Stimson gave his full support. He strongly urged that there was no need to take the plan to Congress; this was, broadly speaking, an exercise of the traditional power of the Executive in foreign affairs, and it met the requirements of the act of June 28, for surely Admiral Stark's conscience must be clear as he surveyed the stature of American naval strength before and after the agreement. As for the statutes on the transfer of naval vessels, Stimson endorsed the Attorney General's decision that these statutes were designed to meet wholly different circumstances—such cases as that of the *Alabama*, in the Civil War; they would not apply to the present case. Stimson further argued against a State Department view that the agreement should include a specific pledge not to surrender the British Fleet. The Churchill government had already made its position eloquently clear, and to require further pledges would be merely an indication of mistrust. As a Republican, Stimson was in frequent communication with William Allen White, who was finally able to assure him that the Republican candidate, Wendell Willkie, would in general support the plan.

Not all of the President's advisers were so bold. At a meeting of these advisers (at which the President was not present) on August 21, "there was some timidity evident in regard to boldly confronting the situation which existed, and there were suggestions from some of them that it would be better to try to transfer the destroyers to Canada rather than to Great Britain. This suggestion gained enough support to arouse me to strongly make a statement to the contrary. I said that no one would believe that to be the fact; that it was not fact, and that it would simply add a discreditable subterfuge to the situation. I pointed out that today the newspapers had been discussing the fact that the British fleet of destroyers had already been reduced to only sixty vessels and that they had been clamoring

for help on this point and that if we should send away from
this country an almost equal fleet of fifty destroyers which
would subsequently turn up in Great Britain, no one on earth
would believe that it had not been intended for Great Britain.
I pointed out that Canada had neither the need nor the men
to man them and that they would be manned by British sea-
men anyhow. My statement put an end to the Canadian suggestion, but the fact that it should actually have been put forward was an evidence of how technical stupidity can get into
these pleasant people." (Diary, August 21, 1940)

As announced on September 3, the destroyer deal transferred fifty American destroyers to Great Britain, in exchange
for a ninety-nine-year lease on bases in six British possessions
in the Western Hemisphere. Two additional leases, in New-
foundland and Bermuda, were freely granted. This represented a concession to the Prime Minister's desire that the
element of trade be entirely removed from the transaction;
unfortunately the element of trade was exactly what was necessary to make the transaction legal under the shackling
American statutes. The agreement was met with strong and
general approval by the country; the professional isolationists
were reduced to unhappy grumbling about "ignoring Congress," for even on the very narrow ground on which these gentlemen chose to consider the security of their country, it was
clear that the President had made a good bargain.

To Stimson the whole affair was enormously encouraging.
It was clear proof that the Commander in Chief understood
high politics; it established a new degree of mutual confidence and friendship among the British, the Americans, and
the Canadians; its solid success at the bar of public opinion
confirmed his view that the American people were ready for
leadership. At a meeting with the President and Prime Minister King of Canada, on August 17, he summed up his feelings. He reminded the others of Franklin's famous remark at
the end of the American Constitutional Convention, that for a
long time he had wondered about a carved image of the sun
which decorated the chair of George Washington, and that
now he was persuaded that it was a rising, not a setting, sun.
"I said I felt that way about this meeting. I felt that it was

very possibly the turning point in the tide of the war, and that from now on we could hope for better things."

Through sheer inadvertence the final agreement, as published, omitted a part of the American obligation—250,000 Enfield rifles with 30,000,000 rounds of ammunition, and 5 B-17 bombers. This was highly embarrassing, but Stimson could see no other course than a frank admission of the error. At a meeting called by the President, "I did my best to point out that I felt that we were committed to the British for it, and that to go back on that commitment would do a great deal of harm to our good name. But the others thought that due consideration could be given in the shape of another transaction which would satisfy the British just as well or better than the flying fortresses, and they persuaded the President to that effect." (Diary, September 13, 1940) A compensating transaction was finally arranged, but it involved a good deal of complicated reasoning, and Stimson was pleasantly surprised by the good temper shown by the British in the face of this American reluctance to admit publicly a simple error.

The destroyer deal was heartening and dramatic, but it unfortunately did not end the problem of aid to Britain. Throughout the summer and autumn of 1940 Stimson was engaged in almost daily labors to speed up the production and transfer of military supplies. Energetic efforts were made to harmonize British and American requirements and types of weapons. British missionaries came in and out of the Secretary's office, and over the weeks a close and intelligent co-operation developed. The Treasury Department under Morgenthau was particularly zealous and effective in finding ways to finance these transactions. But more and more both sides found themselves blocked. The British were running out of dollar exchange and the hands of the Americans were tied by statute; General Marshall with his usual courage was willing to sign the necessary certificate whenever there was any reasonable argument to support it, but there were many laws which left no such loophole and many cases where no honest man could sign. "It is really preposterous to have Congress attempt to tie the hands of the Commander in Chief in such petty respects as they have done recently in this legislation. The chief hold of the Congress on the Executive is their ability to vote or to refuse to vote supplies for an Army and their right to raise and support armies in the Constitution. The more I run over the experiences of this summer, the more I feel that that ought to be substantially the only check; that these other little petty annoying checks placed upon the Commander in Chief do an immense amount more harm than good and they restrict the power of the Commander in Chief in ways in which Congress cannot possibly wisely interfere. They don't know enough." (Diary, September 9, 1940)

On December 17 the President announced his determination to insure all-out aid to Great Britain. On December 29 he presented his case to the people in the "arsenal of democracy" speech. At the start of the new session of Congress there began the great debate which continued for two months, ending with the passage of the Lend-Lease Act, which gave the President the power to "manufacture . . . or procure . . . any defense article for the government of any country whose defense the President deems vital to the defense of the United States," and "to sell, transfer title to, exchange, lease, lend, or otherwise dispose of, to any such government any defense article." In Stimson's view this was one of the most important legislative achievements of the entire war. It was another great Rooseveltian triumph. At one stroke it smashed two bottlenecks: it provided for the financing of the British supply program, and at the same time it gave to the American Government badly needed authority over the whole field of military supplies. It was also a firm declaration of the American intention to block the Nazis; Stimson called it a "declaration of economic war."

Unlike the Selective Service Act, Lend-Lease was in its concept and origin a specifically "administration" measure; it was as members of a united team that the Administration leaders most closely concerned planned their statements to the congressional committees considering the bill. Leaving finance to Morgenthau and foreign policy to Hull, Stimson, as head of the department which would be most directly affected in the execution of any lend-lease program, centered his argument on the practical benefits which would result from passage of the bill.

In prolonged sessions with the House and Senate committees he emphasized that the bill would bring order out of the chaos then surrounding the procurement of munitions for friendly nations. For a dozen different purchasing missions of varying types and sizes it would substitute the trained and experienced military procurement officers of the United States Government. More important, it would permit the American Government to exercise a centralized and effective control over the distribution of weapons produced in the United States, for all such weapons would remain in American hands until they were complete and ready to use. There would be none of the difficulty previously caused by the fact that the same factory often was at work on orders for two or more independent governments.

Most important of all, Lend-Lease was a delegation of power, in the great tradition, to the one man to whom power must always be given in a national emergency—the President. Here Stimson clashed head on with more than one member of his own party, for the Republicans had taken up the chant of "dictatorship." Over and over again he emphasized his conviction that the only sound general principle was to trust the President. "My opinion—and it is one of long standing, and it has come from observation of various men who have held the Presidency during the period of my lifetime, whom I have had the privilege and the honor of observing at close range— my opinion is this: I have been impressed always with the tremendously sobering influence that the terrific responsibility of the Presidency will impose upon any man, and particularly in foreign relations. . . . That has applied to all of the gentlemen whom . . . I have had the opportunity of observing closely. . . . I feel that there is no one else, no other possible person in any official position who can be trusted to make conservatively and cautiously such a tremendous decision as the decisions which would have to be made in a great emergency involving a possible war. . . ."[2]

[2] Hearings on HR 1776, before the House Committee on Foreign Affairs, January 17, 1941.

Five times in the winter of 1941 Stimson went to Capitol Hill to testify in support of the Lend-Lease Act and its first appropriation bill. Five times he found himself involved in warm debate with men who feared the policy proposed and hated its proposer, Mr. Roosevelt. Each time he listened to another set of questions from the well-worn grab bag of isolationism; he had heard them all six months before when he first came to Washington. The answers were still the same. Yes, the United States was in peril; no, he did not think the President was likely to give our Navy away; yes, the Government would administer the act with due regard for the defense of the United States; the whole proposal was in fact designed to do nothing else than improve the security of the United States; no, he did not think it was a breach of neutrality; there was no obligation to be neutral in the face of aggression. It makes a weary tale in the retelling, but the questions were pointed, and so were the answers. Everything that Stimson had said before about the nature of the world crisis he now said again. And each day as he came away worn by the effort of debate he was heartened by the thought that this was a worth-while battle.

The Lend-Lease Act, substantially unweakened by amendment, was signed by the President on March 11, 1941. Congress retained the two controls appropriate to the legislative branch—it reserved the right of appropriation for the program, and it required regular reports. The first seven billions were appropriated shortly after. The administration had made its preparations, and the first supplies were transferred on the same day the bill was passed. Thus the War Department, "in addition to its other duties," became a service of supply to Allied armies everywhere. After the first labors of organization were complete, Stimson turned the job over to Under Secretary Patterson, and the work went ahead like any other program of procurement.

The great labors performed in the administration of Lend-Lease are no part of Stimson's life, and although he came frequently in contact with broad problems of allocation of weapons, this responsibility too was generally in other hands. Throughout the war he never wavered in his belief that the act was a constantly growing force for victory, and in its continued success he read a solid confirmation of his claim that the wise law is the law which gives power to the Executive. At his flexible discretion the President was able to direct where it was most needed the output of the "arsenal of democracy."

As the years passed, the Lend-Lease Act increased in favor in the eyes of Congress. Three times in the war Stimson went up to the Capitol to express his firm conviction that the act should be continued. Each time he found a milder and more friendly audience, until in 1945 he felt as if he must have come to his own funeral, so generous were the praises lavished on his "judgment" and "leadership" four years back. And for his part, as the years passed and the act was constantly renewed, he felt no anger or surprise that he had been so sharply quizzed in 1941. For truly this was a new departure, and in the broad view it was not the fight over the Lend-Lease Act but its eventual successful passage that deserved to be remembered in the record of the Seventy-seventh Congress.

CHAPTER XV

Valley of Doubt

1. A DIFFERENCE WITH THE PRESIDENT

THE Roosevelt administration in 1941 was conducting a struggle on two great fronts. One was the crisis in Europe, with its looming counterpart in the Far East; the other was the battleground of American opinion. During the months that followed the passage of the Lend-Lease Act, the tactics of combat on this second battleground became a point of significant divergence between Stimson and his chief.

To the President and all his leading advisers it was clear that the United States must take an ever increasing part in the resistance of the world against German and Japanese aggression. This could only be done with the approval and support of the bulk of the nation, and perhaps no nation of basically sound spirit has ever been more at a disadvantage in adjusting its thinking to a great crisis than the United States before Pearl Harbor. For the cheap and unworthy beliefs into which it was beguiled in the years between 1918 and 1939 the country paid a great penalty, and the full price has perhaps not even yet been exacted. For twenty years the people of the United States had turned their backs to the rest of the world; complacently they had listened to those who argued that their country could be an island to itself; by an overwhelming majority they had enforced a policy of isolation; it was their pressure that had produced legislation designed on the extraordinary theory that a single nation can keep itself out of war by passing laws. As the storm began to rise in 1931, Americans were indignant, as any decent people must be when they see aggression; they were indignant and inactive. Even in 1939 most of them believed that this war was not theirs. It is therefore not strange that in 1940 and 1941 the nation, turning at last to face the facts of life with action, kept thinking in terms of "measures short of war."

American thinking was thus confused, but Americans have no cause to be ashamed of the basic reason for the confusion, which was nothing more nor less than their hatred of war. Many much less noble feelings were involved in the complex emotional reaction called isolationism, but the ordinary American, the man in the great majority who detested the Nazi system and devoutly hoped for its defeat, held back from urging full participation in the struggle for the simple reason that he hated war. It was to this decent feeling that the more rabid isolationist leaders made indecent appeals, and to this decent feeling President Roosevelt deferred in constantly asserting that he was not advocating war, nor leading his country into an inevitable conflict.

Perhaps no public figure in the country had a clearer record of opposition to the whole cast of thinking that dominated the country between the two world wars than Stimson. He constantly denied that war could be avoided by isolation, and never doubted that the final issue of policy was always one of right and wrong, not peace and war. Yet even Stimson did not publicly preach to the American people the necessity of fighting; any such outright appeal would at once have lost him his hearers; always his statements were framed to preach rather the absolute necessity of preventing a Nazi triumph. Although constantly pressed for such an admission by isolationist members of Congress, Stimson never allowed himself to say that the final result of President Roosevelt's policy would be war.

When he first took office in 1940, and for several months afterward, Stimson himself did not honestly believe that war was the probable *immediate* outcome of the policy of helping the British. A declaration of war was certainly not imminent, nor even remotely possible in view of the temper of the people at the time. And of course the country had almost no weapons or troops. As he gradually became convinced that war was inevitable, he was bound to silence by the requirement of loyalty to his chief.

It was after the election, as the year was ending, that Stimson first noted in his diary his feeling that in the end the United States must fight. On December 16 after a meeting with Knox, General Marshall, and Admiral Stark he noted that "there was a basic agreement among us all. That in itself was very encouraging. All four agreed that this emergency could hardly be passed over without this country being drawn into the war eventually." (Diary, December 16, 1940) This belief Stimson continued to hold, ever more strongly, for the next twelve months. But in this period his thinking passed through several distinct stages.

In the first stage, which lasted more or less through the passage of the Lend-Lease Act, he believed that the President was leading the country into active measures just as fast as it was willing to go. He fully approved of the President's radio address of December 29, in which Mr. Roosevelt made entirely clear his decision not to permit the defeat of Great Britain.

Although Stimson felt certain that young Americans would not permanently be willing to remain "toolmakers for other nations which fight" when they had once appreciated the issue "between right and wrong," he admitted that the time was not ripe for the final step. "That cannot yet be broached but it will come in time I feel certain and the President went as far as he could at the present time." (Diary, December 29, 1940)

The second stage of Stimson's thinking is more complicated; it lasted from April, 1941, until the autumn. During this period it was his strong belief that the situation required more energetic and explicit leadership than President Roosevelt considered wise. There were two central reasons for this feeling. First, he was convinced that if the policy of sustaining Great Britain was to succeed, America must throw the major part of her naval strength into the Atlantic battle. There was no other way to insure the safe delivery of the lend-lease supplies which the nation had decided to send to the British; second, Stimson's whole concept of the duty of the Chief Executive centered on his obligation to act as the leader, and not merely the representative, of public opinion. Of the power of forthright leadership he had a higher opinion than the President. It will be helpful to consider each of these points in some detail.

The winter of 1940-1941 was a period of relative quiet in the European war; the principal objective of both sides was to prepare for the great campaigns anticipated in the following spring and summer. It was expected by the British and American leaders that Hitler would then make a final great effort to conquer the British Isles. Accordingly their major purpose was to insure the defense of the British home islands. The bulk of the burden fell to the British themselves; the task of the Americans was to help insure the safe delivery of a maximum volume of supplies of all kinds. But the constantly increasing rate of successful submarine attacks made it seem clear to Stimson, Marshall, and Knox, even in December, that the Royal Navy must have the assistance of American naval units in defending the Atlantic highway. No halfway measures would do. On December 19, "we had about the longest [Cabinet] meeting yet. The President brought up the question of the sinkings on the oceans of the traffic with Great Britain. The list of these sinkings is terrific, over four million tons so far—a terrific loss to civilization and to commerce, all over the world—and it is now very clear that England will not be able to hold out very much longer against it unless some defense is found. The President discussed various measures of getting new ships, taking the ships that were interned belonging to foreign nations on one side—building new ones on the other. I finally told him the story of my leaky bathtub . . . I told him that I thought it was a pretty high price to put so much new water into the bathtub instead of plugging the leaks, meaning by that that I thought we ought to forcibly stop the German submarines by our intervention. Well, he said he hadn't quite reached that yet." (Diary, December 19, 1940)

Through the winter Stimson's belief in the need for convoys grew constantly stronger, as did that of his military advisers and of the Navy Department. Toward the end of March, in a meeting with Knox, "We both agreed that the crisis is coming very soon and that convoying is the only solution and that it must come practically at once." (Diary, March 24, 1941)

The following day a meeting was held with the senior British officers in Washington. "They agreed, each one of them, that they could not, with present naval forces, assume the entire escort duty that is required to protect the convoys of munitions to Great Britain." (Diary, March 25, 1941)

The President was not less aware than Stimson and Knox of the vital importance of assisting the British in the Atlantic, but his approach to the problem was different. April 10 "was a very long day, mostly spent at the White House. . . . The President had evidently been thinking out things as far as he could to see how far he could go toward the direction [of] protection of the British Transport line. He made up his mind that it was too dangerous to ask the Congress for the power to convoy. He thought that if such a resolution was pressed now it would probably be defeated. On this point I am rather inclined to differ with him, provided that he took the lead vigorously and showed the reasons for it. Nevertheless, he had made a decision and it was an honest one. Therefore he is trying to see how far over in the direction of Great Britain we could get and how would be the best way to do it. We had the atlas out and by drawing a line midway between the westernmost bulge of Africa and the easternmost bulge of Brazil, we found that the median line between the two continents was at about longitude line 25. . . . His plan is then that we shall patrol the high seas west of this median line, all the way down as far as we can furnish the force to do it, and that the British will swing their convoys over westward to the west side of this line, so that they will be within our area. Then by the use of patrol planes and patrol vessels we can patrol and follow the convoys and notify them of any German raiders or German submarines that we may see and give them a chance to escape." (Diary, April 10, 1941)

When it came to the announcement of this patrol system, the President, in agreement with the majority of the Cabinet, chose to portray it as a principally defensive move. In a conference with Stimson and Knox on April 24, "He kept reverting to the fact that the force in the Atlantic was merely going to be a patrol to watch for any aggressor and to report that to America. I answered there, with a smile on my face, saying,

'But you are not going to report the presence of the German Fleet to the Americas. You are going to report it to the British Fleet.' I wanted him to be honest with himself. To me it seems a clearly hostile act to the Germans, and I am prepared to take the responsibility of it. He seems to be trying to hide it into the character of a purely reconnaissance action which it really is not." (Diary, April 24, 1941)

The patrol system proved no final answer to the requirements of the Atlantic, and gradually through the summer and autumn the President was driven to continuously stronger measures, acting each time considerably later than Stimson thought right. This divergence between the President and his Secretary of War on the method of entering the Atlantic contest is a clear specific instance of their general disagreement on the second great issue that occupied Stimson's mind at the time: *the President's duty to lead.*

Stimson had the highest respect for Franklin Roosevelt's political acumen, and at no time was he prepared to assert categorically that the President's method was wrong; all he could say was that it was emphatically not the method he himself would have chosen, and that in his opinion the President would have been an even greater politician if he had been a less artful one. This difference between the two men was basic to their natures. In this particular instance it will perhaps never be possible to say with certainty which was right; our task here is merely to present the issue as Stimson saw it.

The central point was stated to the President by Stimson in a private meeting on April 22. "I warned him in the beginning that I was going to speak very frankly and I hoped that he wouldn't feel that I did not have the real loyalty and affection for him that I did have. He reassured me on that point and then I went over the whole situation of the deterioration in the American political situation toward the war that has taken place since nothing happened immediately after the [Lend-Lease] victory. I cautioned him on the necessity of his taking the lead and that without a lead on his part it was useless to expect the people would voluntarily take the initiative in letting him know whether or not they would follow him if he did take the lead." (Diary, April 22, 1941)

Stimson was certain that if the President were himself to go to the country and say frankly that force was needed and he wanted the country's approval in using it, he would be supported. In contrast to this policy, the President's method seemed to him to be one of cautious waiting for circumstance to get the fight started for him. The President was determined to avoid a setback at the hands of the isolationists, and he seriously feared that any overboldness on his part would lead to such a defeat.

On May 6 Stimson delivered a radio address, the text of which had been seen and passed by the President, expressing his own general view of the crisis, so far as loyalty to the President permitted. He came out flatly for active naval assistance to the British, pointing out that any other course would mean the annulment of the objectives of the Lend-Lease Act. And in the last two paragraphs he stated as clearly as he dared his conviction that war was coming.

". . . I am not one of those who think that the priceless freedom of our country can be saved without sacrifice. It can not. That has not been the way by which during millions of years humanity has slowly and painfully toiled upwards towards a better and more humane civilization. The men who suffered at Valley Forge and won at Yorktown gave more than money to the cause of freedom.

"Today a small group of evil leaders have taught the young men of Germany that the freedom of other men and nations must be destroyed. Today those young men are ready to die for that perverted conviction. Unless we on our side are ready to sacrifice and, if need be, die for the conviction that the freedom of America must be saved, it will not be saved. Only by a readiness for the same sacrifice can that freedom be preserved."

There was no bitterness in Stimson's disagreement with the President. One day at a Cabinet meeting, "the President talked a little about his program of patrol and what he was planning to do, . . . and after narrating what had been done he said, 'Well, it's a step forward.' I at once said to him, 'Well, I hope you will keep on walking, Mr. President. Keep on walking.'

The whole Cabinet burst into a roar of laughter which was joined in by the President." (Diary, April 25, 1941)

Although it was one of the strongest, along with a speech by Secretary Knox, Stimson's speech of May 6 was only one of many by administration leaders in this period. Stimson was interested to discover that he and Knox were not the only members of the Cabinet who were disturbed at the President's apparent failure to follow up more rapidly his victory in the Lend-Lease Act. Jackson and Ickes were also worried. The President had his more cautious advisers, however, notably in the State Department. In Mr. Roosevelt's preparations for his own radio speech of May 27, he faced the contrasting advice of two camps, and although the final speech was much stronger than Stimson had feared it might be, it was not nearly so strong as he had hoped. The President firmly asserted the doctrine of the freedom of the seas, and made it clear that he intended to use "all additional measures necessary" to assure the delivery of supplies to Great Britain. He also declared an "unlimited national emergency," thus giving the administration somewhat broader powers in dealing with the crisis. But when, on the following day in his press conference, he allowed himself to say that this bold and vigorous speech did not mean that he planned to institute convoys, Stimson was deeply discouraged. He had himself urged a very different course; in a letter of May 24 to the President he had suggested that the President ask Congress for power "to use naval, air, and military forces of the United States" in the Atlantic battle.

Throughout June Stimson's anxiety increased, and in the first few days of July it reached its climax. On July 2 he made his only wholly pessimistic diary entry in five years. The Nazi attack on Russia had begun and was going altogether too well; meanwhile America seemed to have lost her way. "Altogether, tonight I feel more up against it than ever before. It is a problem whether this country has it in itself to meet such an emergency. Whether we are really powerful enough and sincere enough and devoted enough to meet the Germans is getting to be more and more of a real problem." (Diary, July 2, 1941)

The next day he wrote the following letter and memorandum to the President, who at the time was considering his message to Congress on the occupation of Iceland.

July 3, 1941

My Dear Mr. President:

My thoughts are deeply with you during these critical days. When the time comes for you to speak, my view is that you should speak to the Congress not by message but face to face and do it with personal and disarming frankness. You are such a master of such intercourse that I hesitate even to suggest the points that you should cover.

The main thing it seems to me is to point out how you have done your best to serve the cause of peace and how events have proved too strong for you. That in my opinion is the most appealing and persuasive line and the one which will produce the following of the whole nation. It is the course which all of your constituents have themselves been obliged to follow.

I enclose merely a memorandum of some of the points to be covered, making no attempt at phraseology.

Faithfully yours,

HENRY L. STIMSON

The President,
Hyde Park, New York

MEMORANDUM FOR ADDRESS TO CONGRESS

"I have sincerely hoped that we should not be drawn into this war. I have earnestly tried to avoid the use of force. I have labored with all my strength to secure a national defense, both naval and military, for this nation which would be sufficient to protect it when fighting alone against any combination of nations that might attack it. But my hope is becoming dim. The effort to avoid the use of force is proving ineffective. Our national defense is as yet far from complete. It has now become abundantly clear that, unless we add our every effort, physical and spiritual as well as material, to the efforts of those free nations who are still fighting for freedom in this world, we shall ourselves be brought to a situation where we shall be fighting alone at an enormously greater danger than we should encounter today with their aid."

The attitude suggested in this memorandum was rejected by the President, although the advice of such men as Stimson and Hopkins was again effective in offsetting more cautious counsel from other sources. In a meeting at the White House on July 6, Stimson told the President's advisers that "the President must be frank. Whether or not he was going to ask the Congress for action, he must in any event tell them exactly what he is doing and what he intends to do." (Diary, July 6, 1941) The President's message of July 7 did at least frankly state that he had moved American forces into Iceland and proposed to defend the sea communications between the United States and that island. In comparison with Stimson's own long draft, prepared on July 5 at Mr. Roosevelt's request, the President's message lacked emphasis on the central and controlling fact that Iceland was important principally as a way station on the North Atlantic route from America to Great Britain. It also omitted any intimation of war as imminent. The President was still content to build his case mainly on the defense of the Western Hemisphere, believing that this was a more palatable argument to the people, and one less subject to violent attack from the isolationists.

This effort in July was Stimson's last active attempt to bring the President to his way of thinking. It was clear that Mr. Roosevelt did not agree with him, and Stimson was inclined to believe after July that the President was so far committed to his own more gradual course that nothing could change him.

Moreover, as the summer wore on, the kind of lifting leadership which Stimson desired became less possible. 'The chance for a trumpet call for a battle to save freedom throughout the world had been sunk in a quibble over the extent of defense and the limits of the Western Hemisphere.' Meanwhile, what words might have accomplished earlier was being achieved by events; one of our patrolling destroyers was attacked, and the President publicly announced that the fleet would shoot on sight Axis vessels in the western Atlantic. While the President accomplished his object of having the war come to him, it should be observed that by this policy he in effect surrendered the initiative to the Nazis. By waiting for Nazi attacks on American vessels the President left it to them to choose their time to fight.

Looking back on this period Stimson could not avoid a comparison between Franklin Roosevelt and his distinguished cousin Theodore. From what he knew of both men, he was forced to believe that in the crisis of 1941 T.R. would have done a better and more clean-cut job than was actually done. Equally with his cousin he would have appreciated the true meaning of the Nazi threat, and there can be no higher praise, for no statesman in the world saw and described the Nazi menace more truly than Franklin Roosevelt. T.R.'s advantage would have been in his natural boldness, his firm conviction that where he led, men would follow. He would, Stimson felt sure, have been able to brush aside the contemptible little group of men who wailed of "warmongers," and in the blunt strokes of a poster painter he would have demonstrated the duty of Americans in a world issue. Franklin Roosevelt was not made that way. With unequaled political skill he could pave the way for any given specific step, but in so doing he was likely to tie his own hands for the future, using honeyed and consoling words that would return to plague him later.

The frame of mind of the American people under this treatment was graphically shown in a Gallup Poll at the end of April, 1941. To three questions the public gave three remarkable answers. Of those expressing an opinion, (1) nearly three-fourths would favor entering the war "if it appeared certain that there was no other way to defeat Germany and Italy," (2) four-fifths thought the United States would sooner or later enter the war, (3) four-fifths were opposed to immediate entry into the war.

The most striking fact about this result was that in the considered view of the leaders of the American Government, and also by facts publicly known, it was already clear that "there was no other way to defeat Germany and Italy" than by American entry into the war. The trouble was that no one in authority had said so.

In Stimson's view these answers exactly reflected the leadership of the President. The first answer showed how far he and others had succeeded in giving the American people a clear understanding of the fascist danger. The second answer reflected a somewhat fatalistic expectation that just as America had participated in every general European conflict for over two hundred years, she would probably get into this one too. The third answer, showing opposition to immediate entry, was the direct result of the fact that no responsible leader, and particularly not the President, had explicitly stated that that was necessary; on the contrary, the President in particular had repeatedly said that it was *not* necessary.

To Stimson it always seemed that the President directed his arguments altogether too much toward his vocal but small isolationist opposition, and not toward the people as a whole. By his continuous assertion that war was *not* a likely result of his policy, he permitted the American people to think themselves into a self-contradictory frame of mind. As Stimson constantly pointed out at the time, only the President could take the lead in a warlike policy. Only he had the right and duty to lead his people in this issue.

If Mr. Roosevelt had been himself a believer in neutrality, as McKinley had been in 1898 or Wilson for so long in 1916, it would have been natural that effective pressure for action should develop in private places. But as the proclaimed and acknowledged champion of the anti-Axis cause, he was necessarily its spearhead in policy, and without word from him the American people could not be expected to consider all-out action necessary.

There are those who will maintain that this explanation of Stimson's feelings merely confirms their view that Franklin Roosevelt dishonestly pulled the American people into a war they never should have fought.[1] Nothing could be farther from Stimson's own position, and it should be emphasized that if this charge is to be leveled against Mr. Roosevelt, it

[1] Quite aside from all other evidence, any argument that the American people were duped is of course wholly refuted by the Gallup Poll quoted above.

must in some degree be leveled at Stimson too. For the difference of policy between him and the President was one of degree, not of kind. Stimson saw war coming in December, 1940; it was not until April, 1941, that he began to feel that the President could successfully preach war to the people—there are always times, in politics, when it is impossible to speak with entire frankness about the future, as all but the most self-righteous will admit. *The essential difference between Stimson and the President was in the value they set on candor as a political weapon.* And as Stimson himself fully recognized, it was a good deal easier to advocate his policy, as Secretary of War, than to carry it out, as President. Certainly the consequences of failure in a bold course would have been extremely serious—no one can say whether the United States could have surmounted the reaction in feeling which would have set in if any proposal by the President had been roundly beaten in Congress or thoroughly disapproved by the people. On the other hand, it was equally true that the impasse into which America had thought herself in 1941 might have continued indefinitely if that had been the will of the Axis, and if this had happened, the President would have had to shoulder a large share of the blame. It did not happen, and all that America lost by her failure to enter the war earlier was time. But time in war means treasure and lives, and through the summer of 1941 Stimson was constantly faced with concrete examples of the losses incurred by delay.

2. THE PRICE OF INDECISION

The Secretary of War was not the only one who suffered from the difficulties of the strange condition, neither peaceful nor wholly warlike, in which the United States found herself in the latter half of 1941. The entire Army suffered, and it was not surprising that during those months there was a problem of "morale" among the troops. The men drafted in the first year of Selective Service faced many discouragements that the later millions did not know in nearly the same degree. Equipment was extremely scanty, and training programs were incomplete. But most of all, the new Army faced the problem that no one could tell it in clear and compelling terms exactly what it was training for, and the bulk of the selectees came to regard their year of service as something to be finished as quickly and painlessly as possible. The act required that they train for twelve months; they would do it, and then go home.

Probably no obviously necessary measure ever passed Congress by so close a margin as the bill to extend the term of service for selectees which was enacted in August, 1941. When Stimson first discussed this bill with leaders of Congress, they were almost unanimous in their assertion that it could never pass. They turned out to be wrong, by a margin of one vote; for this the country could thank George Marshall, who undertook the main burden of advocating and explaining the bill. Without it, the Army would by December 7 have been largely disorganized by discharges and plans for discharges—the meaning of such a disorganization can best be understood by recalling what happened to the American Army when it began to restore its soldiers to civilian life in 1945.

What made this measure so distasteful to Congressmen was that it seemed to involve an unexpected change in a contract between the selectees and the government. The original act clearly stated that the twelve-month term of service could be extended "whenever the Congress has declared that the national interest is imperiled," but this clause had not been emphasized at the time, and Congressmen did not wish to take the onus of making the required declaration. In fact many of them hoped by inaction to force the President to do by trickery what they themselves refused to do openly. On August 7, Representative Walter G. Andrews, of New York, came to see Stimson. Andrews, "a very good man," and a supporter of the bill for extension, "fished out an opinion which he said the opponents were relying on which held that technically, although not morally, the President would have the power to extend the term of service of each man himself after his one year expired by passing him into the Reserve and then calling him out from the Reserve. This is one of those finespun technical interpretations which possibly is legally correct (I think I can say probably) and yet which is contrary to the intention of the Congress at the time when the statutes last summer were made and I am sure it would arouse great resentment against the President if he followed that. Yet that is just what these cowards in the Congress are trying to do. They want to avoid the responsibility themselves . . . and to throw it on the President and then, if he should take this interpretation, they would be the first ones to jump on him as violating the real purpose of the law." (Diary, August 7, 1941) Stimson himself had felt on several occasions that Mr. Roosevelt might well be more frank with Congress than he was, but certainly in the face of this sort of pusillanimous hostility it was not easy for the President to be trustful.

The battle over this bill involved Stimson in a particularly unpleasant clash with Senator Burton K. Wheeler, the man who had described the Lend-Lease Act as a measure designed to plow under every fourth American boy. Under Wheeler's frank, a million antiwar postcards were sent out in July, containing material designed to show the folly of the President's policy. Some of these cards were delivered to soldiers, and in their anger Stimson and the President decided that the former should make a strong statement. Stimson told his press conference that "this comes very near the line of subversive activities against the United States—if not treason." To this accusation Wheeler hotly replied, and he was able to demonstrate that no copies of his card had been sent intentionally to any soldiers. Against the advice of most of his staff Stimson decided to apologize. It was not a pleasant decision, for the extraordinary bitterness of Wheeler's whole course in 1941 had reached one of its highest points in his attack on Stimson. After making the apology "my mind felt very much better," and the surprised and friendly reaction to his statement in the press confirmed his feeling that he had done the right thing. Even Wheeler seemed to think the apology creditable.

As finally passed, the Draft Extension Act provided for the retention in service of all selectees, National Guardsmen, and Reserves for an additional period of not more than eighteen months beyond the year originally specified. On August 15, the day after its passage, Stimson delivered a radio address to the Army in an effort to explain the reasons for the bill. So far as he could, he rehearsed the nature of the danger facing the country. As it was still the government's policy to discuss the peril in terms of defense, his speech was probably not very effective in its purpose, and although it was sound enough, Stimson thought it "poor" and "defensive" when he read it over after the war. But in 1941 nothing short of a radical change in the country's thinking could fully have reconciled drafted soldiers to an extension of their term of involuntary service. The reports of low morale were disturbing, but the root of the difficulty could not be removed by any action of the War Department. "The trouble has come from the fact that we have [been] trying to train an army for war without any declaration of war by Congress and with the country not facing the danger before it." (Diary, September 15, 1941)

The aspect of morale usually regarded by the public as most important was the provision of adequate facilities for the relaxation and recreation of the soldier off duty. The importance of this undertaking Stimson never denied, and particularly in 1941, while the country was at peace, he pressed for speed and co-ordination in its handling. In Frederick Osborn he found an able and imaginative administrator for these matters, and Osborn's services to the Army constantly expanded in scope throughout the war. But nothing in Stimson's nature or experience led him to believe that the morale of an army could be measured by the number of its recreation halls and canteens. In his report for 1941 to the President he called attention to this curious but widely held delusion, which seemed to him wholly at variance with the best American tradition. ". . . At the same time that we leave no stone unturned for the protection and welfare of our soldiers, we must not forget that it is not the American ideal to bribe our young men into the patriotic service of their country by thoughts of comfort and amusement. Moving pictures and soda water fountains have their places, but endurance of hardship, sacrifice, competition, and the knowledge that he is strong and able to inflict blows and overcome obstacles are the factors that in the last analysis give the soldier his morale. And such is the growing morale of our present Army."

Thus Stimson emphasized, in the autumn of 1941, the one finally critical element in the morale of the individual soldier.

It is his skill and self-confidence as a fighting man that is central, not his comforts. His morale depends finally on his military training and his confidence in his military leaders. And in 14,000 miles of inspections Stimson had already seen enough to be sure that in this most important single matter the Army was sound as ever. In maneuvers in Tennessee and New York, Washington and North Carolina he had seen the new divisions, and many of the new commanders. The new Army was starting right, and public disturbance over the morale of the troops never concerned Stimson as much as critics thought it should; he remained certain that as soon as it was in action, the Army would have no basic problem of morale. To one worried friend he remarked that the day would come when the country would draw its own strength of heart from the spirit of the armed forces, and in the years that followed he found this prophecy constantly confirmed.

The national indecision which produced anxiety in Stimson and a serious problem of morale in the Army had its effect too in the field of production. In three areas Stimson and Patterson found themselves at a disadvantage in their constant campaign for more and better equipment.

The first was the government itself. Even within the Army it required civilian insistence to insure that procurement should be based on a more generous objective than merely the exact tables of equipment of projected units. In the Government as a whole the President continued in his refusal to appoint a single executive head for all production and procurement problems. Severely hampered by limitations on his authority, Knudsen was not able to instill in all his manufacturers the necessary sense of urgency. In September the President superimposed on his existing creation an agency called SPAB, the Supply, Priorities, and Allocations Board, with Donald Nelson as executive director. At the time this seemed a step forward, since it did at least give a single agency more power than Knudsen and his competitors in other places had had, but it soon proved to be only one more unsatisfactory makeshift.

Manufacturers remained cautious—not all of them, of

course, but many. Neither industry nor government was ready for a thoroughgoing conversion from peace to war; it continued to be the general practice merely to add military production to the ordinary civilian business of the country, and only the partial attention of such great industries as those making automobiles and rubber and electric machines was given to military production.

The third and as usual the most explosive source of difficulty was labor. Stimson's general view of the labor problem in a time of national emergency is discussed in a later chapter. It is enough here to remark that a united and patriotic response by workingmen depends on the same factors as the attitude of soldiers, government officials, and businessmen, and during the six months before Pearl Harbor there were more strikes and labor stoppages than there would have been if the country had been actively in the war; the climactic event in this period was a coal strike led by John L. Lewis in November, at a time when every standard of good sense and loyalty demanded full production in the mines. Stimson believed in firmness in dealing with strikes that affected the national defense—in this respect he found the President overcautious; but actually the basic difficulty was the absence of the war spirit.

On August 19, in a talk with Harry Hopkins, Stimson summarized his feelings on the American production program. "Hopkins asserted that the United States was not producing munitions as rapidly as it could. I said that was undoubtedly true but that it was making them as rapidly as I thought they could be made in the light of (1) the fact that there was no objective like a war to stimulate production; (2) the complexity of the organization which did not have any single responsible head; and (3) the 'persuasive' handling of labor. I enumerated the different strikes that were now retarding production. I told him that until those three items were changed he could not expect full production." (Diary, August 19, 1941)

CHAPTER XVI

The War Begins

1. PEARL HARBOR

THE Japanese attack on Pearl Harbor which ended the months of indecision has been the subject of more comment and investigation than any other military action in American history. The extraordinary damage there inflicted by the Japanese, at negligible cost to themselves, made the attack a shocking blow not only at American power but at American pride as well. Stimson was as much dismayed as anyone by the incompetence of the American defense at Pearl Harbor, but he also felt that in the hue and cry over the opening engagement of the war insufficient attention was given to the series of events which preceded it. The problem faced by the United States in the Pacific during 1941 was one of unusual complexity, and in the policy pursued by the American Government there was much that deserved close study, for the Pacific crisis was typical of the difficulties faced by a democracy in dealing with dictatorial aggression. The principal responsibility for the execution of American policy in this period rested with President Roosevelt and Secretary Hull. The position we have now to make clear is Stimson's own, and as such it will vary in some particulars from that of the responsible officers, but these very differences may serve to illustrate the nature of the problem presented to the administration.

The primary and overriding principle of American foreign policy when Stimson entered the Roosevelt Cabinet was unyielding opposition to aggression. It was this single, simple, solid rule that was the final touchstone of policy, however much it might be necessary to give or take in specific instances. We have already seen that by December, 1940, Stimson and others in the Government were persuaded that in the end this principle must lead to war. The world was a house divided, and the stand taken by America must in the end be forcefully upheld.

The second great general principle was that the decisive theater of the world conflict was in Europe. In June, 1941, the already dominant importance of this theater was increased by the German attack on Soviet Russia. If the Germans should quickly conquer Russia they would be vastly strengthened. It was the estimate of War Department Intelligence officers, at first, that the campaign could last only one to three months. On the other hand, if the Nazis should be stopped by the Russians and eventually defeated by a coalition of anti-Nazi powers, the world-wide conspiracy of aggression would be fatally weakened. Throughout 1941, therefore, the principal efforts of the American Government were directed toward the support of those resisting aggression in Europe, and with this policy Stimson heartily agreed. His only serious differences with the President arose out of his conviction that America was destined to play a major fighting role in the war. On this ground, from September onward, he strongly urged the claims of the American Air Forces to a larger share in the American output of military aircraft. Admitting that planes allotted to the United States might not be immediately useful in combat, he argued that "it is better for her [Britain] to have in the world a potent, well-armed, friendly American air force than a few additional planes."[1]

It was against the background of these two major American postulates that the Japanese crisis developed. The exact course of that development it was impossible to foretell because the problem of Japan was necessarily subordinate to the larger questions of aggression in general and Nazi Germany in particular. At different times there existed in the Government a number of different views as to the proper line of policy toward the Japanese.

When he arrived in Washington in 1940, Stimson found

[1] Memorandum to the President, October 21, 1941.

the administration engaged in a line of policy well described by the President as "babying them along." Making no secret of its view that the Japanese militarists were morally no better than the Nazis, and refusing absolutely to modify its cordial relations with China, the American Government was nevertheless still permitting the export of war materials to Japan, although finished munitions were under a "moral embargo" which had been established in 1938 and 1939. Both the President and the State Department were somewhat sensitive to criticism of this policy, since they were as well aware as their critics of the wickedness of the Japanese. Their object was simply to prevent the development of a war crisis in the Pacific at a time when the United States was both unprepared and preoccupied by the Nazis.

Since 1937, when the Japanese attacked China, Stimson had been urging, as a private citizen, an embargo on all American trade with Japan, and this attitude he carried with him into the Cabinet. Recognizing the peril of a premature showdown with Japan, he nevertheless believed that the effect of an embargo would be to check and weaken the Japanese, rather than to drive them into open war. His basic feeling, until more than a year after he entered the administration, was that the Japanese would not willingly take the suicidal step of making war on the United States. The folly of such a course had been convincingly described to him by trustworthy Japanese at the London Naval Conference ten years earlier, and although he did not trust the Japanese leaders of 1940 and 1941 any more than he trusted Hitler, he did not accurately appreciate their lack of prudence.

He therefore argued that the best possibility of a successful diplomatic adjustment with Japan lay in a policy of the utmost firmness. In October, 1940, the embargo on exports to Japan was materially extended, and in support of a still more vigorous policy Stimson wrote a memorandum pointing out how Japan had yielded before to American firmness, in her withdrawal from Shantung and Siberia in 1919 and her acceptance of naval inferiority in 1921. The moral of these events, he wrote, was that "Japan has historically shown that she can misinterpret a pacifistic policy of the United States for weakness. She has also historically shown that when the United States indicates by clear language and bold actions that she intends to carry out a clear and affirmative policy in the Far East, Japan will yield to that policy even though it conflicts with her own Asiatic policy and conceived interests. For the United States now to indicate either by soft words or inconsistent actions that she has no such clear and definite policy towards the Far East will only encourage Japan to bolder action." (Memorandum, October 2, 1940) The theory of this memorandum was not borne out by events. When the United States at last became genuinely firm, the Japanese did not yield; whether they would have yielded if Stimson's policy had been tried earlier it is impossible to say. In retrospect he was inclined to think that even by 1940 it was too late to dissuade them, by any line of diplomacy. To be certainly effective a firm policy would have had to begin much earlier, and such a course would have involved military preparations that would hardly have been greeted with favor by the American people.

The line of policy suggested by Stimson and others was predicated on the assumption that the Japanese, however wicked their intentions, would have the good sense not to get involved in war with the United States. The line of policy of the President and Mr. Hull was based rather on the importance of avoiding such a war, and on the admittedly faint hope that Japanese expansion could at least be restrained by some sort of diplomatic *modus vivendi*; Secretary Hull even dared to believe in the possibility of a complete reversal of Japanese policy; to strengthen this possibility he constantly pointed out to the Japanese the advantages to be gained by a realignment in the Pacific under which the Japanese would discard their expansionist dreams in favor of co-operative participation in a general development of peaceful trade. In such hopes Stimson was unable to join; his own attempts at persuasion had failed in far more hopeful circumstances in 1931, and he feared that the attempt to win the Japanese now could only lead to a further misunderstanding of American intentions. It is only fair to add that Hull himself put the possibility of success at one in ten.

In May, 1941, there arose an issue of grand strategy which clearly illustrated the divergence of opinion on Japan within the Government. This was the question of the movement of the United States Fleet from Hawaii to the Atlantic. With their eyes firmly fixed on the all-important struggle to keep open the Atlantic sea lane to Britain, Stimson, Knox, and Marshall became convinced that the bulk of the fleet should be moved to the Atlantic. This proposal was opposed by the State Department, and not viewed with any great sympathy by the admirals of the Navy. On the side of those urging the move it was argued that the European theater was the only one of decisive importance; that the fleet at Hawaii was no real threat to Japan since the Japanese clearly understood that we should never use it offensively without ample warning; that it had little or no defensive value there, since it was powerless to protect the Philippines, while the defense of Hawaii itself against invasion could easily be secured by land and air forces; that, so far from encouraging the Japanese in their expansion, the use of the fleet in the Atlantic would be a clear sign of the American intention to take active measures against aggression, since the Atlantic was the only ocean in which the American Navy could at the time find active employment. To put the fleet into action would prove the United States to be in earnest.

In opposition to the proposal were two major arguments. Hull insisted that the faint chance of an honorable diplomatic settlement with the Japanese was worth pursuing; he believed that any such chance would vanish with the removal from the Pacific of America's principal striking force. Further, he and his advisers believed that the disappearance of the American fleet from the Pacific would be taken by the Japanese as a go-ahead signal for their southward expansion; from such expansion there might well result a situation in which the United States would be forced to fight. In these opinions the Navy under Admiral Stark concurred, at least to some degree; the Pacific Ocean had for years been the Navy's assumed area of combat.

It is worth noting that in this disagreement both sides believed that the Japanese had no present intention of attacking the United States; the central disagreement was on the degree

of restraint imposed on her other ambitions by the United
States Fleet at Hawaii. In the light of later events it may be
argued either that the Japanese laid their basic plans without
any fear of the fleet or that they regarded its neutralization as
an essential prerequisite to their general attack. Certainly its
presence did not in the end deter them, but it may be considered doubtful whether its active employment against the
Nazis would have been any greater deterrent. So far as Stimson individually is concerned, the core of his position was
simply that in the fight against the Nazis no handy weapon
should be left inactive; his preoccupation with Europe made
him more disposed than ever to minimize the danger from
Japan. He simply could not believe that she would dare to
attack southward so long as both the British Empire and the
United States remained major unbeaten naval powers, and in
this, of course, he was wrong—he had been more nearly right
in 1932, when he had foreseen war as the inevitable final
result of Japanese militarism.

The result of the disagreement within the Government was
compromise; the President decided that three battleships and
an appropriate supporting force should be transferred to the
Atlantic. It does not seem that anyone was wholly pleased by
this arrangement, which, however, had the quite fortuitous
effect of reducing by three the number of capital vessels available as Japanese targets on December 7. The President considered the subject closed, and Stimson swallowed his disappointment.

During July and August, 1941, the whole attitude of the
American Government toward Japan was changed. The advance of the Japanese into southern Indo-China, at a time
when conversations looking toward better relations were being
conducted by Hull with the Japanese Ambassador, made it
finally clear that Japan intended to expand her holdings in
southeast Asia whenever and wherever such expansion was
feasible. An abrupt end was put to a line of American policy
which Stimson at the time considered akin to the "appease-
ment" of Neville Chamberlain. On July 26, by freezing Japanese assets, the President completed the embargo he had been
constructing so cautiously and gradually for three years. On

August 12, after a wholly unsatisfactory exchange of notes between the President and the Japanese, Hull made it plain to Stimson and Knox that the situation in the Pacific might at any time develop into a military and not a diplomatic problem.

By a curious coincidence there occurred in this same month of August an important change in the thinking of the General Staff with regard to the defense of the Philippine Islands. For twenty years it had been considered that strategically the Philippines were an unprotected pawn, certain to be easily captured by the Japanese in the early stages of any war between the United States and Japan. Now it began to seem possible to establish in the Philippines a force not only sufficient to hold the Islands but also, and more important, strong enough to make it foolhardy for the Japanese to carry their expansion southward through the China Sea. For this change of view there were two leading causes. One was the contagious optimism of General Douglas MacArthur, who in July had been recalled to active duty in the United States Army after five years of service in building and training the new Philippine Army. MacArthur knew the current situation in the Philippines better than any other American officer, and he was surprisingly hopeful about the capabilities of his forces.

The second reason for the new view of the Philippines was the sudden and startling success of American Flying Fortresses in operations from the British Isles. Stimson found his military advisers swinging to the belief that with an adequate force of these heavy bombers the Philippines could become a self-sustaining fortress capable of blockading the China Sea by air power. The supposed advantage of this new weapon was that it could be delivered in force to the Philippines in spite of Japanese control of the surrounding areas.

Both the optimism of General MacArthur and the establishment of an effective force of B-17's were conditional upon time. Thus the new hope for a strong Philippine defense had the effect of making the War Department a strong proponent of maximum delay in bringing the Japanese crisis to a climax. Where before Stimson and Marshall had relied on the general Japanese unwillingness to start a war with the English-speaking powers, they now hoped to have the much stronger reliance of an effective military force on the spot. In their eyes the Philippines suddenly acquired a wholly new importance and were given the highest priority on all kinds of military equipment. As to how much time would be needed, estimates varied. On October 6 Stimson told Hull that "we needed three months to secure our position."

As it turned out, the State Department was able to get only two months of delay after this October conversation, but Stimson considered that Hull did all that he possibly could, and he was at no time critical of the State Department's inability to string out the negotiations any further. The defense of the Philippines was important, but it was certainly less important than the maintenance intact of basic principles of American policy in respect to China, and Stimson was certain that nothing short of an important compromise of these principles could have delayed the Japanese attack.

In the detailed negotiations of October and November Stimson had no active part. The beginnings of effective reinforcement of the Philippines rekindled briefly his hope that Japan might be persuaded not to force the issue; this new and concrete threat might do what a merely potential threat had failed to do. But in the latter part of November even this cautious hope began to disappear; it became apparent that a showdown could not be long delayed.

On November 26 Hull restated to the Japanese the basic American principles for peace in the Pacific. So deep was the gulf between these principles and the evidently fixed intentions of the Japanese Government that on the following morning Hull told Stimson, "I have washed my hands of it, and it is now in the hands of you and Knox—the Army and the Navy." (Diary, November 27, 1941) On the same day the War and Navy Departments sent war warnings to all United States forces in the Pacific.

During the following days it was learned that a large Japanese force was proceeding southward by sea from Shanghai. News of this force strengthened the conviction of the American Government that the next Japanese move would be an extension southward of the venture already begun in Indo-

China. The target of the force might be Thailand, Singapore, Malaya, the Philippines, or the Dutch East Indies. In any of these cases except an attack on the Philippines it would be necessary for the United States to make a decision as to whether or not to join in resistance to the Japanese advance. The whole Cabinet shared the President's view that the country would support a decision in favor of war.

Thus during the first week of December the attention of the American Government was directed at the Southwest Pacific, and the problems faced by the administration seemed to be two: first, to make it clear to the Japanese that aggression beyond a designated point in that area would mean war with the United States, and second, in the event of such aggression, to insure the support of the American people for a decision to fight Japan. It was still considered unlikely that the Japanese would begin their next set of moves by an open attack on the United States, and it seemed even less probable that any such attack would be directed at the United States Fleet in Hawaii.

The administration paid the Japanese the compliment of assuming that they would take the course best calculated to embarrass their potential enemies. It seemed obvious that by limiting their overt attack to such areas as Thailand or the Dutch East Indies or even Singapore they could insure a serious division of opinion among Americans. Although Mr. Roosevelt and his advisers hoped and believed that the country could be persuaded to fight in such a case, they knew that it would reproduce in the Pacific, and in waters half a world distant from the United States, the same questions that had been presented by Nazi aggression in Europe. There could be no assurance that what had been debated indecisively for eighteen months in one case would be determined overnight in the other. In Stimson's opinion the Japanese aggressors made a serious miscalculation when in this crisis of 1941 they did not try to divide their foes by piecemeal attacks on one of them at a time.

On December 7, at 2:00 P.M., "the President called me up on the telephone and in a rather excited voice to ask me 'Have you heard the news?' I said, 'Well, I have heard the telegrams which have been coming in about the Japanese advances in the

Gulf of Siam.' He said, 'Oh no. I don't mean that. They have attacked Hawaii. They are now bombing Hawaii.' Well, that was an excitement indeed." (Diary, December 7, 1941)

When Stimson recovered from his astonishment at the Japanese choice of the greatest American base as a point of attack, he was filled with confident hope of a major victory; it seemed to him probable that the alerted forces at Hawaii could cause very heavy damage to the attacking Japanese. It was not until evening that he learned how great a tactical success the Japanese had achieved in their strategic folly. The military party in Japan had undertaken a war which could have only one final result, but they had certainly made a good beginning.

The disaster at Pearl Harbor raised questions of responsibility, and even guilt, which occupied the attention of a half-dozen boards and committees during and after the war. That so great and unexpected a defeat should be investigated seemed to Stimson entirely natural and proper, but he was frequently irritated by the strange conclusions reached by some of the investigators. The Army's own Pearl Harbor Board so far misconceived the nature of military responsibility that it pointed a finger of blame at General Marshall himself, on the curious theory that the Chief of Staff is directly at fault whenever one of his subordinate staff officers fails to do a thorough job. Only General Marshall himself was seriously upset by this preposterous charge, but Stimson regarded it as outrageous that the reputation of the Army's finest soldier should be unnecessarily subjected to attack, and the answers which Stimson himself was forced to prepare for this and other accusations seemed to him hardly the best conceivable wartime employment of a Cabinet officer's energy.

His own view of Pearl Harbor was fully set forth during these investigations and need not be repeated here in detail. He was satisfied that the major responsibility for the catastrophe rested on the two officers commanding on the spot— Admiral Kimmel and General Short. It was true that the War and Navy Departments were not fully efficient in evaluating the information available to them, and of course it was also true that no one in Washington had correctly assessed

Japanese intentions and capabilities. Stimson like everyone else was painfully surprised by the skill and boldness displayed by all branches of the Japanese war machine from December 7 onward. Further, Washington had not adequately appreciated the importance of keeping its field commanders fully informed. "The novelty of the imminence of war and the fact that our outpost commanders were untried in their positions now indicate that more details and repeated emphasis would have been a safer policy."[2] In so far as these later views were not matched by foresight in 1941, Stimson along with his associates missed a chance to mitigate or prevent the Pearl Harbor disaster. The men in Washington did not foresee this attack, and they did not take the additional actions suggested by a retrospective view. But the basic fact remained: the officers commanding at Hawaii had been alerted like other outpost commanders; unlike other outpost commanders they proved on December 7 to be far from alert. It did not excuse them that Washington did not anticipate that they would be attacked. Washington's belief was based, among other things, on its quite natural assumption that they would be alert. It was on this assumption that Stimson and others based their initial satisfaction with the news that the Japanese had dared to attack Pearl Harbor. "The outpost commander," Stimson pointed out to the Joint Committee of Congress, "is like a sentinel on duty in the face of the enemy. His fundamental duties are clear and precise. . . . It is not the duty of the outpost commander to speculate or rely on the possibilities of the enemy attacking at some other outpost instead of his own. It is his duty to meet him at his post at any time and to make the best possible fight that can be made against him with the weapons with which he has been supplied."[2] In this duty the commanders in Hawaii failed.

Much of the discussion of Pearl Harbor was confused and embittered by a preposterous effort to demonstrate that President Roosevelt and his advisers had for some unfathomable but nefarious reason "planned it that way." There was also a marked disposition to believe that men friendly to the President were hiding something of crucial importance. Stimson

[2] Statement to the Joint Committee of Congress. March 21, 1946.

for one submitted without reservation every relevant passage
from his private diary, and in addition wrote two long statements. In the end the prolonged and exhaustive investigation
by a Joint Committee of Congress produced a majority report
which Stimson considered both fair and intelligent. While it
gave him, with the President and other high officials, a general
approval for discharging their responsibilities with "distinction, ability, and foresight," it by no means exonerated War
Department officials, and the responsibility which it inferen-
tially placed on him, as head of the War Department, he was
quite willing to accept. The twisted and malicious views of
the minority report he considered sufficiently answered by
the majority.

Even on December 7, in the midst of the first overwhelming
reports of disaster, Stimson never doubted that the central
importance of the Pearl Harbor attack lay not in the tactical
victory carried off by the Japanese but in the simple fact
that the months of hesitation and relative inaction were ended
at a stroke. No single blow could have been better calculated
to put an end to American indecision. "When the news first
came that Japan had attacked us, my first feeling was of relief
that the indecision was over and that a crisis had come in a
way which would unite all our people. This continued to be
my dominant feeling in spite of the news of catastrophes which
quickly developed. For I feel that this country united has
practically nothing to fear, while the apathy and divisions
stirred up by unpatriotic men have been hitherto very discouraging." (Diary, December 7, 1941)

In the attack on Pearl Harbor a curtain of fire was lowered
over the problems and anxieties of the preceding months. No
longer would the secret war plans of the Army's General Staff
be freely published by a major newspaper—as the Chicago
Tribune had done three days before Pearl Harbor; no longer
would it be a question whether Congress would permit American vessels to carry arms to Britain—by a narrow margin,
in mid-November, the Neutrality Act had been amended to
permit such action; no longer would the administration be
faced with the awful task of producing on a wartime scale
with a peacetime attitude; no longer would there be any foolish

doubts about the morale of the American armed forces; no longer would the loud and bitter voices of a small minority be raised in horror at every forward step to block aggression. The die was cast, and Stimson knew that America at war would have unity, courage, strength, and will.

In the four years that followed he suffered often from the cares of wartime office, and over every day was cast the growing shadow of the casualty lists. But to a man whose temperament was that of a soldier, these things were easier to bear than the fearful former sight of America half-asleep. On December 7, 1941, for the first time in more than twenty years, the United States of America was placed in a position to take unified action for the peace and security of herself and the world. The Japanese attack at Pearl Harbor restored to America the freedom of action she had lost by many cunning bonds of her own citizens' contriving. The self-imprisoned giant was set free.

2. MISSION OF DELAY

"All students of history know that every war has three periods . . . the period of the 'onset,' the period of the 'drag' (when the war begins to weigh on the nations involved), and the 'finish.' During the first period it is inevitable that the free government, the government which depends on the consent of the people, . . . should be at a distinct disadvantage." Thus Stimson to his press conference on December 11, 1941. The American people and their leaders were suddenly face to face with the humiliating fact of defeat, and the testing prospect of still further unavoidable reverses. The galvanic awakening of the nation after Pearl Harbor made final victory seem certain, but the "distinct disadvantage" of the present could not be removed overnight.

It quickly became apparent that the skill and boldness shown by the Japanese at Pearl Harbor were not a single isolated phenomenon. At Guam and Wake, Singapore and Hong Kong the enemy victories began. On December 10 came the first landing in the Philippines, to be followed in twelve days by a much larger landing, in the classically anticipated area of the

Lingayen Gulf. Everywhere the enemy's advance was unex-
pectedly successful, and with the destruction of the *Prince of
Wales* and the *Repulse*—again on December 10—it became
apparent that in their technique as well as their power the
Japanese were for the time being masters of the Southwest
Pacific.

For Stimson as Secretary of War the point of focal interest
was the Philippines. It was quickly apparent that the hopes
of the previous autumn could not be realized; there would
be no successful defense of the Philippines by air power.
The preparations had not been completed; the Japanese were
too strong; most important of all, there had been no adequate
realization of the degree to which air power is dependent on
other things than unsupported airplanes. American planes by
scores were lost on the ground, in the Philippines as in Hawaii.
Nor could there be any major reinforcement through the air,
which, like the sea, came swiftly under Japanese control. Thus
the defense of the Philippines became once more the desperate
and losing struggle which had been forecast in the planning
of earlier years.

Thus coldly stated, the problem was one which the American
high command might have been expected to accept regretfully
as insoluble, writing off the Philippines and preparing to
defend the defensible. This point of view was not absent from
the General Staff, and it was forcefully urged by some naval
leaders. But neither strategically nor politically was the problem so simple as it appeared. Strategically it was of very great
importance that the Army in the Philippines should prolong
its resistance to the limit. Politically it was still more important
that this defense be supported as strongly as possible, for neither
the Filipino people nor the rest of the Far Eastern world could
be expected to have a high opinion of the United States if she
adopted a policy of "scuttle." On these grounds Stimson and
Marshall reacted strongly against any defeatist attitude. They
argued "that we could not give up the Philippines in that way;
that we must make every effort at whatever risk to keep Mac-
Arthur's line open and that otherwise we would paralyze the
activities of everybody in the Far East." (Diary, December
14, 1941) Taking his troubles to the White House, Stimson

found to his "great joy" that the President fully agreed with him and Marshall "as against the Navy"; Mr. Roosevelt called in the Acting Secretary of the Navy (Knox was in Hawaii) and "told him his position—told him that he was bound to help the Philippines and that the Navy had got to help in it." (Diary, December 14, 1941)

This difference of opinion with the Navy (which largely disappeared after the appointment of Admiral King as Naval Commander in Chief) was less a matter of strategy than one of attitude. Stimson fully understood that the fleet after Pearl Harbor was in no condition to mount any major counter-offensive, and he admitted too the Navy's right of decision as to acceptable and unacceptable risks for its carriers and remaining battleships. What he and the President opposed was the Navy's apparent lack of aggressive spirit. Frank Knox was a fighter, and his spirit was not broken by the disaster at Pearl Harbor, but the naval high command as a whole was shaken and nervous. The issue was really a broader one than the defense of the Philippines; it was the basic and critical issue between what Stimson called an "aggressive defense" and a "defensive defense." He summarized the matter in his diary after a discussion with McCloy, Lovett, and Bundy on December 17. "I laid before them the issue which was now pending before us, namely as to whether we should make every effort possible in the Far East or whether, like the Navy, we should treat that as doomed and let it go. We all agreed that the first course was the one to follow; that we have a very good chance of making a successful defense, taking the southwestern Pacific as a whole. If we are driven out of the Philippines and Singapore, we can still fall back on the Netherlands East Indies and Australia; and with the cooperation of China—if we can keep that going—we can strike good counterblows at Japan. While if we yielded to the defeatist theory, it would have not only the disastrous effect on our material policy of letting Japan get strongly ensconced in the southwestern Pacific which would be a terribly hard job to get her out of, but it would psychologically do even more in the discouragement of China and in fact all of the four powers who are now fighting very well together. Also it would have a very bad effect on Russia. So this theory goes. It has been accepted by the President, and the Army is taking steps to make a solid base at Port Darwin in Australia." (Diary, December 17, 1941)

Events were to prove that even the aggressive defense adopted by the President and his advisers succeeded only in holding Australia and a small foothold in New Guinea. The attempt to reinforce the Philippines, although undertaken with the firmness and conviction described above, was a failure. The Japanese sea and air blockade was almost complete, and although blockade running was energetically organized, very little reached General MacArthur. Only by submarine could a tenuous connection be maintained. The securing of delay, and the maintenance of American honor in the Philippines, thus fell to the gallant and isolated Philippine and American forces under President Quezon and General MacArthur.

Through December and January Stimson watched with a full heart the skillful and vastly courageous operations of MacArthur's forces. Hopelessly outnumbered, and under-equipped as no American Army force would be again, they exacted losses from the enemy that left no doubt in any mind of the quality of the American soldier. Even more heartening was the overwhelming proof of the loyalty of the Filipinos. By the Japanese attack forty years of American trusteeship were put to the acid test of courage, and the test was triumphantly passed. But even these great considerations were over-shadowed by the need for facing "the agonizing experience of seeing the doomed garrison gradually pulled down." (Diary, January 2, 1942)

And what was "agonizing" for Stimson and others in Washington must necessarily be still more trying for Quezon and MacArthur in the Philippines. These two men were in the battle; they could see, as Washington could not, the tragic sufferings of soldiers and civilians alike under the invasion; they could not see, as Washington could, that it was not for lack of effort that the Philippines were not reinforced. Message after message came from them asking for help, and words seemed to be the only answer. Finally, on February 8, Quezon, with the unanimous approval of his Cabinet, sent a message to the President proposing that the Philippines receive immediate and unconditional independence from the United States, and that they be forthwith neutralized by agreement between Japan and the United States; all troops were to be withdrawn and the Philippine Army disbanded. Quezon's message also contained strictures against the American failure to reinforce the Philippines, in terms as unfair as they were wholly understandable. With his message came one from High Commissioner Sayre stating that, "If the premise of President Quezon is correct that American help cannot or will not arrive here in time to be availing," Sayre would support his proposal. General MacArthur, in forwarding these two messages, added his own. After describing in detail the extremely precarious position of his command, he warned that, "Since I have no air or sea protection you must be prepared at any time to figure on the complete destruction of this command. You must determine whether the mission of delay would be better furthered by the temporizing plan of Quezon or by my continued battle effort. The temper of the Filipinos is one of almost violent resentment against the United States. Every one of them expected help and when it has not been forthcoming they believe they have been betrayed in favor of others. . . . So far as the military angle is concerned, the problem presents itself as to whether the plan of President Quezon might offer the best possible solution of what is about to be a disastrous debacle. It would not affect the ultimate situation in the Philippines for that would be determined by the results in other theatres. If the Japanese Government rejects President Quezon's proposition it would psychologically strengthen our hold because of their Prime Minister's public statement offering independence. If it accepts it, we lose no military advantage because we would still secure at least equal delay. Please instruct me."

Arriving in the War Department, these messages were a serious shock to Marshall and Stimson. Quezon's message seemed to assume that the Japanese were in fact attacking the United States but not the Philippines, and that the Filipino people had no interest in the war, a position which Quezon himself had repeatedly repudiated in public, and to which he could only have been driven by the pressure of his wholly distorted view of the American attitude toward supporting the Philippine campaign. Worse than that, Commissioner Sayre and General MacArthur appeared to have made no effort to dissuade Quezon from his position and had even given it some support in their messages. To Stimson and Marshall it seemed obvious that any such proposal as Quezon's would simply play into the hands of the Japanese. It would completely destroy the historic friendship between the Philippines and the United States. It involved an acceptance of the entirely disproved notion that the Japanese could be trusted to keep an agreement for "neutralization," and worst of all it would treat the "two great powers," Japan and America, as equally guilty of the destruction of the Philippines. "It was a wholly unreal message, taking no account [of] what the war was for or what the well known characteristics of Japan towards conquered people were." (Diary, February 9, 1942)

Stimson and Marshall took the messages to the President at once; "Sumner Welles was present, Cordell Hull being sick. The President read the message and then asked Marshall what we proposed doing about it. Marshall said that I could state our views better than he could and I then gave my views in full and as carefully as I could. In order to be more sure of no interruption, I arose from my seat and gave my views standing as if before the court. The President listened very attentively and, when I got through, he said he agreed with us. Sumner Welles . . . said that he agreed fully." Marshall and Stimson returned to the War Department, where the soldier drafted a reply to MacArthur while the civilian answered Quezon. "We barely finished by two-thirty when we went back again to the White House and there met Welles again, and also this time Stark and King. We spent an hour or more going over the drafts which of course were rather rough. The President was very quick and helpful in his suggestions and by four o'clock we had them completed and took them back to the Department to have written out for sending. It had been a pretty hard day, for the taking of the decision which we reached was a difficult one, consigning as it did a brave garrison to a fight to the finish and at the same time trying to send to Quezon a message which would put our attitude to the

Philippines upon a correct and elevated basis." (Diary, February 9, 1942)

Out of this day's work came the following radiogram to the Philippines.

MESSAGE SENT TO GENERAL MACARTHUR
February 9, 1942

"In the second section of this message I am making, through you, an immediate reply to President Quezon's proposals of February eight. My reply must emphatically deny the possibility of this Government's agreement to the political aspects of President Quezon's proposal. I authorize you to arrange for the capitulation of the Filipino elements of the defending forces, when and if in your opinion that course appears necessary and always having in mind that the Filipino troops are in the service of the United States. Details of all necessary arrangements will be left in your hands, including plans for segregation of forces and the withdrawal, if your judgment so dictates, of American elements to Fort Mills. The timing also will be left to you.

"American forces will continue to keep our flag flying in the Philippines so long as there remains any possibility of resistance. I have made these decisions in complete understanding of your military estimate that accompanied President Quezon's message to me. The duty and the necessity of resisting Japanese aggression to the last transcends in importance any other obligation now facing us in the Philippines.

"There has been gradually welded into a common front a globe encircling opposition to the predatory powers that are seeking the destruction of individual liberty and freedom of government. We cannot afford to have this line broken in any particular theater. As the most powerful member of this coalition we cannot display weakness in fact or in spirit anywhere. It is mandatory that there be established once and for all in the minds of all peoples complete evidence that the American determination and indomitable will to win carries on down to the last unit.

"I therefore give you this most difficult mission in full understanding of the desperate situation to which you may shortly be reduced. The service that you and the American members of your command can render to your country in the titanic struggle now developing is beyond all possibility of appraisement. I particularly request that you proceed rapidly to the organization of your forces and your defenses so as to make your resistance as effective as circumstances will permit and as prolonged as humanly possible.

"If the evacuation of President Quezon and his Cabinet appears reasonably safe they would be honored and greatly welcomed in the United States. They should come here via Australia. This applies also to the High Commissioner. Mrs. Sayre and your family should be given this opportunity if you consider it advisable. You yourself however must determine action to be taken in view of circumstances.

"Please inform Sayre of this message to you and to Quezon.

"Submit by radio the essentials of your plans in accordance with these instructions.

"Second section of message.

"Please convey the following message to President Quezon:

"I have just received your message sent through General MacArthur. From my message to you of January thirty, you must realize that I am not lacking in understanding of or sympathy with the situation of yourself and the Commonwealth Government today. The immediate crisis certainly seems desperate but such crises and their treatment must be judged by a more accurate measure than the anxieties and sufferings of the present, however acute. For over forty years the American government has been carrying out to the people of the Philippines a pledge to help them successfully, however long it might take, in their aspirations to become a self governing and independent people with individual freedom and economic strength which that lofty aim makes requisite. You yourself have participated in and are familiar with the many carefully planned steps by which that pledge of self government has been carried out and also the steps by which the economic independence of your islands is to be made effective. May I remind you now that in the loftiness of its aim and the fidelity with which it has been executed, this program of the United States towards another people has been unique in the history of the family of nations. In the Tydings McDuffie Act of one nine three four, to which you refer, the Congress of the United States finally fixed the year one nine four six as the date in which the Philippine Islands established by that Act should finally reach the goal of its hopes for political and economic independence.

"By a malign conspiracy of a few depraved but powerful governments this hope is now being frustrated and delayed. An organized attack upon individual freedom and governmental independence throughout the entire world, beginning in Europe, has now spread and been carried to the southwestern Pacific by Japan. The basic principles which have guided the United States in its conduct toward the Philippines have been violated in the rape of Czechoslovakia, Poland, Holland, Belgium, Luxembourg, Denmark, Norway, Albania, Greece, Yugoslavia, Manchukuo, China, Thailand and finally the Philippines. Could the people of any of these nations honestly look forward to true restoration of their independent sovereignty under the dominance of Germany, Italy, or Japan? You refer in your telegram to the announcement by the Japanese Prime Minister of Japan's willingness to grant to the Philippines her independence. I only have to refer you to the present condition of Korea, Manchukuo, North China, Indo China, and all other countries which have fallen under the brutal sway of the Japanese government, to point out the hollow duplicity of such an announcement. The present sufferings of the Filipino people, cruel as they may be, are infinitely less than the sufferings and permanent enslavement which will inevitably follow acceptance of Japanese promises. In any event is it longer possible for any reasonable person to rely upon Japanese offer or promise?

"The United States today is engaged with all its resources and in company with the governments of twenty-six other nations in an effort to defeat the aggression of Japan and its Axis partners. This effort will never be abandoned until the complete and thorough overthrow of the entire Axis system and the governments which maintain it. We are engaged now in laying the foundations in the southwest Pacific of a development in air, naval, and military power which shall become sufficient to meet and overthrow the widely extended and arrogant attempts of the Japanese. Military and naval operations call for recognition of realities. What we are doing there constitutes the best and surest help that we can render to the Philippines at this time.

"By the terms of our pledge to the Philippines implicit in our forty years of conduct towards your people and expressly recognized in the terms of the Tydings McDuffie Act, we have undertaken to protect you to the uttermost of our power until the time of your ultimate independence had arrived. Our soldiers in the Philippines are now engaged in fulfilling that purpose. The honor of the United States is pledged to its fulfillment. We propose that it be carried out regardless of its cost. Those Americans who are fighting now will continue to fight until the bitter end. Filipino soldiers have been rendering voluntary and gallant service in defense of their own homeland.

"So long as the flag of the United States flies on Filipino soil as a pledge of our duty to your people, it will be defended by our own men to the death. Whatever happens to the present American garrison we shall not relax our efforts until the forces which we are now marshaling outside the Philippine Islands return to the Philippines and drive the last remnant of the invaders from your soil."

FRANKLIN D. ROOSEVELT.

Thus the order was given, with its reasons, for the continuance of a battle which in the end accomplished all that was desired by the writers of this message. The response from Quezon was prompt and definite. In his autobiography he has described the effect of the President's message as "overwhelming"; he answered at once that he fully understood the reasons for the President's decision and would abide by it. General MacArthur replied with even greater firmness that he would resist to the end, and that he had not the least intention of surrendering Filipino elements of his command. "I count on them equally with the Americans to hold fast to the end," said his message. As for evacuation, his family would remain with him, and it was not safe that Quezon should leave, as his health would not permit the trials of the necessary voyage. Later, at the direct order of the President (an order fully approved by Stimson and Marshall), MacArthur, with his family, would leave the Philippines, to undertake the great task of leading the Allied forces north from Australia, and Quezon too would be persuaded to take his government into temporary exile. But the spirit of resistance symbolized by the two leaders would endure, in the Philippines and in history.

In this interchange of messages there were many of the complex elements that lay at the heart of World War II. Here was the leader of a colonial people, after two months of gallant resistance to aggression, driven in his resentment of what seemed a policy of nonsupport to repudiate the role of willing sacrifice. His American commander, unable to understand the failure of his government to give him needed help, was balancing the alternative of resistance against what he himself called a "temporizing plan." Both of these men had already amply proved their skill and courage; both had repeatedly demonstrated their devotion to the common cause of the free world. Yet neither appeared to appreciate the moral abdication involved in the proposal of a neutralized Philippines.

To the men in Washington the proper reply seemed clear, but to make it was a test of their own resolution. Not for the first or last time, Stimson and Marshall took courage from each other and found themselves fully supported by the President. The central problem here was moral, far transcending in its meaning any question of the "mission of delay." It was a part of the necessary tragedy of war that this moral issue must be met by a command to other men to die. Noble Romans might find such orders easy, but the men who met in the White House that day were ordinary Americans in their feelings about human life. To give the order was a matter of duty, but it was in its loyal execution that the true glory would be found. And so on February 13 Stimson sent General Mac-Arthur his final message in acknowledgment of the replies received from the Philippines: "The superb courage and fidelity of you and Quezon are fully recognized by the President and every one of us."

The decision of December, reiterated in the radiograms of February, reached its appointed ending in the final surrender of the battered remnants of the American and Filipino forces on Corregidor in early May. There followed three more years of suffering for the survivors and for all who honored their achievement. The best statement of the service of these men to America, the Philippines, and themselves was made by General Wainwright in his last message from the Rock: "We have done our best, both here and on Bataan, and although beaten we are still unashamed."[3]

The advance of the Japanese suffered serious delay only in the Philippines. Singapore fell on February 15; in April the Japanese easily took Batavia, capital of the Netherlands East Indies. Stimson like other Americans could only watch in gloomy frustration while the Japanese filled the vacuum created by their initial victories of sea and air. It was fortunate that the decision to reinforce Australia had been taken in December, for the distance of that continent, and American unfamiliarity with wartime logistics, made the execution of that decision painfully slow. One shipment of light bombers was anxiously watched by Stimson and Marshall as it arrived in December in Brisbane. Six weeks later they were still waiting in vain for word that the planes were ready to fight.

Meanwhile Stimson's own attention was turned to problems of defense closer at home. The losses at Pearl Harbor temporarily so weakened the Navy that the defense of the west coast became an Army assignment, and in December the War Department executed an unprecedented deployment of troops to protect that area. In May, when the Japanese Fleet disappeared eastward on a combat mission, Marshall made a swift and skillful personal inspection of the western defenses, for he joined in Stimson's belief that the famous Doolittle raid— a pet project of the President, and a remarkable psychological victory in a period when such victories were valuable—might provoke retaliation governed more by pride than by strategy.

[3] Biennial report of the Chief of Staff, July 1, 1943, p. 12.

At the same time, mindful of its duty to be prepared for any emergency, the War Department ordered the evacuation of more than a hundred thousand persons of Japanese origin from strategic areas on the west coast. This decision was widely criticized as an unconstitutional invasion of the rights of individuals many of whom were American citizens, but it was eventually approved by the Supreme Court as a legitimate exercise of the war powers of the President. What critics ignored was the situation that led to the evacuation. Japanese raids on the west coast seemed not only possible but probable in the first months of the war, and it was quite impossible to be sure that the raiders would not receive important help from individuals of Japanese origin. More than that, anti-Japanese feeling on the west coast had reached a level which endangered the lives of all such individuals; incidents of extra-legal violence were increasingly frequent. So, with the President's approval, Stimson ordered and McCloy supervised a general evacuation of Japanese and Japanese-Americans from strategic coastal areas, and they believed in 1947 that the eventual result of this evacuation, in the resettlement of a conspicuous minority in many dispersed communities throughout the country, was to produce a distinctly healthier atmosphere for both Japanese and Americans.

It remained a fact that to loyal citizens this forced evacuation was a personal injustice, and Stimson fully appreciated their feelings. He and McCloy were strong advocates of the later formation of combat units of Japanese-American troops; the magnificent record of the 442nd Combat Team justified their advocacy. By their superb courage and devotion to duty, the men of that force won for all Japanese-Americans a clear right to the gratitude and comradeship of their American countrymen.

While the attention of the War Department was necessarily focused in large measure on the threat to the west coast, there were in the early months of 1942 other areas almost equally menaced. Stimson himself was principally interested in the Panama Canal. An attack in California might be extremely disturbing to Californians, and a failure to repel it would be intolerable, but if the Japanese were interested in securing important results, the best target in the Western Hemisphere was the

Canal. A breach in the Gatun Lake Dam or Locks would put the Canal out of service for an estimated two years, and on an inspection trip to Panama in March Stimson found that the officers in charge of the defenses believed that such damage could be effectively prevented only by intercepting enemy aircraft carriers before they had discharged their planes. In retrospect he believed that the Canal would have been a better target than Pearl Harbor for the initial Japanese attack. Even in March, after three months of energetic and able preparation, the Canal defenses were far from perfect, and on his return to Washington he was able to give a considerable stimulus to the varied elements of the new defense system, which was based on a constant patrol of radar-equipped long-range planes, together with an inner patrol and a modern aircraft warning service. Radar equipment and technique were the central requirements, and in his work to supply both to Panama Stimson learned how important it was that the two go together.

One vital element in the defense of the Canal had already been provided shortly after December 7. The attack at Pearl Harbor emphasized again the importance of unity of command; all the armed forces in any one area must have a single commander. Stimson was ashamed that the lesson had to be so painfully learned; for months he had read it in the experience of the British in North Africa, Crete, and Greece. Incautiously he had assumed that it was equally well learned by others, but even after Pearl Harbor it was only by the force and tact of General Marshall that unity of command was quickly established in all the outposts, and even then there were compromises—as in the Atlantic approaches to the Canal, where the naval commander was independent of General Andrews at Panama.

Neither the west coast nor Panama was ever attacked by the Japanese (if we except a brief shelling by a single submarine off California, and the remarkable wind-blown fire bombs of the last year of the war). In the naval victories of the Coral Sea and Midway, the onset was ended. At Guadalcanal in August the initiative passed to the Americans, and in September and October General MacArthur reversed the enemy advance in New Guinea. But months before these events the emphasis in Stimson's thinking had shifted. Having been among the first to insist on the establishment of an effective line of resistance in the Pacific, he became, in February and March, one of the earliest to emphasize that the Pacific theater was and must remain secondary. But this attitude was the result of his thinking on larger matters of strategy, and it may well be left to a later chapter.

3. WAR SECRETARY

The existence of a state of war radically revises the functions of a Secretary of War. In time of peace he is ordinarily one of the most independent and least noticed of Cabinet officers; once or twice a year he takes the stage to make his plea for funds; occasionally the public will be somewhat surprised to discover that he has other than military functions. In a time of approaching crisis he becomes somewhat more important; he must tell what his Department needs, always in terms of defense, and his counsel will have weight in diplomatic problems. In wartime all this changes; suddenly his branch of the Government becomes central. This shift will please some and annoy others of his colleagues, but it is inevitable. He finds himself in constant contact with the President, whose function as Commander in Chief takes precedence over all his other responsibilities; the nature of this relationship depends entirely on the individuals concerned, for it has no constitutional rule, and no set tradition. Only a part of the Secretary's duties concerns directly military questions, for in wartime the demands of the Army enter into every aspect of national life. Furthermore the enhanced prestige of the War Department will often operate to draw its officials into activities which even in wartime are no central part of their business, and frequently the men who mutter most about "military dominance" will be among the first to seek military support when they think they can get it; others, reluctant to accept the responsibility for unpopular decisions, will secure War Department approval for their action and then let it be understood that they have acted only under military pressure.

Within the Army, war brings more changes still. In the making of a citizen army the central issue is leadership; of such leadership war is the final test. But this leadership must be military; the confidence of the Army and the country must be confidence in soldiers. If the generals are successful, they will receive the credit they deserve, and they will receive in addition an uncritical emotional support that has no counterpart in peacetime democratic life. If they fail or seem to fail they will be quickly forgotten, but the fear their failure makes will spread to the whole military establishment. The pearl of highest price for a democracy at war is well-placed confidence in its military leadership. It thus becomes the duty of the Secretary of War to support, protect, and defend his generals. Those who fail must be quietly removed; those who succeed must be publicly acclaimed; those who come under attack, even when the attack is justified, must, if they are skillful fighting officers, be sustained and encouraged—for the first-rate field commander cannot be replaced by formal requisition. A rule which is sound for all administration everywhere thus becomes vital in an army at war. You discipline and reprimand in private; you praise and promote in public; and *you back your subordinates*. The function of the civilian Secretary is dual: as a responsible public official, it is his duty to insure that the Army serves the broad public interest; as the Army's chief it is his duty to act as the defender of the Army against its enemies and detractors.

These, then, were the duties to which Stimson addressed himself after Pearl Harbor. The core of the high command in the War Department did not change between December 7, 1941, and August 15, 1945. To Stimson's staff were added, from time to time, civilians of special qualifications who became members of his small personal circle of assistants. In the General Staff officers came and went, but the atmosphere of that body remained an atmosphere inspired by George Marshall. The unity and harmony at the top remained unbroken, and it was a team of men whose single object was to win the war. The proper record of the men who served there can be written only in terms of the whole accomplishment, and the whole accomplishment cannot yet be assessed as history. In the chapters that follow there will be many a story only half-told, for the decisions and policies in which Stimson had a part have not yet been fully connected in the records with their results. And it is not always easy to be sure—even with the aid of diaries and recollection—whether an idea or a decision started in Stimson's mind or in Marshall's, or in the civil or the military staff. The story that follows is personal, and not official, but the distinction is arbitrary in the extreme. At no other time in his life was Stimson so thoroughly surrounded by loyal, understanding, and able men as during the forty-four months of World War II.

The worst mistake of all would be to assume that in what follows there is any adequate record of the labors of the War Department high command. If there is a man whose personal history parallels that whole vast record it is General Marshall and not Stimson, but probably there is not such a man. For where there is mutual confidence, there can be decentralization, and where there is initiative, decentralization will produce programs and policies and results which no higher commander need expect to find in his biography. In a sense it was Stimson's greatest administrative success that he kept his desk free for those problems which, by their importance or peculiarity, only he could undertake.

This was a necessity for more than one reason. Stimson's mind was so constructed that it could hold only one major problem at a time. He disliked interruptions; he liked thoroughness. Traits of this kind do not grow weaker as a man grows older; if Stimson had not trusted those around him he must inevitably have become a dangerous bottleneck. His value to the War Department must come from the application of his principles and experience to major matters. His friend Grenville Clark used to tell him that he could do his job in four hours a day; this was an optimistic estimate, but the principle was correct.

Neither custom nor statute is based on this theory of a Cabinet officer's functions, and many a man has been buried by the mass of detailed work which will cross a government official's desk if he lets it. From the ordinary details Stimson was protected by the devoted skill of John W. Martyn, the

War Department's senior civil servant. With almost flawless discrimination Martyn separated the wheat from the chaff, calling to Stimson's attention only what it was necessary that he handle. From the thousands of signatures required by law he was relieved by a machine which reproduced his signature in lifelike form. For the mass of visitors who were certain that their business could only be handled by the Secretary of War in person there were two techniques. If possible, they were kept away; if not, then Stimson would hear them briefly and sympathetically, delivering them as quickly as possible into the hands of the appropriate subordinate. If they were then disappointed in their quest, he had still been polite; it was a technique that Stimson would have liked to be able to teach to Franklin Roosevelt, whose natural good will often took the shape of quick and unredeemable promises.

Stimson's concern for his private affairs was cut to a minimum by the painstaking work of his old law firm, the insight and experience of his personal secretary, Elizabeth Neary, and the loyal help of his successive military aides. Most of all, he had the care and support of Mrs. Stimson.

The work that remained was not light. Each day he rose at six-thirty, had a short walk before breakfast, and dictated for an hour or more before proceeding to the Department. There he remained through the day until the late afternoon, returning when he could for a game of deck tennis around five-thirty. In the evening he was usually alone with Mrs. Stimson, reading the "easier" official papers, or at dinner with one of his small circle of close friends; but often when problems were pressing the evening too was given to work.

Washington was a city whose climate he considered designed for the destruction of the sanity of government officials, and he found two ways of escape. He could fly to Highhold for the week end; the small problems of a farm in wartime were a welcome relaxation, and in the intimacy of home he could talk with old friends like a soldier on leave from the front. Or he could go on an inspection trip. Stimson believed that the visits of a Secretary of War were on the whole encouraging to the troops, though this belief was somewhat shaken by the evident disappointment of a group of lieutenants in New-foundland who had been expecting Hedy Lamarr. In any case he was certain that they were encouraging to him. On four overseas tours and frequent journeys to camps and airfields in the United States he invariably found new strength, and often new ideas, for the work in Washington.

A similar source of encouragement was available in Washington, in the constant stream of men from the war theaters. These were always welcome visitors in the Secretary's office; liaison officers, foreign emissaries, and returning troop leaders he eagerly questioned, and in their answers there was a directness of contact that the daily cables could not give him. In the generally high quality of the officers fresh from the wars there was renewed assurance that the war was in safe hands; it was heartening to find that the major general of 1943 had fulfilled the promise of the major of 1940.

There is terror in the very name of war, and the responsibilities of wartime leadership are wearing beyond the knowledge of those who have not carried them. But in righteous war there is also strength for the spirit, and it comes mainly from the front lines backward. In the needs of the men who were fighting, the undying challenge of their death, and the constant proof of their quality as men and soldiers there was an ever growing source of inspiration for all at home. And this inspiration was greater for Stimson than for the ordinary citizen, for he was closer to the Army, more directly aware of its work, and accountable for its support. In the force of this feeling is not merely the explanation of his continued strength to serve but also the motivation for many of the policies and purposes which we are about to discuss.

CHAPTER XVII

The Army and Grand Strategy

---

1. PEARL HARBOR TO NORTH AFRICA

IMMEDIATELY after Pearl Harbor it became necessary for the United States and Great Britain to concert their strategy. In the week before Christmas, 1941, Winston Churchill and his principal military advisers arrived in Washington for the first of the great wartime meetings with the President and American advisers.

The most important single accomplishment of this meeting was that it laid the groundwork for the establishment of an effectively unified Allied high command. The Combined Chiefs of Staff, set up in Washington in early 1942, rapidly became a fully developed instrument for the co-ordination of land, sea, and air warfare in a world-wide war. Its seven members, four Americans and three Britons, gradually developed an authority and influence exceeded only by the decisive meetings between the President and the Prime Minister. For their success there were several causes, but in Stimson's mind these could in the main be reduced to two. One was the inflexible determination of Mr. Roosevelt and Mr. Churchill to fight the war as a unified team. The other was the organizing genius and diplomatic skill of George Marshall. It was Marshall who insisted that the Combined Chiefs should in fact be chiefs, and not merely elders of the council; the British members were the direct representatives of the military chiefs of the British armed forces, while the American members were themselves the responsible leaders of the services which they represented. It was Marshall too who guided the development of the staff work of the Combined Chiefs, insisting on a continuous record of consideration and decision and directive. Finally, it was Marshall, with the particular assistance and support of an equally disinterested and farsighted soldier-statesman, Field Marshal Sir John Dill, who made it possible for the Combined Chiefs to act not as a mere collecting point for the inevitable rivalries between services and nations but as an executive committee for the prosecution of a global war.

Marshall was also the primary agent in the establishment and operation of the strictly American counterpart to the Combined Chiefs; in spite of the urging of Stimson and others, the President for some time hesitated to approve an executive agency of this type for co-ordinating the American military effort; he was particularly doubtful about the wisdom of appointing any officer as Chief of Staff to himself. Marshall combined his advocacy of such an appointment with a refusal to accept it for himself, arguing that it would only be acceptable to the Navy if an admiral received the appointment. The Joint Chiefs of Staff, when finally organized, included four officers: the President's Chief of Staff and the senior officers of the Army, Navy, and Army Air Forces; these were the same men who served as American members of the Combined Chiefs, and they exercised direct supervision over the American share of the Allied military effort. The Joint Chiefs became the President's direct military advisers.

As it became gradually more effective, this formal organization of the staffs had, in Stimson's view, a most salutary effect on the President's weakness for snap decisions; it thus offset a characteristic which might otherwise have been a serious handicap to his basically sound strategic instincts. Both in the December meeting of 1941 and in the following June the President made suggestions to the Prime Minister which if seriously pursued must have disrupted the American military effort. Mr. Roosevelt was fond of "trial balloons," and perhaps Stimson's fear of this technique was due largely to its complete dissimilarity from his own method of thought, but he nevertheless felt certain that both Mr. Roosevelt and Mr. Churchill were men whose great talents required the balancing restraint of carefully organized staff advice.

Stimson, as Secretary of War, was neither a professional

soldier nor the finally responsible political leader, and the organization which made the Chiefs of Staff directly responsible to the President left him with no formal responsibility in matters of military strategy. This arrangement might have disturbed him seriously if he had not continued to enjoy a relationship of complete mutual confidence with the President and with Generals Marshall and Arnold. He continued to be called in, as the advocate of the War Department and as a constitutionally recognized adviser to the President, and he thus became an active participant in the two years of Anglo-American discussion over the grand strategy of their European campaigns.

The detailed discussions in the meeting of December, 1941, were largely devoted to the problems of the Pacific, where the situation was immediately critical, but even in the face of the Japanese advance there was no deviation from the principle already accepted by both sides before Pearl Harbor—only the European theater was decisive. In the language of a memorandum prepared by Stimson and used by the President as the agenda for the first general meeting of the conference, "Our joint war plans have recognized the North Atlantic as our principal theatre of operations should America become involved in the war. Therefore it should now be given primary consideration and carefully reviewed in order to see whether our position there is safe." The first essential was "the preservation of our communications across the North Atlantic with our fortress in the British Isles covering the British Fleet." It was accordingly decided that an immediate beginning should be made in the establishment of an American force in Great Britain.

By itself the decision of December was not definitive, since the general agreement on the central importance of Great Britain did not include any strategic plan for the use of that fortress as a base for offensive operations. In the middle of February Stimson began to feel that the absence of such a plan was a serious weakness; without it there was no firm commitment that could prevent a series of diversionary shipments of

troops and supplies to other areas more immediately threatened. In March his fears were strikingly confirmed by the
arrival in Washington of a gloomy message from Mr. Churchill suggesting increased American commitments in non-European areas of the globe, to meet the Axis threat developing in
Africa, southeastern Europe, and the Far East. At a White
House meeting Stimson argued that the proper policy was that
of avoiding such dispersion, and instead, "sending an overwhelming force to the British Isles and threatening an attack
on the Germans in France; that this was the proper and orthodox line of our help in the war as it had always been recognized and that it would now have the effect of giving Hitler
two fronts to fight on if it could be done in time while the
Russians were still in. It would also heavily stimulate British
sagging morale." (Diary, March 5, 1942) Stimson found on
the following day that his view was fully confirmed by the
detailed military analysis of the War Plans Division under
Brigadier General Eisenhower, and the same general position
was taken by all the President's advisers, the Navy accepting
primary responsibility for the necessary labors in the Pacific.
On March 8 the President replied to the Prime Minister
proposing as a general rule that the British alone should assume the responsibility for the Middle East, the Americans
the responsibility for the Pacific, while both nations jointly
should operate in the critical Atlantic theater. At the same
time it was decided that the American planners should prepare in detail a plan for invading Europe across the English
Channel.

On March 25, "At one o'clock we lunched with the President in the Cabinet room. Knox, King, Harry Hopkins and
Arnold, Marshall and I were there. The subject of discussion
was the Joint Planners' report. The President started out and
disappointed, and at first staggered, me by a résumé of what he
thought the situation was, in which he looked like he was
going off on the wildest kind of dispersion debauch; but, after
he had toyed a while with the Middle East and the Mediterranean basin, which last he seemed to be quite charmed with,
Marshall and I edged the discussion over into the Atlantic and
held him there. Marshall made a very fine presentation. . . .

Towards the end of the meeting when the President suggested that the subject be now turned over to the Combined Chiefs of Staff organization (British and American), Hopkins took up the ball and made a strong plea that it should not go to that organization at all where it would simply be pulled to pieces and emasculated; but, as soon as the Joint American Army and Navy Chiefs of Staff had perfected it, someone (and he meant Marshall as he had told me before) should take it directly over to Churchill, Pound, Portal, and Brooke, who are the highest British authorities, and get it through them directly. This stopped the President's suggestion and we came away with his mandate to put this in shape if possible over this week end." (Diary, March 25, 1942)

Stimson's own strong distaste for the "charming" Mediterranean basin no doubt contributed to his alarm at the President's interest in it. In any case, this meeting made it clear that although Mr. Roosevelt had agreed to support the idea of a trans-Channel attack, the concept was not yet his own. Two days later, with the warm approval of Hopkins and Marshall, Stimson wrote the President a letter designed to persuade him to take a firm and final position.

Confidential

March 27, 1942

Dear Mr. President:

John Sherman said in 1877, "The only way to resume specie payments is to resume." Similarly, the only way to get the initiative in this war is to take it.

My advice is: As soon as your Chiefs of Staff have completed the plans for the northern offensive to your satisfaction, you should send them by a most trusted messenger and advocate to Churchill and his War Council as the American plan which you propose and intend to go ahead with if accepted by Britain. You should not submit it to the secondary British Chiefs of Staff here for amendment. They know about it and, if they have comment, they can send their comment independently to Great Britain.

And then having done that, you should lean with all your

strength on the ruthless rearrangement of shipping allotments and the preparation of landing gear for the ultimate invasion. That latter work is now going on at a rather dilettante pace. It should be pushed with the fever of war action, aimed at a definite date of completion not later than September. The rate of construction of a number of landing barges should not be allowed to lose the crisis of the World War. And yet that is the only objection to the offensive that, after talks with British critics here, I have heard made.

If such decisive action is once taken by you, further successful dispersion of our strength will automatically be terminated. We shall have an affirmative answer against which to measure all such demands; while, on the other hand, so long as we remain without our own plan of offensive, our forces will inevitably be dispersed and wasted.

Faithfully yours,

HENRY L. STIMSON
Secretary of War.

The President,
Hyde Park, New York

The plan for which Stimson and Marshall were arguing went under the code name of BOLERO. It contemplated a maximum build-up of American strength in Great Britain, looking toward a full-scale invasion in the spring of 1943, with fifty divisions, 60 per cent of them American, on the continent of Europe by the end of that summer. In the event of a desperate crisis on the Russian front in 1942, it also included the alternative possibility of a much smaller "beachhead" invasion in the autumn of that year, but this alternative, known as SLEDGE-HAMMER, was conceded to be less desirable. Concern over the plan SLEDGEHAMMER was in the end the cause of the abandonment of BOLERO; to Stimson, SLEDGEHAMMER'S possible dangers did not seem so important. His objective was to secure a decision to invade Europe from the British base at the earliest practicable moment; only developing events could show whether that moment would be in 1942 or 1943.

On April 1 the President accepted the BOLERO plan and dispatched Hopkins and Marshall to London to secure the approval of the British. The emissaries were in the main successful and returned to Washington with an agreement to proceed on the basis of BOLERO. Stimson was delighted. But the agreement held for less than two months.

BOLERO was the brain child of the United States Army; the President and the Prime Minister had accepted it, but neither of the two had been fully and finally persuaded. Stimson never knew which of them was responsible for the Washington meetings in June at which the whole question was reopened. The initiative for the meeting came from Mr. Churchill, but he might well have acted on the basis of an indication that the President was not completely certain about the wisdom of BOLERO. Mr Roosevelt continued to lean toward an operation in North Africa, known in this period as GYMNAST, and on June 17 he reopened the subject with his advisers. "The President sprung on us a proposition which worried me very much. It looked as if he was going to jump the traces [after] all that we have been doing in regard to BOLERO and to imperil really our strategy of the whole situation. He wants to take up the case of GYMNAST again, thinking that he can bring additional pressure to save Russia. The only hope I have about it at all is that I think he may be doing it in his foxy way to forestall trouble that is now on the ocean coming towards us in the shape of a new British visitor. But he met with a rather robust opposition for the GYMNAST proposition. Marshall had a paper already prepared against it for he had a premonition of what was coming. I spoke very vigorously against it." The Navy was noncommittal but not nearly so vigorous in opposition as Stimson would have liked. "Altogether it was a disappointing afternoon." (Diary, June 17, 1942)

In the following two days Stimson prepared his brief in defense of BOLERO. The Prime Minister and his team had arrived, and it was evident that they were discussing new diversions. All of Stimson's experience as an advocate, and all of his conviction that the war would be won only by a cross-Channel campaign went into a letter written on June 19 and dispatched to the President with the unanimous endorsement of General Marshall and his staff.

Personal and Secret

June 19, 1942

Dear Mr. President:

While your military advisers are working out the logistics of the problem which you presented to us on Wednesday, may I very briefly recall to your memory the sequence of events which led to and the background which surrounds this problem. I hope it may be helpful to you.

1. Up to the time when America entered the war, the British Empire had, by force of circumstances, been fighting a series of uphill defensive campaigns with insufficient resources and almost hopeless logistics. The entry of Japan into the war and the naval disasters at Pearl Harbor and the Malay Peninsula imposed new defensive campaigns in the theatres of the Far East.

2. After the discussions with Mr. Churchill's party here last December the need for a carefully planned offensive became very evident. Russia had successfully fought off the entire German Army for six months. Winter had begun and the shaken and battered German Army would be helpless to renew its offensive for nearly six months more. The one thing Hitler rightly dreaded was a second front. In establishing such a front lay the best hope of keeping the Russian Army in the war and thus ultimately defeating Hitler. To apply the rapidly developing manpower and industrial strength of America promptly to the opening of such a front was manifestly the only way it could be accomplished.

3. But the effective application of America's strength required prompt, rapid and safe transportation overseas. The allied naval power controlled the seas by only a narrow margin. With one exception the Axis Powers controlled every feasible landing spot in Europe. By fortunate coincidence one of the shortest routes to Europe from America led through the only safe base not yet controlled by our enemies, the British Isles.

4. Out of these factors originated the BOLERO plan. The British Isles constituted the one spot (a) where we could safely and easily land our ground forces without the aid of carrier-based air cover. (b) through which we could without the aid of ships fly both bomber and fighting planes from America to Europe. (c) where we could safely and without interruption develop an adequate base for invading armies of great strength. Any other base in western Europe or north-west Africa could be obtained only by a risky attack and the long delay of development and fortification. (d) where we could safely develop air superiority over our chief enemy in northern France and force him either to fight us on equal terms or leave a bridgehead to France undefended.

5. The psychological advantages of BOLERO also were manifest. The menace of the establishment of American military power in the British Isles would be immediately evident to Hitler. It at once tended to remove the possibility of a successful invasion of Britain, Hitler's chief and last weapon. It awoke in every German mind the recollections of 1917 and 1918.

6. A steady, rapid, and unrelenting prosecution of the BOLERO plan was thus manifestly the surest road, first to the shaking of Hitler's anti-Russian campaign of '42, and second, to the ultimate defeat of his armies and the victorious termination of the war. Geographically and historically BOLERO was the easiest road to the center of our chief enemy's heart. The base was sure. The water barrier of the Channel under the support of Britain-based air power is far easier than either the Mediterranean or the Atlantic. The subsequent over-land route into Germany is easier than any alternate. Over the Low Countries has run the historic path of armies between Germany and France.

7. Since the BOLERO plan was adopted, subsequent events have tended to facilitate our position and justify its wisdom. (a) The greatest danger to America's prosecution of the BOLERO plan lay in the Pacific from Japan where our then inferiority in aircraft carriers subjected us to the dangers of enemy raids which might seriously cripple the vital airplane production upon which a prompt BOLERO offensive primarily

rests. The recent victory in the mid-Pacific [at Midway] has greatly alleviated that danger. Our rear in the west is now at least temporarily safe. (b) The psychological pressure of our preparation for BOLERO is already becoming manifest. There are unmistakable signs of uneasiness in Germany as well as increasing unrest in the subject populations of France, Holland, Czechoslovakia, Yugoslavia, Poland and Norway. This restlessness patently is encouraged by the growing American threat to Germany.

8. Under these circumstances an immense burden of proof rests upon any proposition which may impose the slightest risk of weakening BOLERO. Every day brings us further evidence of the great importance of unremittingly pressing forward that plan. When one is engaged in a tug of war, it is highly risky to spit on one's hands even for the purpose of getting a better grip. No new plan should even be whispered to friend or enemy unless it was so sure of immediate success and so manifestly helpful to BOLERO that it could not possibly be taken as evidence of doubt or vacillation in the prosecution of BOLERO. Enemies would be prompt to jump at one or the other of these conclusions.

9. While I have no intention of intruding on any discussion of logistics by the staff, one or two possible contingencies have occurred to me which would bear upon the wisdom of now embarking upon another trans-Atlantic expedition such as GYMNAST. (a) Assume the worst contingency possible; Assume a prompt victory over Russia which left a large German force free for other enterprises. It is conceivable that Germany might then make a surprise attempt at the invasion of Britain. She would have the force to attempt it. She may well have available the equipment for both air-borne and water-borne invasion. One of our most reliable military attachés believes emphatically that this is her plan—a surprise air-borne invasion from beyond the German boundaries producing a confusion in Britain which would be immediately followed up by an invasion by sea. Our observers in Britain have frequently advised us of their concern as to the inadequacy of British defenses against such an attempt. Obviously in case of such an attempt it would be imperative for us to push our

forces into Britain at top speed and by means of shipping additional to that already allocated to the project. In case a large percentage of allied commercial shipping had been tied up with an expedition to GYMNAST, such additional reenforcement of Britain would be impossible. (b) On the other hand, if German invasion of Russia is prolonged, even if it is slowly successful, the increasing involvement of Germany in the east tends to make increasingly easy an Allied invasion into France and the acquisition of safe bases therein against Germany. (c) Thus German success against Russia, whether fast or slow, would seem to make requisite not a diversion from BOLERO but an increase in BOLERO as rapidly as possible. (d) Furthermore, BOLERO is one overseas project which brings no further strain upon our aircraft carrier forces. GYMNAST would necessarily bring such a strain and risk. It could not fail to diminish the superiority over Japan which we now precariously hold in the Pacific.

10. To my mind BOLERO in inception and in its present development is an essentially American project, brought into this war as the vitalizing contribution of our fresh and unwearied leaders and forces. My own view is that it would be a mistake to hazard it by any additional expeditionary proposal as yet brought to my attention.

Faithfully yours,

HENRY L. STIMSON
Secretary of War.

The President,
The White House.

On June 21 there was "a good deal of pow-wow and a rumpus up at the White House." Stimson was not there, but he got a full report from Marshall. It appeared that the Prime Minister, who had never really liked BOLERO, was particularly disturbed by some casual remarks the President had made to Lord Mountbatten some time earlier about the possibility of having to make a "sacrifice" cross-Channel landing in 1942 to help the Russians. "According to Marshall, Churchill started out with a terrific attack on BOLERO as we had expected. . . . The President, however, stood pretty firm. I found out afterwards through Harry Hopkins that he [the President] showed my letter, with which Harry said he had been much pleased, to the Prime Minister. I had not anticipated that because I said some very plain things in it about the British. Finally, with the aid of Marshall who came into the conversation as a reserve after lunch, the storm was broken and, according to Harry Hopkins, Marshall made a very powerful argument for BOLERO, disposing of all the clouds that had been woven about it by the Mountbatten incident. At any rate towards the end it was agreed that we should go ahead full blast on BOLERO until the first of September. At that time the Prime Minister wanted to have a résumé of the situation to see whether a real attack could be made [in 1942] without the danger of disaster. If not, why then we could reconsider the rest of the field. At any rate that seems to have been the substance so far." (Diary, June 21, 1942) This was still the decision when the Prime Minister returned in haste to Great Britain as a result of unexpected British reverses in the Near East, where the fall of Tobruk on June 21 had shifted the attention of the Washington meeting from grand strategy to immediate repair work.

On July 10, "Marshall told me of a new and rather staggering crisis that is coming up in our war strategy. A telegram has come from Great Britain indicating that the British war Cabinet are weakening and going back on BOLERO and are seeking to revive GYMNAST—in other words, they are seeking now to reverse the decision which was so laboriously accomplished when Mr. Churchill was here a short time ago. This would be simply another way of diverting our strength into a channel in which we cannot effectively use it, namely the Middle East. I found Marshall very stirred up and emphatic over it. He is very naturally tired of these constant decisions which do not stay made. This is the third time this question will have been brought up by the persistent British and he proposed a showdown which I cordially endorsed. As the British won't go through with what they agreed to, we will turn our backs on them and take up the war with Japan." (Diary, July 10, 1942)

Although this drastic threat was designed mainly as a plan to bring the British into agreement with BOLERO, Stimson in retrospect was not altogether pleased with his part in it; he thought it a rather hasty proposal which showed how sorely the patience of the Americans had been tried by constant appeals for reconsideration. Although the bluff was supported by the British Chiefs of Staff in Washington, who had been converted to BOLERO, it did not appeal to the President. "The President asserted that he himself was absolutely sound on BOLERO which must go ahead unremittingly, but he did not like the manner of the memorandum [a further paper from Marshall, King, and Arnold] in regard to the Pacific, saying that was a little like 'taking up your dishes and going away.' I told him that I appreciated the truth in that but it was absolutely essential to use it as a threat of our sincerity in regard to BOLERO if we expected to get through the hides of the British and he agreed to that." (Diary, July 15, 1942)

Mr. Roosevelt was not persuaded, and the bluff was never tried. It would not have worked in any case, for there was no real intention of carrying it out, and Stimson supposed that the British knew this as well as he did. Furthermore, Stimson knew that the President had a lingering predilection for the Mediterranean, and the Prime Minister had shown on his last visit that he too knew the President's feeling; back on June 21 he "had taken up GYMNAST, knowing full well I am sure that it was the President's great secret baby." In spite of Mr. Roosevelt's renewed assurances of his support for BOLERO, therefore, it was with considerable concern that Stimson watched Hopkins, Marshall, and King leave for London to undertake a final series of discussions on Anglo-American strategy for 1942. He was not surprised—although very deeply disappointed—when these discussions resulted in a decision to launch a North African attack in the autumn. GYMNAST, rebaptized TORCH, replaced BOLERO.

The TORCH decision was the result of two absolutely definite and final rulings, one by the British, and the other by the President. Mr. Churchill and his advisers categorically refused to accept the notion of a cross-Channel invasion in 1942. Mr. Roosevelt categorically insisted that there must be *some* operation in 1942. The only operation that satisfied both of these conditions was TORCH. Stimson admitted that there was considerable force in both of these rulings. His own interest in BOLERO had never blinded him to the dangers of SLEDGE-HAMMER, the 1942 version of that operation. On the other hand, he could understand that for many reasons it was important that American troops should come to grips with the German enemy somewhere, as soon as possible.

But in July, 1942, neither of these considerations seemed to him as important as the fact that TORCH would obviously force an indefinite postponement of effective action in the only decisive theater outside Russia, and he pushed his disagreement with the President to the limits prescribed by loyalty. Again and again he emphasized the unwelcome fact that TORCH destroyed BOLERO even for 1943. The July agreement paid lip service to the build-up in Britain, but an operation in execution will always take priority over one merely in contemplation, especially when the one in contemplation is not viewed with a friendly eye by one-half of the team.

Stimson's disapproval of TORCH was fully shared by the War Department staff, but after a final protest to the President on July 24, during which the two men offered to bet each other about the wisdom of the operation, Stimson limited himself to extracting a promise from Marshall that he would make a stand against the final execution of the operation if at any time "it seemed clearly headed for disaster." (Diary, August 10, 1942) This time never came, for with his usual skill and energy Marshall organized the Army's part of the operation to a point at which he was himself prepared to endorse it. TORCH had what BOLERO had never had, the enthusiastic support of the highest authorities, and it was therefore possible to give it priorities and exclusive rights with the kind of ruthlessness that Stimson had so ardently and fruitlessly urged for BOLERO.

Confessing his doubts only to Marshall, Stimson too gave his full support to the prosecution of TORCH. "We are embarked on a risky undertaking but it is not at all hopeless and, the Commander in Chief having made the decision, we must do our best to make it a success." (Diary, September 17, 1942)

He was particularly delighted with the selection of his old friend George Patton to command the Casablanca landing force; Patton's realistic appreciation of the dangers ahead was matched by his burning determination to overcome them. The work of the General Staff in preparation Stimson considered admirable; so far as possible the dangers he foresaw were minimized. But, as he had feared, the necessary shipping and air support for TORCH were obtained at the expense of the BOLERO build-up in Great Britain.

In October and November there occurred two great and unforeseen events which still further reduced the dangers of TORCH. One was the successful Russian stand at Stalingrad. The shift of the Russians from the defense to a massive counterattack, in the following weeks, finally banished the specter of a German victory in Russia, which had haunted the council table of the Western Allies for a year and a half. At the same time, in the battle of Alamein, the British Eighth Army achieved a definitive victory over the Afrika Korps. To these two major areas Hitler was forced to give new attention, and the prospect of a counterattack through Spain against TORCH was diminished. Stimson nevertheless continued to be greatly concerned with the dangers of such a riposte to the North African attack, and through the early weeks of the invasion he lent his weight to the provision of adequate protective forces opposite Gibraltar. But the attack through Spain did not develop. Providential and unexpected good weather at Casablanca speeded that critical landing, and the heavy submarine and air losses which had been anticipated did not occur. Stimson always considered TORCH the luckiest Allied operation of the war, but he was prepared to admit that those who had advocated the operation could not be expected to see it in that light; the President had won his bet.

The tactical success of TORCH does not of itself dispose of the broader questions of strategy which lay behind the difference between the War Department and the President. The great commitment in North Africa led inexorably to later operations in the Mediterranean theater which were certainly a great contribution to victory; equally certainly these operations were unimportant in comparison with the land and air offensive finally launched from Great Britain. If Stimson or Marshall had been Commander in Chief, the invasion of France would in all probability have been launched in 1943, one year earlier than it actually occurred. Would the war have been ended sooner? This is a problem in a dozen unknowns. No certain answer is possible, and the matter is here left open. All that Stimson could say was that if he were faced with the problems of 1942, he would argue again as he had then.

2. THE GREAT DECISION

As the North African campaign progressed, the joint operations of the British and American forces led to increasing daily co-operation and understanding in the higher echelons, but the basic differences in strategy remained. At Casablanca in January, 1943, the British again refused to go ahead with any cross-Channel operation in the coming year, and it was therefore agreed that the next great move would be to Sicily, in a campaign whose name was HUSKY. In May, at Washington, there was made the first of three binding decisions to launch a cross-Channel invasion in 1944. For the first time the President himself took the stand for which Stimson had argued a year before—he insisted that the first problem was to plan the landing in northern France; when that had been done, it would be possible to see what supplies and troops were available for other operations. The Prime Minister finally accepted this position, although part of his price was that General Marshall should be assigned to him for a tour of North Africa —ruefully Marshall remarked that he seemed to be merely a piece of baggage useful as a trading point. Stimson suspected that his wily English friend, knowing that in Marshall he faced the most powerful single advocate of the Channel attack, was hoping to convert him to the Mediterranean, but he knew that the Prime Minister was also indulging his great respect and affection for General Marshall. And he was not surprised to find that Marshall returned safe, and unconverted, to the Pentagon.

Thus in midsummer, 1943, it was understood that there should be a cross-Channel attack in 1944. A staff was at work in London planning this attack, which was to have a British supreme commander. Meanwhile the invasion of Sicily had begun on July 10, and the question of further Mediterranean operations was still under debate. This was the situation when Stimson arrived in England, on the first of his three wartime visits to the European theater. What happened there is best described in his report of August 4, 1943, to the President. This report records Stimson's side of a prolonged debate with Mr. Churchill, from which he returned to Washington with more definite ideas than ever about the necessity of fighting hard for a cross-Channel invasion in 1944. The term used at the time by Stimson for this invasion was ROUNDHAMMER. (Its official name had become OVERLORD, but Stimson preferred not to mention this new name in his reports. OVERLORD was the final name for the invasion when executed.) The report to Mr. Roosevelt was outspoken, and it must be remembered that this paper, like all of Stimson's comments in this period, was predicated on the assumption that differences with the British were differences between friends.

"My principal objective had been to visit troops. But when I reached London the P.M. virtually took possession of my movements for the first week and I found myself launched in the discussion of subjects and with people which I had not expected. These unexpected subjects were so important that I devoted the bulk of my time to their consideration and altered my trip accordingly.

"Although I have known the P.M. for many years and had talked freely with him, I have never had such a series of important and confidential discussions as this time. He was extremely kind and, although we discussed subjects on which we differed with extreme frankness, I think the result was to achieve a relation between us of greater mutual respect and friendship than ever before. I know that was the case on my side. Although I differed with him with the utmost freedom and outspokenness, he never took offense and seemed to respect my position. At the end I felt that I had achieved a better understanding with him than ever before. . . .

"I told him that the American people did not hate the Italians but took them rather as a joke as fighters; that only by an intellectual effort had they been convinced that Germany was their most dangerous enemy and should be disposed of before Japan; that the enemy whom the American people really hated, if they hated anyone, was Japan which had dealt them a foul blow. After setting out all the details upon which my conclusion was predicated, I asserted that it was my considered opinion that, if we allow ourselves to become so entangled with matters of the Balkans, Greece, and the Middle East that we could not fulfill our purpose of ROUNDHAMMER in 1944, that situation would be a serious blow to the prestige of the President's war policy and therefore to the interests of the United States.

"The P.M. apparently had not had that matter presented to him in that light before. He had no answer to it except that any such blow could be cured by victories. I answered that that would not be so if the victories were such that the people were not interested in and could not see any really strategic importance for them. Towards the end he confined his position to favoring a march on Rome with its prestige and the possibility of knocking Italy out of the war. Eden on the other hand continued to contend for carrying the war into the Balkans and Greece. At the end the P.M. reaffirmed his fidelity to the pledge of ROUNDHAMMER 'unless his military advisers could present him with some better opportunity' not yet disclosed. . . .

"On Thursday, July 15th, I called at the office which had been set up to prepare plans for ROUNDHAMMER under Lt. Gen. Morgan of the British Army as Chief of Staff and Maj. Gen. Ray W. Barker of the U.S.A. as his deputy. . . . I was much impressed with General Morgan's directness and sincerity. He gave us his mature opinion on the operation, with carefully stated provisos, to the effect that he believed that with the present allocated forces it could be successfully accomplished. He was very frank, however, in stating his fear of delays which might be caused by getting too deep into commitments in the Mediterranean. . . . Barker who explained the details of the plan to us shared the same fear. In other words, they both felt that the plan was sound and safe but there might be a subsequent yielding to temptation to undertake new activities which would interfere with the long stage of preparation in the false hope that such interference could be atoned for by subsequent speeding up.

"During the fortnight that I spent in England I found the same fear pervaded our own officers who were engaged in ROUNDHAMMER preparations. . . . They were all confident that the plan was feasible. On one particular danger which the P.M. had frequently urged upon me, namely the fear of a successful German counterattack after the landing had been made, the airmen were confident that they could by their overwhelming superiority in the air block the advances of the German reinforcements and thus defeat the counterattack. The matter had been carefully studied by them. They told me that their confidence was shared by the officers of the RAF. . . .

"I saw the P.M. again at a dinner given by Devers on Wednesday where I sat beside him, and again on Saturday I was with him nearly all day when he took me to Dover with a smaller family party in his special train. . . . During the trip back he brought me with evident delight a telegram which he had just received from the Combined Chiefs of Staff in Washington, telling him that General Marshall had proposed that a study be made of the operation known as AVALANCHE. [This was the landing executed in the following September at Salerno on the west coast of Italy near Naples.] He took this as an endorsement by Marshall of his whole Italian policy and was greatly delighted. I pointed out to him that it probably meant that Marshall had proposed this as a short cut intended to hasten the completion of the Italian adventure so that there would be no danger of clashing with the preparations for ROUNDHAMMER. . . .

"On Monday, July 19, I talked over the new telephone with Marshall and found that my assumption of Marshall's position was correct and that he had only suggested AVALANCHE so as to leave more time for ROUNDHAMMER and to obviate the danger of a long slow progress 'up the leg' [of Italy] which might eliminate ROUNDHAMMER altogether. I told him also of my talks with the P.M. and with the other military men, including particularly Morgan, and at the close of my statement he suggested to me that I should go as promptly as possible to Africa to see Eisenhower, where I should be able to round out what I had gotten in London with the views of the people in Africa. He said, 'Then you will have all sides and I think it is very important for you to go and to go quickly.' Information which I subsequently received from the P.M. as to his proposed early visit to America caused me to understand why Marshall urged haste. . . .

"I told the P.M. of my talk with Marshall and his confirmation of my interpretation of his support of AVALANCHE, namely that he favored it only for the purpose of expediting the march up the peninsula and that he was still as firmly in favor of ROUNDHAMMER as ever. I pointed out to the P.M. that Marshall's view as to ROUNDHAMMER had always been supported by the whole Operations Division of the American General Staff. I also told him of my talk with Generals Morgan and Barker and of their full support of the ROUNDHAMMER proposition.

"He at once broke out into a new attack upon ROUNDHAMMER. The check received by the British attack at Catania, Sicily, during the past few days had evidently alarmed him. He referred to it and praised the superlative fighting ability of the Germans. He said that if he had fifty thousand men ashore on the French Channel coast, he would not have an easy moment because he would feel that the Germans could rush up sufficient forces to drive them back into the sea. He repeated assertions he had made to me in previous conversations as to the disastrous effect of having the Channel full of corpses of defeated allies. This stirred me up and for a few minutes we had it hammer and tongs. I directly charged him that he was not in favor of the ROUNDHAMMER operation and that such statements as he made were 'like hitting us in the eye' in respect to a project which we had all deliberately adopted and in which we were comrades. . . . On this he said that, while he admitted that if he was C-in-C he would not set up the ROUNDHAMMER operation, yet having made his pledge he would go through with it loyally. I then told him that, while I did not at all question the sincerity of his promise to go with us, I was afraid he did not make sufficient allowance for the necessary long-distance planning and I feared that fatal curtailments might be made impulsively in the vain hope that those curtailments could be later repaid. I stressed the dangers of too great entanglement in an Italian expedition and the loss of time to ROUNDHAMMER which it would involve. He then told me that he was not insisting on going further than Rome unless we should by good luck obtain a complete Italian capitulation throwing open the whole of Italy as far as the north boundary. He asserted that he was not in favor of entering the Balkans with troops but merely wished to supply them with munitions and supplies. He told me that they were now doing magnificently when only being supplied ten tons a month. (*Note:* In these limitations he thus took a more conservative position than Eden had taken at the dinner on July 12.)

"When I parted with him, I felt that, if pressed by us, he would sincerely go ahead with the ROUNDHAMMER commitment but that he was looking so constantly and vigorously for an easy way of ending the war without a trans-Channel assault that, if we expected to be ready for a ROUNDHAMMER which would be early enough in 1944 to avoid the dangers of bad weather, we must be constantly on the lookout against Mediterranean diversions. I think it was at this meeting that he told me of his intention of coming to America and that he expected to come in the first half of August. I then understood what Marshall had meant in his telephone message as to the promptness on my part and I thereafter aimed my movements so as to be able to return to America in time to report to the President before such meeting."

From England Stimson flew to Africa to consult General Eisenhower, so as to have a clear understanding of the present potentialities of the Mediterranean theater. There he found that Eisenhower, in agreement with American officers in London and Washington, was in favor of a limited attack on Italy, having for its main object the capture of air bases in the Foggia area which were vitally needed for the prosecution of the air offensive against Germany; the air forces based in Great Britain were finding themselves severely limited by their distance from southeastern Germany and by the adverse weather conditions of the British Isles. In Stimson's report on this view he concluded:

"Such a project if feasible would not only not impair ROUNDHAMMER but it would greatly aid and facilitate it and would have the maximum advantage in effect upon Germany both psychologically and materially.

"This conception of the American staff of an Italian operation is entirely different from the conception put forward at times to me by the P.M. and Eden and also made by certain others, notably General Smuts in a letter to the P.M. This last, which for brevity I will call the British conception, is not put forward as an aid to ROUNDHAMMER but as a substitute to supplant it. It contemplates an invasion from the south—in the direction of the Balkans and Greece or possibly towards southern France though this last suggestion has not been pressed. Such a southern invasion and the ROUNDHAMMER invasion cannot be both maintained. On the contrary, if they are both held in contemplation, they will be in constant interference and will tend to neutralize each other. For example, under the American conception it is absolutely essential to have a speedy daring operation which will not draw upon or interfere with the mounting of ROUNDHAMMER. A slow progressive infiltration of the Italian boot from the bottom, time consuming and costly, would be sure to make ROUNDHAMMER impossible.

"The main thing therefore to keep constantly in mind is that the Italian effort must be strictly confined to the objective of securing bases for an air attack and there must be no further diversions of forces or matériel which will interfere with the coincident mounting of the ROUNDHAMMER project."

This memorandum of August 4 was sent to Harry Hopkins for delivery to the President at Shangri-La, Mr. Roosevelt's place of escape from Washington. Stimson went to Highhold for three days of rest. The President sent him a message that he had read it and "would see me as soon as he returned to Washington." Back at the Pentagon, Stimson received word "that he would see me tomorrow, Tuesday, at lunch. In order to prepare for my talk with him I invited Harry Hopkins over to lunch and talked over with him my memorandum, which he had read and also my conclusion. . . . I was very much interested to find as I went over with Harry Hopkins the suggestions in my own mind that he agreed with every step and with my final conclusion." (Diary, August 9, 1943)

The diary entry for the next day is as follows:

"Last night was the hottest night that I can ever recall in Woodley and I did not sleep very well as a consequence, particularly as I was tired with the hard day.

"Nevertheless I got up and dictated immediately after breakfast a proposed report of my conclusions on the events stated in the memorandum which I had already sent to the President. I decided that it would be better to present them to the President in writing. The decisions that I have recommended are among the most serious that I have had to make since I have been in this Department and I have found that a good written report gets further and lasts longer than a verbal conference with the President. It was hard work grinding my mind down to the summary of such important matters when I was feeling as tired as I was this morning. Nevertheless I managed to do it."

Later in the morning, when these recommendations had been typed as a letter to the President, "I read them over and signed it. Then I called in Marshall and let him read them, telling him that that was going to be my report to the President and I wanted him to know what I was going to say in case he had any serious objections to it. He said he had none but he did not want to have it appear that I had consulted him about it. I told him that for that very reason I had signed the paper before I showed it to him or anyone else and that I proposed to send it in unless there was some vital objection which I had been unable to conjure up myself. . . .

"Then at one o'clock I went to the White House and had one of the most satisfactory conferences I have ever had with the President. He was very cordial and insisted on hearing about my trip. Then we plunged into the ROUNDHAMMER matter and, after recalling to his memory some of the matters which were in my memorandum and which as a whole he had very thoroughly in his mind, I produced my letter of conclusions and handed it over to him and told him that I thought that was better than my trying to explain verbally."

August 10, 1943.

Dear Mr. President:

In my memorandum of last week, which was intended to be as factual as possible, I did not include certain conclusions to which I was driven by the experiences of my trip. For a year and a half they have been looming more and more clearly through the fog of our successive conferences with the British. The personal contacts, talks, and observations of my visit made them very distinct.

First: We cannot now rationally hope to be able to cross the Channel and come to grips with our German enemy under a British commander. His Prime Minister and his Chief of the Imperial Staff are frankly at variance with such a proposal. The shadows of Passchendaele and Dunkerque still hang too heavily over the imagination of these leaders of his government. Though they have rendered lip service to the operation, their hearts are not in it and it will require more independence, more faith, and more vigor than it is reasonable to expect we can find in any British commander to overcome the natural difficulties of such an operation carried on in such an atmosphere of his government. There are too many natural obstacles to be overcome, too many possible side avenues of diversion which are capable of stalling and thus thwarting such an operation.

Second: The difference between us is a vital difference of faith. The American staff believes that only by massing the immense vigor and power of the American and British nations under the overwhelming mastery of the air, which they already exercise far into the north of France and which can be made to cover our subsequent advance in France just as it has in Tunis and Sicily, can Germany be really defeated and the war brought to a real victory.

On the other side, the British theory (which cropped out again and again in unguarded sentences of the British leaders with whom I have just been talking) is that Germany can be beaten by a series of attritions in northern Italy, in the eastern Mediterranean, in Greece, in the Balkans, in Rumania and other satellite countries. . . .

To me, in the light of the postwar problems which we shall face, that attitude . . . seems terribly dangerous. We are pledged quite as clearly as Great Britain to the opening of a real second front. None of these methods of pinprick warfare can be counted on by us to fool Stalin into the belief that we have kept that pledge.

Third: I believe therefore that the time has come for you to decide that your government must assume the responsibility of leadership in this great final movement of the European war which is now confronting us. We cannot afford to confer again and close with a lip tribute to BOLERO which we have tried twice and failed to carry out. We cannot afford to begin the most dangerous operation of the war under halfhearted leadership which will invite failure or at least disappointing results. Nearly two years ago the British offered us this command. I think that now it should be accepted—if necessary, insisted on.

We are facing a difficult year at home with timid and hostile hearts ready to seize and exploit any wavering on the part of our war leadership. A firm resolute leadership, on the other hand, will go far to silence such voices. The American people showed this in the terrible year of 1864, when the firm unfaltering tactics of the Virginia campaign were endorsed by the people of the United States in spite of the hideous losses of the Wilderness, Spottsylvania, and Cold Harbor.

Finally, I believe that the time has come when we must put our most commanding soldier in charge of this critical operation at this critical time. You are far more fortunate than was Mr. Lincoln or Mr. Wilson in the ease with which that selection can be made. Mr. Lincoln had to fumble through a process of trial and error with dreadful losses until he was able to discover the right choice. Mr. Wilson had to choose a man who was virtually unknown to the American people and to the foreign armies with which he was to serve. General Marshall already has a towering eminence of reputation as a tried soldier and as a broad-minded and skillful administrator. This was shown by the suggestion of him on the part of the British for this very post a year and a half ago. I believe that he is the man who most surely can now by his character and skill furnish the military leadership which is necessary to bring our two nations together in confident joint action in this great operation. No one knows better than I the loss in the problems of organization and world-wide strategy centered in Washington which such a solution would cause, but I see no other alternative to which we can turn in the great effort which confronts us.

Faithfully yours,
HENRY L. STIMSON
Secretary of War

The President,
The White House

The President "read it through with very apparent interest, approving each step after step and saying finally that I had announced the conclusions which he had just come to himself. We discussed the matter in its many aspects and then passed on to" other matters, among them current negotiations about the atomic bomb. By the time these matters were disposed of, "the time had come for a conference which he was going to have with the Joint Chiefs of Staff and he invited me to stay and sit in on the conference. Generals Marshall and Arnold and Admirals King and Leahy then came in together with Colonel Deane. We then had a very interesting conference on the subject of the coming conference with the Prime Minister and with the British Chiefs of Staff. The President went the whole hog on the subject of ROUNDHAMMER. He was more clear and definite than I have ever seen him since we have been in this war and he took the policy that the American staff have been fighting for fully. He was for going no further into Italy than Rome and then for the purpose of establishing bases. He was for setting up as rapidly as possible a larger force in Great Britain for the purpose of ROUNDHAMMER so that as soon as possible and before the actual time of landing we should have more soldiers in Britain dedicated to that purpose than the British. It then became evident what the purpose was and he announced it. He said he wanted to have an American commander and he thought that would make it easier if we had more men in the expedition at the beginning. I could see that the military and naval conferees were astonished and delighted at his definiteness. . . . It was very interesting and satisfactory to me to find him going over with the Joint Chiefs of Staff the very matters which I had taken up with him and announcing his own support of the various positions which I had urged, and I came away with a very much lighter heart on the subject of our military policy than I have had for a long time. If he can only hold it through in the conferences which he is going to have with the Prime Minister, it will greatly clear up the situation."

The President held it through. The cross-Channel attack had at last become wholly his own, and it developed at Quebec two weeks later that the Prime Minister too was preparing to face the inevitable. Winston Churchill was as magnanimous in reconciliation as he was stubborn and eloquent in opposition, and when Stimson was called to Quebec from his vacation on August 22, he found that the President's scheme for moving troops to England had proved unnecessary. "He told me that Churchill had voluntarily come to him and offered to accept Marshall for the OVERLORD operation." In a later conversation Mr. Churchill "said he had done this in spite of the fact that he had previously promised the position to [Field Marshal] Brooke and that this would embarrass him somewhat, but he showed no evidence of retreating from his suggestion to the President. I was of course greatly cheered up. . . ." (Diary notes on vacation trip, August, 1943)

The decisions of Quebec were not quite final, but from this time onward OVERLORD held the inside track. There were further alarms from the Prime Minister during the Moscow Conference of Foreign Ministers in October, and in November at Teheran he made a last great effort to urge the importance of operations in the eastern Mediterranean, even at the cost of delay in OVERLORD. But at Teheran the President was reinforced by the blunt firmness of Marshal Stalin, whose comments on the doubts and diversionary suggestions of Mr.

Churchill Stimson followed in the minutes of the meetings with great interest. OVERLORD became at last a settled commitment, and in his press conference on December 9 Stimson allowed himself the following comment:

"The principal event of the past week has been the conference at Teheran. I have received and carefully studied the minutes of the military discussions and the records of the decisions at that conference. While, of course, the nature and details of those decisions cannot be made public, I can say that the presence of Premier Stalin and of his companion at the conference, Marshal Voroshilov, has contributed mightily to the success of the conference. Marshall Stalin's power of lucid analysis and the fairness of his attitude contributed strongly to the solution of several long-standing problems."

It was after Teheran, at Cairo, that the question of the supreme commander for OVERLORD was finally settled. It had been understood since Quebec that this commander should be an American, but objections had arisen in the United States to the selection of General Marshall. The news of his prospective appointment leaked to the press and persons eager to discredit the administration claimed that it was a British plot to remove his influence from the central direction of the war. Others dared to suggest that he was being sent away from Washington so that the President could replace him with General Somervell and insure the use of Army contracts to support his campaign for re-election. To this suggestion, an outrageous libel against all concerned, Stimson promptly gave a stern denial, but it was not so easy to quiet those who sincerely felt that Marshall was indispensable as Chief of Staff. None of this questioning would have been important if it had arisen *after* a definite announcement of Marshall's new position, for the enormous significance of his duties as supreme commander would then have been concrete and self-evident, not merely potential. But, as it was, Stimson could see that the President was disturbed.

Nor was the matter made easier by Marshall's own attitude. His sensitive personal integrity kept him completely silent about the question. Except on one occasion when Stimson drove him to a reluctant admission that 'any soldier would prefer a field command,' he firmly refused to discuss the matter and the President was therefore cut off from the counsel of the man whose advice he had learned to accept without hesitation on all major Army appointments. Feeling himself at least in part the originator of the move to make Marshall supreme commander, Stimson did what he could to help the President to a final conclusion. He even urged that Mr. Roosevelt might persuade the British to accept Marshall as commander of both the European and the Mediterranean theaters; but the British, like the Americans, had public opinion to deal with, and this plan proved impracticable. Furthermore, Marshall's appointment would involve complex readjustments of the command in other theaters and there remained the difficult problem of selecting a man to act in his place as Chief of Staff. When the President departed for Teheran, the matter was still unsettled.

Marshal Stalin emphatically stated at Teheran that he could not consider the OVERLORD promise definite until a supreme commander had been appointed, and under this spur the President reached his decision in a meeting with Marshall at Cairo. Stimson learned from the cables what the President finally decided, but he did not hear the full story until Mr. Roosevelt returned to Washington. On December 18 he had lunch with the President and received a detailed account of the matter.

"He described his luncheon with Marshall after the conference was over and they had returned to Cairo. He let drop the fact, which I had supposed to be true, that Churchill wanted Marshall for the commander and had assumed that it was settled as, in fact, it had been agreed on in Quebec. The President described, however, how he reopened this matter with Marshall at their solitary luncheon together and tried to get Marshall to tell him whether he preferred to hold the command of OVERLORD (now that a general supreme commander was not feasible) or whether he preferred to remain as Chief of Staff. He was very explicit in telling me that he urged Marshall to tell him which one of the two he personally preferred, intimating that he would be very glad to give him the one that he did. He said that Marshall stubbornly refused,

saying that it was for the President to decide and that he,
Marshall, would do with equal cheerfulness whichever one
he was selected for. The President said that he got the impression that Marshall was not only impartial between the two but
perhaps really preferred to remain as Chief of Staff. Finally,
having been unable to get him to tell his preference, the President said that he decided on a mathematical basis that if Marshall took OVERLORD it would mean that Eisenhower would
become Chief of Staff but, while Eisenhower was a very good
soldier and familiar with the European Theater, he was unfamiliar with what had been going on in the Pacific and he
also would be far less able than Marshall to handle the Congress; that, therefore, he, the President, decided that he would
be more comfortable if he kept Marshall at his elbow in Washington and turned over OVERLORD to Eisenhower. I thanked
him for his frank narration of the facts. I said that frankly I
was staggered when I heard of the change for I thought that
the other arrangement was thoroughly settled at Quebec. I
said that I had chosen to recommend Marshall in my letter to
the President last summer for two reasons: first, because I was
confident that he was our best man for OVERLORD and he would
be able to push through the operation in spite of the obstacles
and delays which I felt certain it would meet in Great Britain
on account of the attitude of the Prime Minister and the British Staff; but, secondly, I said that I knew that in the bottom
of his heart it was Marshall's secret desire above all things to
command this invasion force into Europe; that I had had very
hard work to wring out of Marshall that this was so, but I had
done so finally beyond the possibility of misunderstanding,
and I said, laughingly, to the President: 'I wish I had been
along with you in Cairo. I could have made that point clear.'
And I told the President that, like him, I had had great difficulty in getting Marshall to speak on such a subject of his
personal preference, but that I had finally accomplished it and
that when he was on the point of leaving for this Teheran
conference I had begged him not to sacrifice what I considered
the interests of the country to the undue sensitiveness of his
own conscience in seeming to seek a post." (Diary, December
18, 1943)

THE ARMY AND GRAND STRATEGY

The appointment of Eisenhower was a disappointment to
Stimson, but only in that it was not the appointment of Marshall. This feeling he promptly explained in a letter to the new
supreme commander in order that there might be no shadow
of misunderstanding; he assured Eisenhower of his confident
and wholehearted support and received a reply of disarming
sincerity:

"I have always agreed with you that General Marshall was
the logical choice to do the OVERLORD job, but as long as it has
been assigned to me you need have no fear but that I will do
my best. It is heartening indeed to have your expression of
confidence."

As for Marshall himself, never by any sign did he show
that he was not wholly satisfied with the President's decision.
It seemed indeed quite possible that Marshall had himself
independently concluded that whatever his desires, his duty
lay in Washington, and that he had refused to say so to the
President or to Stimson because any such claim would have
seemed immodest—it would have been as unlike Marshall as
the contrary course of seeking field command. Many times in
the war Stimson had cause to wonder at the quality of this
American, but perhaps no other incident showed more clearly
his utter selflessness. As Stimson had remarked in speaking of
him a year before, the proverb truly applied: "He that ruleth
his spirit is better than he that taketh a city."

Events confirmed the President's judgment. General Eisenhower fully justified the confidence placed in him, and General Marshall continued to serve in Washington as only he
could do. By the middle of June, 1944, Stimson was happy to
acknowledge to his diary that the two men were in the right
place after all.

The decisions of Cairo and Teheran ended two years of discussion. At their meeting of December 18 the President had
remarked to Stimson, "I have thus brought OVERLORD back to
you safe and sound on the ways for accomplishment." And so
it proved. Occasionally during the months that followed Stimson felt concern lest continued British caution might adversely
affect the operation, but events belied his fears. When the time

came in the following summer to mount the supporting invasion of southern France, there was one further contest with British advocates of a Balkan operation, but in this Stimson was only a satisfied observer of the firmness of the President and the Joint Chiefs of Staff. His major part in Operation OVERLORD had come to its victorious ending six months before the English Channel was crossed.

Through those six months the men in the War Department waited with a growing sense of tense anticipation. The game for them was now afoot, and they knew that OVERLORD would be a full test of their Army. They had argued for this campaign in the conviction that a properly equipped and well-trained Army could fight on equal terms with the best forces of an experienced enemy *in its first battle*—most of the divisions in the invasion would have no previous experience. More than that, the whole theory of victory by ground force superiority—supported by air mastery—was one in which the War Department had been a lonely advocate. The victories of North Africa and Italy had not dispelled the caution with which many Allied officers looked at the new American Army, nor were there many Americans outside the General Staff and the Ground Forces who wholeheartedly believed that the Army could produce explosive victories against the battle-tested Germans. In 1947, when the great American victories of the OVERLORD campaign were history, it seemed important to Stimson to recall that the Army which won those victories was born of George Marshall's faith, trained under Leslie McNair in the great maneuver grounds of the United States, and commanded by generals few of whom had commanded troops in battle anywhere before D-day.

It was no wonder, then, that as the eyes of all the world turned toward the English Channel in the spring of 1944, the senior officers of the War Department waited with especial anxiety for news from the Supreme Commander. What they heard needs no retelling here—the unprecedented sweep across France in the summer of 1944 is recognized as one of the great campaigns of all military history.

As the anxiety of the last days before the landing gave way to cautious satisfaction at its first success, and to full confi-

dence after the first great victory at Cherbourg, Stimson realized that OVERLORD was destined to succeed, and he gave himself the satisfaction of going over to see it for himself. In a
flying visit to England and Normandy in mid-July, he saw
in action the magnificent forces of General Eisenhower and
stood in wonder, like any private soldier, at the colossal scope
of the undertaking, with its vast bases in Great Britain, its
great fleets and beehive beaches on the other side, its overwhelming air support, its first-rate fighting troops, and above
all its calm and supremely competent field leadership. At
General Bradley's headquarters he heard the plan that later
exploded the American Third Army through the enemy lines
to clear the way for the liberation of all France, and, observing
the troops and equipment which packed the narrow Cotentin
Peninsula, he knew that Bradley had what he needed for the
execution of this bold and brilliant plan. The brief visit with
its sharply etched impressions was a clear demonstration to
Stimson that in his unwearied assertion of the powers of the
fresh and vigorous American Army he had, if anything, un-
derstated his case. It was not often that a man could see so
clearly as a triumphant fact what he had argued as a theory
not many months before. In England Stimson exchanged con-
gratulations with his friend and former adversary, the Prime
Minister. 'It is wonderful, a great triumph,' said the P.M.,
and Stimson did not see any need to quarrel when Mr. Churchill added, 'But we could never have done it last year.'

The foregoing account represents with complete frankness
Stimson's part in the long deliberations which reached their
climax in the final decisions of Cairo, and their fruition in the
year of victories which began on the following sixth of June
in Normandy. As an important part of Stimson's life this
account has been a necessary chapter of our book, and it has
seemed proper not to curb or moderate the story by any retrospective comment until it should be fully told. It is a story of
persistent and deep-seated differences between partners in
a great undertaking. Of Stimson's own share in it he found
no reason later to be ashamed. If any advocacy of his had

been helpful in securing the adoption of the Operation OVER-
LORD he was proud.

But this accomplishment would become unimportant, and
it would be far better that it should not have been discussed,
if the reader should conclude from the foregoing that Stimson
considered these differences to be indicative of any basic cleavage between the British and the American leaders and peoples.
Still less would it be his wish that any small-minded conclusions should be drawn about the character or purposes of the
greathearted and brilliant Englishman who was the leader in
opposing the final decision. The great fact is not the differences but their settlement, and in the execution of OVERLORD
after Cairo there was no one more energetic or more determined than the Prime Minister, and no one more delighted
by its success.

The reluctance of British leaders to accept a cross-Channel
operation seemed far less remarkable to Stimson than the
courage with which they finally supported it. To the British
the Channel had been for centuries a barrier of special import,
and if it had protected them so long, might it not now protect
their enemies? Beyond the Channel lay France, where a generation before the British people had paid a ghastly price of
youth and strength in years of massive stalemate. From World
War II there were the further painful memories of Dunkirk
and Dieppe. The British Prime Minister had himself been a
farsighted and incisive opponent of the bloody futility of the
western front in 1915 and afterward; it was wholly natural
that he should be fearful lest there be a repetition of that
slaughter. If the Americans had suffered similar losses in the
First World War or faced similar succeeding dangers, would
they have felt differently? There was here no need for criticism. Americans could rest content with the fact that in their
freshness and their vast material strength they naturally
argued for the bold and forceful course, and in action justified
their argument.

After the war some writers plentifully endowed with misinformation chose to make capital out of "revelations" of disagreement between America and Great Britain; these men
demonstrated only their own special purposes. In America

some of these writings took the shape of personal attacks on Mr. Churchill. These could well be left to Mr. Churchill himself, for that doughty warrior had never yet required help in defending his policies. But this much it seemed proper for Stimson to say: It was his considered opinion that with the single exception of Franklin Roosevelt no man in any country had been a greater factor than Mr. Churchill in the construction of the grand alliance that destroyed the Nazis; no man had been quicker to leap the gulf of mutual suspicion and strike fellowship with Russia; none had more steadfastly sustained the allies of his nation while remaining frankly and explicitly "the King's first minister"; with no man at times had Stimson had sharper differences and for none had he higher admiration.

One of the postwar conclusions reached by some American writers was that the British opposition to OVERLORD was mainly guided by a desire to block Soviet Russia by an invasion farther east. This view seemed to Stimson wholly erroneous. Never in any of his long and frank discussions with the British leaders was any such argument advanced, and he saw no need whatever to assume any such grounds for the British position. Not only did the British have many good grounds to fear a cross-Channel undertaking, but Mr. Churchill had been for nearly thirty years a believer in what he called the "right hook." In 1943 he retained all his long-held strategic convictions, combined with a natural British concern for the Mediterranean theater, and in Stimson's view that was all there was to it.

Far more serious than any personal vilification, even of so great a man as Mr. Churchill, was the possibility that Americans of good will might be unduly affected by postwar discussion of differences and disagreements between their leaders and the leaders of Great Britain. Naturally and inevitably British and American interests had frequently diverged in specific areas of the world and disputes on these matters had frequently become warm. To draw broad and bitter conclusions from such disagreements would be mean and self-righteous folly.

Stimson's disagreement with Mr. Churchill over the cross-

Channel invasion was not his only difference with British leaders during the war. Sometimes he took issue with the British government and sometimes with individual Englishmen, and such differences of opinion were not new to him. As Secretary of State he had faced similar difficulties and as a private observer throughout his life he found points in British policy of which he could not approve. It would have been remarkable if it had been otherwise. But all of these differences were trivial compared to his underlying conviction that the final interests of both the United States and Great Britain required the two nations to live together in constantly closer association. The re-establishment of such cordial relations had been his first object as Secretary of State in 1929, and in World War II it was only on the basis of the solid mutual confidence established under the pressure of a common emergency that he was able to be bluntly frank in his disagreements with the British.

In the relationship between the British and American peoples Stimson found no place for pettiness. The true purposes and convictions of the two nations made it inevitable that they should be friends. On the basis of such friendship they might often frankly disagree, for it would be as unbecoming to avoid necessary disagreements as it would be foolish to rejoice in them. But in casting back through his thirty years of close relationship with the British nation it seemed to Stimson that the courage and honor of the Highland Division in 1918, the outstretched hand of Ramsay MacDonald in 1929, the invincible spirit of the whole nation under Churchill in World War II, and a score of other personal memories of Great Britain as a land of hope and glory and friendship— these things, and not specific disagreements, were of final importance.

The real lesson of World War II therefore was not to be found in any revelations of disagreement. Franklin Roosevelt and Winston Churchill established and sustained a wartime collaboration which grew ever stronger in the settlement of successive differences. When all the arguments have been forgotten, this central fact will remain. The two nations fought a single war, and their quarrels were the quarrels of brothers.

CHAPTER XVIII

The Wartime Army

IN LATE November, 1942, after the Joint and the Combined Chiefs of Staff had been created and had begun to function, one of the less tactful hangers-on of the administration asked Stimson how he liked being relegated to the position of housekeeper for the Army. The question was a foolish one, betraying a fundamental ignorance of the functions of a Secretary of War; in recording Stimson's work from Pearl Harbor to VJ-day, only this one chapter can be given to problems of War Department administration. A further foolishness lay in the assumption that Stimson did not like Army housekeeping, or thought it unimportant.

I. REORGANIZATION

The first and greatest wartime administrative achievement of the War Department was the reorganization made effective by Presidential order on March 9, 1942. In General Marshall's words, this reorganization "established three great commands under the direct supervision of the Chief of Staff—the Army Air Forces, the Army Ground Forces, and the Services of Supply (later designated as the Army Service Forces)."[1]

Decentralization of authority was an imperative requirement for effective war expansion. Whereas previously the chiefs of all the Army's arms and services had been largely autonomous officers, each with the right of direct appeal to the Chief of Staff, the Army inside the United States was now to be controlled by three officers, each clothed with full authority

[1] Biennial Report of the Chief of Staff, July 1, 1943, p. 33.

within his own field. This meant, for the Air Forces, a formal recognition of the increased measure of autonomy which had been agreed on in the previous summer, for the Ground Forces a centralized direction of the organization and training of the great new armies, and for the Service Forces, a more efficient co-ordination of the procurement and technical employment of the weapons and equipment of a technological war. But to Stimson the most important result of all was that the reorganization freed the General Staff for the broad duties of planning and supervision which were its proper assignment.

Since it is often argued that the Army is not capable of reforming itself, it is of some importance to note that Stimson's personal activity in this broad field of Army organization was more important in limiting change than in encouraging it. Twice he used his veto power to prevent suggested changes. During the preparation of the reorganization of 1942 he insisted on a rigorous adherence to the traditional conception of the duties and authority of the Chief of Staff, and in 1943 he prevented a further "streamlining" of the Army Service Forces. Both of these actions deserve attention; both originated in Stimson's memory of the issues involved in the great Root reorganization of 1903.

The title of Chief of Staff, borrowed by Root from Europe, was not lightly chosen; it was a deliberate statement of the fact that the highest military officer of the Army exercises his authority only by direction of the President. The name was designed by Root to implant a conception of military responsibility wholly different from that which had led "Commanding Generals" after the Civil War to believe that they were independent of the ignorant whims of presidents and secretaries of war. To Stimson it seemed vital that this reform should not be jeopardized, even unintentionally, by any change in the title and function of the Chief of Staff in 1942, and he accordingly vetoed the Staff's proposal to vest the Chief of Staff with the title of Commander. In the case of a man like General Marshall, fully alive to his responsibility both to the Secretary of War and to the President, the matter was quite unimportant, and Stimson certainly intended no disparagement of that great officer. It was further obvious that in the course of his duties,

the Chief of Staff must inevitably exercise many of the functions of a commander, and Stimson was the first to insist that
his authority must be unconditionally recognized by every
other officer in the Army. But this authority must be that of
the President's representative—under the Constitution there
could be only one Commander in Chief, and to recognize any
lesser officer with such a title was either insubordination or
flagrant misuse of language. The Army was an instrument of
the President; there must be no repetition of the state of mind
which had led General Sherman, as "Commanding General"
in 1874, to move his headquarters away from the wickedness
of Washington to St. Louis.

The "streamlining" suggested for the Service Forces in
1943 was a brain child of General Somervell. The changes of
1942 had abolished the Chief of Infantry and the other chiefs
of the arms, turning over their functions to the Commanding
General of the Ground Forces, with a view to insuring the
development of a fully co-ordinated training program for the
combined arms. The chiefs of the administrative services, however—Ordnance, Quartermaster, Engineers, and so on—had
survived with most of their traditional duties intact, under the
direction of the Commanding General of the Service Forces.
In September, 1943, General Somervell proposed that the
functions and prerogatives of these branches be turned over
to a set of new directors, mostly with new names, and with
powers organized on more functional and less traditional lines.
At the same time he proposed a redistricting of the Army's
nine Service Commands. Stimson was prepared in general to
accept Somervell's judgment that his proposed changes would
in the end increase the efficiency of the Service Forces, but it
was a grave question whether the improvement would outweigh its concomitant disadvantages in the creation of bad
feeling. On September 21, Stimson discussed the matter with
McCloy and Patterson. "We three had a very satisfactory talk
about it. I have been tending to feel that this reorganization is
ill advised . . . because it proposes to wipe out the existence of
the administrative services such as the Engineers, the Ordnance, the Quartermaster's Department, and the Signal Corps.
. . . This proposition brings up to me poignant memories of my

experience in 1911-12 when I learned only too well how deeply imbedded in sentiment the services of the Engineers, Ordnance, and Quartermaster are in the memories of all the people that belonged to them, and the tremendous uproar that would be created if we tried to destroy all that sentiment by wiping out the distinction of the services with their insignia, etc. I found in this talk with Patterson that under the present organization the work of production and procurement is going satisfactorily. Whatever critics may say, we have done an almost miraculous job and I therefore am *prima facie* against stirring up a hornet's nest right in the middle of a war when things are going well. . . . Patterson and McCloy shared my views." (Diary, September 21, 1943)

The next day Stimson had the matter out in a conference with the soldiers, and the proposal was killed. Remembering his experiences in supporting Leonard Wood, "who was not unlike General Somervell in his temperament and other characteristics," Stimson saw no reason to create bitterness which could be avoided. Nor was it as if the service branches, like General Ainsworth in the olden time, had shown themselves insubordinate or un-co-operative. There had been slow and unimaginative work in the early days of the emergency, but Stimson had observed with satisfaction the high quality of the work done by such men as Campbell in Ordnance, and the Chief of Engineers and Quartermaster General were men of whom Somervell himself thought well enough to intend giving them new and enlarged responsibilities in his reorganization. General Somervell's driving energy was an enormous asset to the Army, but in this case it seemed better that it should be curbed. His plans were formally disapproved in a letter written by Stimson on October 5, and in succeeding weeks as belated rumors of the proposed changes began to produce a series of worried and disapproving questions from the President, Congress, and such knowing observers as Bernard Baruch, Stimson was confirmed in his belief that this decision against "reform" had been a wise one.

2. "DIPPING DOWN"

The reorganization of March, 1942, was the only major wartime change in the administrative setup of the War Department. The increased decentralization which it insured somewhat shifted the function of the Secretary of War, who retained direct control only over the Bureau of Public Relations and the administration of his own office. There remained, however, supervisory responsibilities which necessarily though occasionally involved Stimson in direct dealings with all the other branches. The principle on which he exercised these functions he explained to Somervell on May 27, 1943. "I gave him a long discourse on my views of the duties of the Secretary of War based on my experience with two great executives—Theodore Roosevelt and Franklin Roosevelt. I told him I did not intend to make the mistakes which Franklin had made of establishing a lot of independent agencies reporting only to himself; but on the other hand I did intend to do what Theodore Roosevelt did, which was to feel perfectly free to dip down into the lower echelons, so to speak, and interest myself keenly and directly with what is going on in exceptional cases." Giving as an example his work for the advancement of radar, Stimson assured the General, for whom he had the highest regard, that he had no intention of abusing this prerogative. Both Somervell and General Marshall fully understood this position, and there is no record of any significant cleavage between the Secretary's office and the chief military leaders of the War Department.

Most of the cases of such "dipping down" were of the kind that suggest themselves to a senior officer in a tour of inspection; either Stimson or someone whom he trusted would observe a failing or apparent failing, and the result would be a memorandum to General Marshall or a short inquiry directed straight to the officer in charge of the matter. Stimson had been on the receiving end of inspectorial comments often enough to know that in many cases they were based on an incomplete understanding of the problem, but he also knew the value of such criticisms in stimulating increased efforts to find a satisfactory solution.

In other cases, the activities of the Secretary were the result of some nonmilitary aspect of the matter. The appointment of a Surgeon General, or a Chief of Chaplains, for example, involved a decision in the Secretary's office because, especially in wartime, these offices attracted the close interest and attention of civilian doctors and clergymen, who felt that the normal methods of military selection could not be counted on to produce men with the desired standing as professionals. The Medical Department, furthermore, was a matter of special interest to Stimson on account of his personal experience in the tropics, and particularly after the appointment of Major General Norman T. Kirk, whom he had first known in the Philippines, he took an active part in supporting its labors.

Another department to which Stimson's attention was given, in accordance with the requirements of the law, was that of the Judge Advocate General. As wartime pressure increased, he was gradually released by new statutes from much of the labor of reviewing court-martial records, but throughout his years in the War Department he was forced from time to time to give his close attention to specific cases, particularly those involving the death sentence. In spite of the strong tendency of a humane reviewing authority to exercise leniency, Stimson fully understood the close relationship between military justice and military discipline; it was not easy, for example, to approve the dismissal of proved combat fliers who, returning from battle, insisted on disregarding the safety regulations of the continental United States, but he cheerfully accepted General Marshall's recommendation that mercy should be subordinated to justice—and the public safety.

Another section of the War Department to which his personal attention was frequently directed was Military Intelligence. By a curious irony, the matter of principal importance here was the development of the very operation of attacking foreign codes and ciphers which Stimson had banished from the State Department in 1929. In 1940 and after, the world was no longer in a condition to be able to act on the principle of mutual trust which had guided him as Secretary of State, and as Secretary of War he fully supported the extraordinary operations that were later revealed to have broken the Japanese codes. In early 1942, with McCloy's assistance, he established a special unit for the analysis and interpretation of this sort of material. This unit, under the direction of Alfred Mc-Cormack, a New York lawyer turned colonel, did its work with remarkable insight and skill. As investigation of the Pearl Harbor catastrophe later revealed, such a unit, if it had existed in 1941, might well have given warning of the degree of Japanese interest in the fleet at Hawaii. It was not Pearl Harbor, however, but the natural development of studies begun months before that led to the establishment of the unit, and if it came into existence too late to help in the prevention of that calamity, it made invaluable contributions in other matters of at least comparable significance during the war.

Stimson also did what he could to insure the effective exchange of military information among different branches of the Government and with America's allies, particularly the British. He backed General Marshall's efforts to break down American resistance to co-operation with the British, and he was insistent that no impatience with its occasional eccentricities should deprive the Army of the benefits of co-operation with General Donovan's Office of Strategic Services. Throughout the war the intelligence activities of the United States Government remained incompletely co-ordinated, but here again it was necessary to measure the benefits of reorganization against its dislocations, and on the whole Stimson felt that the American achievement in this field, measured against the conditions of 1940, was more than satisfactory. A full reorganization belonged to the postwar period.

3. THE PLACE OF SPECIALISTS

Stimson inherited, from the comments of his father on the subject of the "bombproof" officers of the Civil War, and from his own experience with 'the uniform-wearing civilians doing morale duty in the back areas' of World War I, a strong feeling that the dignity of the uniform should as far as possible be reserved for those who in fact did the fighting. It was true that this conviction flew in the face of the developing complexity of war; perhaps not half of the men who served usefully in the Army of World War II would have satisfied Dr. Lewis Stimson's definition of a genuine combatant. As one of those constantly urging the advantages of new weapons and techniques, his son was fully aware of the difference between Marshall's army and Grant's; but he was also, from his own experience, well aware of the constant pressure exerted by men anxious 'to obtain the kudos of having worn a combatant uniform without having performed combatant duty.' It was this experience that had made him lay down in 1940 a rigid set of requirements for appointments to commissioned rank.

In 1942, as he observed the increasing requirement for wholly noncombatant specialists in military operations, Stimson turned to the creation of an Army Specialist Corps, which should recruit for service with the Army the scientists and technical experts who were so much needed in all branches. The men of this corps were to be selected for nonmilitary qualifications and would serve as civilians but with military grades, in a uniform unlike that of the Army but designed to satisfy their self-respect and give them protection under the rules of war, if captured. Other armies, notably the German Army, had used and demonstrated the value of such an organized civilian corps.

But in the American Army the effort failed. Several months passed while the Specialist Corps was being formed, and before it was ready to carry out its assignment events had made that assignment impossible; civilians had already been commissioned in the Army of the United States in very large numbers, and the men of the Specialist Corps found themselves at a hopeless disadvantage in comparison with these other civilians who were already wearing the Army uniform.

Army commanders who needed high-class men for specialist civilian duty, and needed them in a hurry, 'found it so much easier to get them by pandering to the itch to wear the Army uniform that they threw their influence against the Specialist Corps and failed to support the effort to preserve the dignity of their own uniform.' In the face of this combination of disadvantages—the greatly increased complexity of civilian duties in the Army, the belated organization, and the reluctance of military commanders to run the risk of losing picked

civilian aides—it was decided to abandon the new organization and to incorporate its recruits so far as possible in the
Army itself.

Nevertheless the work which it had accomplished under the
direction of a former Secretary of War, Dwight Davis, was
far from wasted. The more than 200,000 applications it had
processed became a useful part of the Army's file on available
civilians. And from its experience came much of the knowledge and technique which made the Officer Procurement
Service an outstanding success.

With the failure of the Specialist Corps—"an experiment
noble in purpose"—Stimson ended his effort to distinguish
between combat soldiers and rear-area troops; it was not that
kind of war, and even a successful Specialist Corps would not
have solved the problem. World War II saw the full development of the usual resentment of company for regiment, regiment for corps, corps for supply troops, and everyone overseas
for everyone at home. But there was no denying that all of
these resented echelons were necessary parts of the American
Army.

4. STUDENT SOLDIERS

A wartime Secretary of War frequently finds himself the
unhappy arbiter between the conflicting requirements of
"military necessity" and "the long view." In no case during
the war was this conflict more trying than in the complex task of adjusting the relationship of the Army to the
colleges.

The basic decision of 1941 had been to find the bulk of the
junior officers for the new army inside the Army itself. To this
position the War Department adhered throughout the war;
for a variety of reasons it was the only satisfactory general
principle. But as the expanding demands of the growing Army
remorselessly reduced the draft age in gradual stages from
twenty-one to eighteen, it became apparent that special
arrangements must be made to provide for a proper wartime
employment of the nation's colleges. Without yielding to the
extreme view of some educators that college training for general leadership was of such pressing importance as to justify

wholesale deferment, Stimson fully accepted the more balanced view of most college presidents that the values of academic training must not be wholly disregarded in the general mobilization of American youth. He was irritated by the apparent willingness of the Navy to promise commissions to selected students without prior service and competition in the enlisted ranks, but part of this annoyance stemmed from his certainty that in the colleges of early 1942 there was a large reservoir of officer material from which the Army stood in danger of being cut off.

The first attempt at a solution to the problem was the establishment in the colleges of a program for students recruited into the Army Enlisted Reserve. Under this program college men were to be deferred as students to continue their studies, and upon their entry on active service they were to have an opportunity to *compete* for a commission. They were not, at Stimson's insistence, to be formally recognized cadets; they were potential, not designated, officer candidates.

The Army Enlisted Reserve lasted only a few months. As the demand for men increased, it became rapidly more difficult to justify the deferment of college students, either to the General Staff or to the general public. The program lacked justice in that it dealt kindly with men whose presence in college was the result largely of their happy choice of parents; there was no true answer to the charge that the deferment of such men was inconsistent with the Army's policy of democratic selection of officers. In August, 1942, Stimson announced that all members of the Enlisted Reserve would be called to active service as soon as they reached draft age.

There remained the colleges. Educators insisted that it was unwise to leave unemployed the nation's greatest engines for the instruction of young men of Army age, and Stimson and his advisers tried again. At the end of 1942 they established the Army Specialized Training Program (ASTP), under which selected younger soldiers of promise were to be sent, as soldiers, to continue at the colleges such studies as might be judged useful in their later military service. There was no connection between this training and a commission, except in so far as their added training might make these students more worthy of promotion, and the very small demand for new officers after 1943 in the end prevented all but a few from winning bars. Many ASTP students undoubtedly felt cheated at this result; they had however allowed their hopes to outrun the Army's promise. The novelty and breadth of this program made its organization and administration unusually difficult, but during 1943 it became gradually more and more effective. And then, in February, 1944, it was decided to end the program on the following April 1.

The ASTP was killed by the manpower shortage. At the end of 1943 the General Staff, finding itself in desperate need of additional troops for the great campaigns of the coming year, no longer accepted as controlling the argument that in the long run college training for selected men was a necessary investment in leadership. Although he took pains to make it entirely clear to the Staff that his interest in such training was personal and intense, Stimson himself felt unable to deny that the need for fighting soldiers must take precedence. The 140,000 men in the ASTP were needed more as present effective troops of ideal combat age than as future experts and officers.

Each step of this story tied in with ups and downs in the Army's estimates of its manpower requirements. In all such changes, the college training program, as a marginal undertaking, was very sharply affected. Factors to which we must give more attention in the next chapter limited the Army to a choice, in the end, between specialized training and an adequate combatant force. It would have been better to have both, but that would have meant fewer civilians, and a still heavier draft. The requirement of a sufficient fighting Army was overriding, but the true question for the Specialized Training Program was whether it should be continued at the expense of further drafts of fathers, deferred workers, and other civilians. Here the choice lay not with the War Department but with Congress, and the verdict of the people's representatives on this point was not a matter of doubt. The Army of early 1944 was forced to cannibalize itself, and the soldiers of the ASTP were among the first victims. Their consolation is to be found in the

all but unanimous opinions of their new combat commanders—
they made unusually fine troops.

Of all the dislocations of the war this one perhaps was the
most disturbing to Stimson; on this issue of continuing college
training he came very close to serious disagreement with
his military staff. But there is no sensible answer to a professional decision on wartime troop requirements. If you
trust your generals, you must give them the men they demand;
Stimson had too often made that point to other citizens not
to feel its force when applied to his own desires. When the
President expressed his chagrin at the decision, Stimson explained "that General Marshall had made it clear to me that
we faced the alternative of either making this immediate cut
in ASTP or losing ten divisions from the forces which were
necessary this summer."[2] In the face of such a warning there
could be no hesitation.

Nor could Stimson sympathize with those who argued that
a wartime suspension of academic activity would do irrepa-
rable damage to the long future of liberal education. He was
content to rest in 1947 on a statement issued December 17,
1942, in defense of the military and "illiberal" curriculum of
the ASTP:

"In reply to the question, 'Does not the Army Educational
Plan go a long way to destroy liberal education in America?'
the Honorable Henry L. Stimson, Secretary of War, today
authorized the following statement:

"Temporarily, yes, so far as the able bodied men of college
age are concerned, but in the long run, emphatically no. The
immediate necessity is to win this war and unless we do that
there is no hope for liberal education in this country. To win
this war and win it as quickly as possible, we must have large
numbers of young men in the Army. We must use every opportunity to train our soldiers for the immediate task ahead. The
Army College Program is designed for that purpose and for
that purpose alone. This training is of necessity primarily
technical and other training must remain in abeyance.

"I am Chairman of the Trustees of one of the leading boys'
schools and all my life I have been a devoted supporter of

[2] Notes after Cabinet meeting, February 18, 1944.

liberal education in school and college. So have my principal assistants, and the necessity of limiting such education in the colleges during the war is very painful. It has been accepted as a necessity. . . .

"It is of enormous importance to make plans ahead for the restoration of liberal education for the period after the war is won and during the period of demobilization. I should like to call your attention to the fact that this problem is already under careful consideration. . . . We hope and believe that many of the soldiers of today will return to become tomorrow the students and leaders in the field of liberal education."

So far as Stimson could see, in 1947, this was exactly what the soldiers were doing.

5. THE ARMY AND THE NEGRO

"We are suffering from the persistent legacy of the original crime of slavery." (Diary, January 17, 1942) There is no deeper or more difficult problem in America than that of the Negro, and the impact of this problem on the wartime Army (and vice versa) brought out its complexities in forms sometimes discouraging and sometimes hopeful.

Each man who comes in contact with "the Negro problem" brings to it his own deep-set beliefs. Stimson's convictions were those of a northern conservative born in the abolitionist tradition. He believed in full freedom, political and economic, for all men of all colors; he did not believe in the present desirability, for either race, of social intermixture. These two views were inconsistent, he believed, only in the opinion of those who *desired* them to be inconsistent. The man who would "keep the nigger in his place" and the man who wished to jump at one bound from complex reality to unattainable Utopia were in Stimson's opinion the twin devils of the situation. He had his troubles with both.

"The persistent legacy" as it came before the War Department in 1940 was a complex mixture of facts and attitudes. It was a fact that most white people would not sanction intermixture of whites and Negroes in the intimate association of military life; it was equally a fact that segregation was repellent to almost all educated Negroes and to an increasing number of the colored rank and file. It was a final fact that segregation was the tradition of the Army, and, in one form or another, of most of civilian America; it was the *modus vivendi*, and the Army followed it, except in its Officer Candidate Schools.

Negro troops had not in the main won glory for themselves in combat during World War I. Yet certain units, under particularly competent and sympathetic white leadership, had fought with distinction. Should the Army now have colored fighting troops? The War Department said it should, and the training given to Negroes in two infantry divisions and a number of other combatant units was more patient and careful and time-consuming than anything required by white units.

The Army contained Negroes in their due proportion to the rest of the nation's population. But wherever Negroes were trained or sent abroad, there was difficulty. Most training camps were in the South, and the South had feelings which seemed wholly wrong to the northern Secretary. Still more disturbing were its actions. A Negro in the Army was a United States soldier, and Stimson was deeply angered when it proved impossible to bring to justice southern police who murdered a colored M.P. Southern bus companies enforced the peculiar rules of the region in serving Army camps; as often happens under these rules, insufficient space was provided for Negroes. Stimson insisted to his deputies that this sort of blatant unfairness must be stopped.

More perplexing still was the problem of the Negro abroad. Theater commanders were co-operative but not enthusiastic in accepting Negro units; in each theater there were special considerations which made Negro troops a problem. To all alike the Negro was an additional complication in a full-time war. But fair-minded soldiers agreed that the Army must make full use of what Stimson called the "great asset of the colored men of the nation." The difficulties of the Negro were not, in the main, of his own making, and in neither justice nor policy could he be excluded from participation in the war.

As he wrestled with the problem Stimson found his own sympathies shifting. On three tours of inspection he saw Negro units in training; each time he was impressed by the progress achieved by intelligent white leaders and colored soldiers working together. In such an officer as Colonel Benjamin O. Davis, Jr., he found the direct refutation of the common belief that all colored officers were incompetent. Davis was exceptional, but in the development of more such exceptions lay the hope of the Negro people. Having at first opposed as unwise the training of colored officers, Stimson shifted his emphasis to an insistence that such officers should be selected and trained with the greatest care. He explained to the 99th Pursuit squadron, the first unit of colored combat fliers, "how the eyes of everybody were on them, and how their government and people of all races and colors were behind them." (Diary, October 5, 1942) In similar fashion, Stimson's early mistrust of the use of the Army as an agency of social reform dissolved under the impact of the manpower shortage, and was turned into enthusiasm by direct observation of the accomplishments of soldiers in attacking illiteracy among Negroes (and whites) at Fort Benning.

In the sharp tragedy of the Negro in America there was no place for bitterness in reply to bitterness, but Stimson occasionally lost patience with Negro leaders whose opinions he found radical and impractical. A further trial lay in the fact that at first the Communists and later both Japanese and Nazi agents made energetic efforts to use the race problem as an apple of discord. In Stimson's view the complaints of Negro leaders fell into three categories: the remediable, about which he was eager to hear, the trivial, rising generally from pride offended by the thoughtless slights of the ordinary white man, and the impossible—those which took no account of a heritage of injustice deeply imbedded in the mores of the nation. The deliberate use of the war emergency to stir unrest and force new policies for which the Negroes themselves were unprepared seemed to Stimson blind folly, and he felt that this hotheaded pressure was partly responsible for the rising racial tension which produced such ugly outbreaks as the Detroit riots of June, 1943. On the other hand, he was equally irritated by the "childishness" of his friends in the Navy, whose rigid restriction of Negroes to service as messboys was only modified on the personal insistence of the President. And Stimson himself pointed out to Army leaders that pictures of the Detroit outbreak showed young white thugs to be in almost every case the aggressors.

There could be no denial of the patriotism and the idealism of the "radical" Negro leaders, and their criticisms sometimes opened the eyes of the War Department, but their general attitude was hardly constructive. The attitudes and opinions advanced by most Negro newspapers, too, were shockingly biased and unreliable; as little as their white opponents would the Negro editors look for the mote in their own eye. It was more helpful to deal with such Negroes as Dr. Frederick Patterson of Tuskegee Institute, or Truman Gibson, Stimson's aide for Negro affairs after 1943. These men made suggestions and recommendations that were of great practical value to their people, and without the least disloyalty to their race they were prepared to face squarely the fact that oppression and injustice have left their mark on the bulk of American Negroes. For his honesty and courage Gibson was called bitter names by some other Negroes; to Stimson he was a trusted associate and a distinguished public servant.

The final reckoning on the Negro and the wartime Army was not clear when Stimson left the War Department. The performance of the only Negro infantry division sent into combat as a whole was disappointing, but smaller units (including elements of the same division) did better. The whole story was to be found only by a study of all the hundreds of Negro units—combatant, service, and training troops—and the man who generalized from a partial experience, even the experience of a Secretary of War, was on dangerous ground. Both the Army and the Negro, Stimson believed, did better than their respective enemies would admit, but from a thorough and dispassionate study of their work in all its aspects there would surely come ways for both to do still better in the future, and it was with great satisfaction that Stimson saw such studies promptly begun by his successor.

6. SCIENCE AND NEW WEAPONS

There was perhaps no more striking success in the American management of World War II than the marriage of science and the military, the basic outlines of which have now been recorded by James Phinney Baxter in *Scientists Against Time*.[3] The two principal agents of this triumph, in Stimson's view, were Vannevar Bush and James B. Conant, two distinguished scientists and administrators whose persuasive foresight had won the confidence of President Roosevelt at the beginning of the national emergency. These men and their associates from the beginning set a standard of effort which in its combination of soundness and daring left open for such officers as Stimson no intelligent course but full and hearty collaboration.

The service a Secretary of War could perform here was a triple one. The easiest, and at the same time perhaps the most important, was simply to make it clear to his Department and to scientific leaders that it was War Department policy to make the fullest possible use of scientific help in every part of the Army's work. This attitude, fully shared by General Marshall, did not always permeate to every level of the Army, and in occasional officers of otherwise outstanding ability there persisted a blind spot on the subject of "outside advice." But after one or two officers had been replaced, largely on account of their inability to make full use of modern techniques, the notion of fighting an up-to-date war began to spread, and it was a notable characteristic of the men whom General Marshall brought rapidly forward during the war that they were not frightened by new ideas.

There remained a real difficulty in establishing proper methods for the development of effective continuous contact between the Army and the scientists, and Stimson's second service was in choosing the men and establishing the organization which could do this job. His principal assistant in this work was Bundy, who was not a scientist but possessed the lawyer's talent for appreciation of the other man's problem. With Bundy and Bush, Stimson worked out in the spring of 1942 an organization, in which the Navy joined, whereby Bush and an officer from each service department became a committee of three for the education of the Joint Chiefs of Staff in scientific problems. To supplement this organization

[3] The Atlantic Monthly Press, Little, Brown & Co., 1946.

there was set up in November, 1942, a special section for new weapons in the G-4 division of the General Staff. Both of these moves were useful, but the latter particularly proved insufficient, and Stimson responded quickly to the suggestion of Bush and Bundy, in September, 1943, that new weapons must become an independent section of the Staff.

The work that followed is an excellent example of the proper functions of the Secretary of War, as Stimson understood that office. By constant but friendly pressure he and his friend Bush won Marshall's support for the new idea, an essential part of which was the selection for the new job of an officer with a solid reputation as a first-class soldier. When this officer had been selected, in the person of Major General Stephen G. Henry, Stimson provided him with a full-dress recital of the importance of his new assignment. The diary entry tells the story:

"I found that General Stephen Henry, whom I had selected for appointment to the new scientific weapons staff post, was here and he and McNarney [Marshall's deputy] came in and I tried to explain to him as well as I could what I wanted of him. I did this by telling him of my own experience with radar beginning with the time of my visit to Panama. Then Dr. Bush came in and joined the talk and gave him a talk on the new weapons which were being developed. Henry's job is to smooth the path of new weapons into use in the Army. It is pretty hard to define it because it is a new job. He is to do the work that it was intended that General Moses should do under G-4 but it has never been done because of interruption of other duties. While we were still talking, I called in Dr. Bowles to add his testimony of what was to be done and gradually the picture unfolded to General Henry and he became more and more interested. Of course he had come to Washington in a rather dejected and disappointed frame of mind because we were taking him away from his division— an armored division, to which he had recently been appointed, but gradually the picture of the greater importance of the new position I was offering him in the war effort had developed before him and he became more and more interested. He has had a very fine record for several years as head of the Armored

Force School at Fort Knox. I heard of him when I was there nearly two years ago and met him then and I had not forgotten the impression his work had made on me.

"Then while we were still talking we had another influx of people from Britain. This was a group headed by Sir Robert Renwick who has just come over to talk of the importance of radar to our Staff. . . . Renwick was a very forceful intelligent man who, although a civilian, holds a very high position in the actual war work in England in precisely the similar lines for which I am seeking Henry. Renwick launched into a vigorous talk about how far behind we were to the place where we ought to be if our effort was to be successful next year. I told him not to pull his punches but to let us have all he had in criticism and he did so, and when he painted the picture of the development that the British had already made in radar and how far we were behind that in our Air Forces, it made a profound impression on Henry. The whole job with Henry took from 10:25 until lunchtime at one o'clock. But it was a job well done for he has accepted his new post with vigor and enthusiasm." (Diary, October 11, 1943)

This process of indoctrination was one which Stimson frequently employed when advancing his favorite ideas. Occasionally, he feared, it left his auditors with the feeling that they had been subjected to an old man's lecturing, but in this case at least the results were thoroughly satisfactory.

Under General Henry, the new Developments Division of the Staff performed with outstanding success. The basic reasons for this success were two: first, the ready acceptance by the Army of such a division at the special staff level, and second, the selection of a director for that division out of the top drawer of the Army. Henry's success eventually priced him out of the market, and he was "stolen" by General Marshall a year later for the unconscionably difficult job of directing the redeployment and demobilization of Army personnel, but the standards he had set were maintained by his successor.

The third important service of the Secretary, and the most arduous, was his personal advocacy of specific new techniques and weapons. The most important single instance of this kind was the use of radar. Stimson's interest in the electronic eye was first kindled in 1940 by the enthusiasm of his relative, Alfred Loomis, and throughout the war it remained an object of his particular attention. In April, 1942, he selected Dr. Edward L. Bowles to serve as his special consultant "for the purpose of getting radar upon a thoroughly sound and competent basis as to installation, training, and maintenance." (Diary, April 1, 1942) Bowles possessed in high degree the knack of winning the confidence and arousing the interest of the military, and his services in the new and difficult business of co-ordinating electronics with tactics were of the first order.

Other matters in which Stimson's personal interest was keen were: artillery—Stimson and McCloy, indulging the inclination of two former artillerists, took a lively interest in all new developments, giving particular support to the development of self-propelled mounts and more powerful antitank guns; antiaircraft—an early slowness in this field drew Stimson's eye and he watched it carefully throughout the war, being personally responsible for a highly successful visit of British gunners from Malta in 1943; tanks—his own first inclination was in favor of heavier tanks than the General Sherman, but on the basis of reports from the party principally interested (General Patton) he stoutly defended the Sherman when it was attacked by critics in 1944 and after; aircraft— this was Lovett's field, and Stimson confined his labors mainly to the vigorous support of the Air Forces' theory of strategic bombing; bacteriological warfare—this purely defensive and precautionary undertaking required Stimson's personal attention in its organizational stages, but after the appointment of George Merck it ceased to give him concern, for Merck combined administrative skill with a keen appreciation of the peculiarly sensitive nature of his assignment; medical science —here Stimson's interest was keen and strong, and his direct contact with the Surgeon General, on the problems of wartime medicine, was probably greater than with any other single bureau chief (the subject, after all, had the strongest of human appeal to any civilian, and especially to a doctor's son) ; atomic energy—mentioned only in low voices behind closed doors for four years, this subject ceased to be an undertaking apart and became the center of Stimson's official life after March, 1945.

The close understanding which Stimson and Marshall maintained with their scientific advisers and the impressive achievements of wartime science combined in the end to produce a wholly new atmosphere in the Army. By March, 1944, it was clear to Stimson that scientists "are now thoroughly in vogue with our Army." For this result the main credit belonged to the scientific leaders who had constantly asserted and proved the value of their services; for his part Stimson was more than content with the generous encomium he later received from the scientists' historian: "It would be hard to exaggerate the role played by Secretary Stimson in ensuring effective cooperation between the civilian scientists and the huge organization over which he presided. No one in the War Department approached with keener zest the problem of extracting from scientific research the maximum contribution to the war effort. Again and again he provided the impetus which broke log jams and speeded major problems on their way to solution."[4]

[4] Baxter, *op. cit.*, pp. 32-33.

CHAPTER XIX

The Effort for Total Mobilization

IT MAY fairly be doubted whether anyone in America fully appreciated, in December, 1941, the size and scope of the war effort which would be necessary in the next four years. In every respect but one—the absence of fighting on American soil—the Second World War for Americans dwarfed all its predecessors, and the exception itself added to the magnitude of the task, for the distance of the front inevitably lent psychological support to those who wished to fight as easy a war as possible.

The extraordinary wartime accomplishment of the American nation left, in Stimson's view, no room for doubt as to the essential soundness and strength of American society. It had been his conviction, throughout his life, that there was no discernible limit to the power of the American people when they were firmly united in purpose. But the strength of Americans was only equaled by their ignorance, both of war and of high politics, and without the leadership of a firm and stouthearted President they could never have been mobilized for victory. The people themselves seemed often to have a willingness for sacrifice and effort which outpaced the actions of Washington, but they tolerated in their Congressmen an attitude of hesitation which frequently delayed and sometimes blocked the measures needed for an all-out prosecution of the war.

To Stimson the residents of wartime Washington broke down broadly into two classifications: those whose first and central object was to win the war, as quickly and thoroughly as a truly total effort would permit, and those who had other

conflicting purposes to which they sometimes gave a prior
allegiance. The men whose whole mind was on victory were
always a minority, but fortunately this minority usually included the President. Yet it was from feelings for or against
Mr. Roosevelt's own New Deal that much of the waste and
suspicion of the war developed. Stimson would have found it
hard to decide which angered him most, the congressional
rear guard which looked at every wartime act through the
distorted lenses of a rancorous mistrust, or the self-righteous
ideologists who had multiplied around the President in the
brave new years after 1933 and who now would not understand
that the natural enemy was in Germany and Japan, not in
Wall Street or among the brass hats. Why the right could not
behave like Jim Wadsworth, and the left like Harry Hopkins,
Stimson never understood. He had foreseen this sort of trouble
in 1939 when he wrote, in supporting Mr. Roosevelt's firm
stand against aggression, that "National unity is not . . . pro-
moted by methods which tend to disrupt the patriotism of
either party or the effective co-operation of the two."[1] Nevertheless he had hoped that war would produce a far greater degree of forbearance and unity than it did. Only in the first few
months after Pearl Harbor was there any appreciable relief
from the stale battles of a past age. Afterwards the New Deal
"cherubs" returned with all their ancient zest to the struggle,
and Stimson once estimated that antiadministration "trouble-
makers" in Congress added to his troubles about one-hundred-
fold.

Now no doubt some of Stimson's feeling was merely a
healthy annoyance at the inevitable disagreements and difficulties of war; he was never, in his private feelings, a man of
overwhelming patience. But he could not avoid the conclusion
that in very large part his objections to the atmosphere of wartime Washington rose from two convictions which he deeply
held and which were not generally shared. The first was his
complete dedication, emotional and intellectual, to the proposition that the only way to fight a war is to fight it with your
whole and undiluted strength. Discussion about what it would
take to win seemed to him meaningless. Such considerations

[1] Letter to the New York *Times*, March 6, 1939.

might be appropriate in small campaigns like those of the Spanish-American War, but in the world conflicts of the twentieth century they were wholly out of place. The only way to minimize the final ghastly price of World War II was to shorten the struggle, and the only way to shorten it was to devote the entire strength of the nation to its relentless prosecution. Every sign of division was an encouragement to the enemy, and every concession to self-indulgence was a shot fired in folly at your own troops. The only important goal of the war was victory, and the only proper test of wartime action was whether it would help to win.

In the mind of a fanatic, of course, the convictions set out in the last paragraph might well have led to absurdity. But Stimson thought he understood that the best soldier is the balanced and healthy one, and neither for the troops nor for the nation did he advocate any ridiculous and unprofitable wearing of hair shirts—he continued to get his own rest and sport whenever possible, and his principal concern for his War Department friends was that they must do the same.

It was obvious, furthermore, that in the kind of war that America faced it would not do for every man to grab a rifle and start walking toward Berlin. Although critics sometimes seemed to doubt it, the War Department was fully aware of the degree to which World War II must be fought "in factory and farm." In the complex organization that was demanded of the United States, there must be balanced the demands of the Army and Navy, of allies in every continent, and of the American economy itself. All this Stimson understood—he had supported Lend-Lease on precisely this theory of America's role in the war. What he held was simply that every man and every dollar and every factory should be so employed as to contribute its maximum strength to the war.

Matched with his conviction that the war deserved the country's whole attention was a complete lack of apprehension lest war destroy any of the lasting values of American democracy. He could not share the fears of either right or left; from his knowledge of the country and its leaders, he was certain beyond doubt or fear that there would be no war-spawned dictatorship in America; nothing in his experience justified the laments of Mr. Roosevelt's opponents over the increased authority of the Executive. Even less was he alarmed by the bogy of "militarism." Only in the fantastic human and economic cost of war did he see important danger, and this cost could be cut down only by a policy of "war to the uttermost."

The general statement of these two convictions would probably have been accepted by most Americans throughout the war; but the application of principles to the terrain and the situation frequently brings to light major latent differences of emphasis, and in order to make Stimson's position wholly clear we shall have to study specific issues of his wartime years. The most fruitful field for such a study is the wartime use of manpower. Nothing touches more closely upon the opinions and interests of a man than the demands of his government with respect to the use of his person, and there is nothing more inextricably a part of modern war than the existence of such demands.

1. MILITARY MANPOWER

The American Army of December, 1941, was composed of those men who by inclination or availability had been most readily and painlessly detached from civilian life. Although the Selective Service Act of 1940 had given definite and conclusive recognition to the principle of the obligation of the citizen to serve as might be directed by his government, the limitations surrounding this principle were such that during the first year of the war Stimson and other administration leaders were involved in a series of moves to strengthen and broaden the Selective Service System. And after 1943, when the manpower requirements of the armed services had been mainly satisfied, these same leaders, by an extension of thinking as logical to them as it was fearsome to their opponents, became ardent advocates of a National Service Act for directing the assignment of the country's labor force, a measure which America alone of major fighting nations never enacted. At each of the different stages of this continuing struggle there were interesting episodes.

The first major improvement in Selective Service after Pearl Harbor was the reduction of the draft age from twenty to eighteen. In retrospect Stimson was astonished that it should have taken the nation almost a year to give legal recognition to the fact that war is a young man's game, but in the records there was ample evidence that this delay was forced not by a lack of foresight on the part of the Army and its leaders but by the reluctance of Congress to accept until absolutely necessary the drafting of younger men. Both before and after Pearl Harbor Army recommendations for a reduction in the draft age were ignored by Congress, and by April, 1942, the War Department had decided to wait until the pressure of events strengthened its case. The rising draft calls of the spring and summer finally provided the required pressure, and in October, 1942, explaining the Army's bitter needs to a House committee, Stimson emphasized the unpleasant fact that the draft was reaching the end of its present resources, and that it was now a choice between men under twenty and men palpably unfit for extended combat service (or else the family men who all agreed should come last). Such a choice was really no choice at all. The argument was unanswerable, although protests were heard from educators, clergymen, and others.

In November, after a month of delay and after the elections had safely passed, over the protests of many and with the reluctant support of others, the draft was at last extended to those who should by all the principles of effective warmaking have been the very first to be called. When General Marshall reported to the nation in 1945 that "men of eighteen, nineteen, and twenty make our finest soldiers" he was only re-emphasizing what troop leaders have known for generations. Yet throughout the war there was a considerable group of men in Congress who continued to be suspicious of the Army's use of younger men, and time after time Stimson was forced to re-emphasize that the War Department was not planning some sort of infant slaughter.

A somewhat contrasting problem was the issue of volunteer enlistments, which also reached its solution at the end of 1942. It was clear that no orderly manpower policy could be worked out while unrestricted volunteering was permitted, but here the advocates of control met strong opposition from the United States Navy, of whose many proud traditions not the least was its reliance upon volunteer sailors and marines. And one of the best-indoctrinated friends of the Navy was Franklin Roosevelt. The President supported with courage and force the reduction of the draft age, but throughout the early months of the war he backed the Navy in its insistence on maintaining a volunteer system. Stimson knew when he was outmatched; even late in 1942, when the question was urgent, he approached it gently. In a letter to the President on November 18 he asked for counsel as to the position he should take before Congress on manpower legislation: "My feeling, as you know, is that sooner or later we should come to a single selective process without any volunteering. But I have a vivid recollection of a letter written by yourself to the Navy painting an attractive picture of the superhuman character of a Navy built upon volunteering. . . ."

Circumstances caught up with the Navy and its friend, however, and on December 5, 1942, the President issued an Executive Order suspending all voluntary enlistments except for seventeen-year-olds. Later, after the usual interservice difficulties, an agreement was reached under which the Army and Navy shared in fair proportion the peaches and lemons produced by the draft. The change was overdue, for a year of delay had thrown the two services seriously out of balance in their relative average ages; figures for September, 1942, showed the average age of Navy enlisted men to be under twenty-three while the corresponding figure for the Army was over twenty-six. Whatever the reason—and the reasons given by Army and Navy supporters were as far apart as the poles— it was a fact that a disproportionate number of young volunteers preferred the naval service. Once more only the pressure of events had forced the correction of an essentially wasteful and inequitable policy. The Navy's desire for volunteers was natural—just as natural as the reluctance of matriarchal America to draft her eighteen-year-olds. But both were attitudes that insufficiently recognized the requirements of the war.

Reducing the draft age and ending volunteer enlistments were minor matters compared to the battle that ebbed and flowed throughout the war over the size of the Army. This was a subject upon which Stimson was more vehement than most of his military advisers; it seemed to him to involve very urgent questions as to the strength of America's wartime resolution.

Questions about the Army's size fell into two categories, one technical, the other almost entirely a matter of attitude. Technically, the problem was one of assessing the various components of the war effort so as to define their relative positions. The useful size of the Army depended upon the weapons and munitions that could be produced to arm it and the ships that could be built to transport and supply it, and the whole program of the Army in turn must be related to the undertakings of the Navy and the requirements of America's allies. A calculus so complex would have no undebatable answer, but some sort of conclusion was urgently required, if only as a basis for action. In this technical problem Stimson took no active part; the matter was one for professionals. The Army's projected strength, based on extended discussions in the Joint Chiefs of Staff and with administration leaders responsible for production and manpower, was fixed in 1942 at 8,200,000 officers and enlisted men. A downward revision in 1943 was offset in 1944 by rising casualty lists, and total strength of the Army on VE-day was approximately 8,300,000. The figure thus projected and defended against heavy opposition in 1942 proved to be both accurate and sufficient. For this Stimson could claim only the credit of never having lost confidence in General Marshall. His own feeling had been, throughout, that the cloth might well be cut too fine; in early 1944 and again a year later he urged Marshall to reconsider and if necessary expand his estimates. Both times the Chief of Staff rehearsed his thinking and stuck to his decision, and his judgment was vindicated in victory.

Stimson, believing that the projected army was perhaps too small, naturally plunged with considerable zest into the task of defending it against those who argued that it was too big. The facts and figures upon which the administration discussion was based were necessarily secret, and it was therefore not possible to undertake a detailed explanation of the situation. But in Stimson's view much of the national doubt about the size of the Army was due not to any difference on the facts but to a widespread misunderstanding of the nature of war. To this problem he addressed himself on March 9, 1943, in a radio speech which clearly demonstrated his broad view of the war, its prosecution, and the Army's critics.

First he addressed himself to a problem of "mental attitude." "Tonight I wish to speak to you about the subtle danger which, unless guarded against, may destroy our present bright hopes for a decisive victory. It arises out of a mental attitude which is quite prevalent among our people, including many of the best of them, and has danger of which most of them are quite unconscious. . . . It is hard to analyze the attitude to which I refer. . . . Very often it appears in patriotic people who do not realize what we are up against and who honestly do not understand the purpose and necessity of some of the war measures which their government is taking. But the attitude is just as dangerous even when it is innocent. I think it can accurately be called the attitude of trying to win the war—the most fierce and dangerous war which has ever confronted the United States—in some easy manner and without too much trouble and sacrifice. Abraham Lincoln met it in the Civil War even after that war had been going on for over a year and many bloody battles had been fought. He said to a caller at the White House in September 1862, 'The fact is the people have not made up their minds that we are at war with the South. They have not buckled down to the determination to fight this war through; or they have got the idea into their heads that we are going to get out of this fix somehow by strategy. . . . They have no idea that this war is to be carried on and put through by hard, tough fighting; that it will hurt somebody; and no headway is going to be made while this delusion lasts.'[2]

"Today this attitude which Lincoln described, manifests itself when we say: 'The Russians have destroyed so many Germans that Germany will not be able to carry on any more offensives'; or when we say: 'The German people are cracking'; or when we say: 'The best way to win the war is to give our Allies plenty of weapons to fight for us'; or when we say:

[2] Stimson had found this quotation in Carl Sandburg's *Abraham Lincoln, The War Years*, I, 553. This book was one in which Stimson found both consolation and instruction during 1943. It was good to know that many of the troubles of World War II had been faced and surmounted, in far more trying circumstances, eighty years before.

'If we make too big a military effort we shall so dislocate our economy that we shall never recover; we shall create a permanent dictatorship and lose our historic freedom'; or when we say other things which at bottom represent merely wishful thinking or the dread of personal sacrifices and the desire to find a better way out. I believe that this attitude towards hard fighting on our part really underlies much of the criticism which is being directed today against the proposed size of our Army."

Yet this attempt to dodge "tough fighting" was the surest way to lengthen the war and almost the only way to put victory in doubt. The people who held this attitude, and who questioned the need, in a time of rising success, for ever greater armies, "do not understand the psychology of combat. They do not realize that battles are won by continuous rapid blows upon an enemy and that when an enemy begins to show signs of demoralization these blows must be continued and, if possible, redoubled in order that he may not have time to re-form his forces. Once the enemy is checked or shaken on the field of battle, he must be constantly pursued and hammered until he is completely beaten or surrenders. The very fact that it is known that we have trained forces ready to do this tends towards his demoralization."

And Stimson cited the contrasting examples of Meade at Gettysburg and Foch in 1918. Hesitation in the one case had lengthened a war beyond expectation, while the remorseless aggressiveness of Foch, in the other, had brought victory months ahead of schedule.

Supporting the general tendency to think up easy ways to win the war were other misconceptions drawn from too hasty observation of the newfangled thing called total war. For if it was true that World War II was in scope and complexity unlike any previous struggle, placing demands upon all of society far exceeding those of simpler wars, it was emphatically not true that war had reduced the importance of armed forces. The lines of effort, for all their increased ramifications, still ended in regiments, ships, and aircraft manned by military men. It was not antediluvian to raise an army, and Stimson addressed himself cheerfully to his duty of explaining the

Army to the people. The first and most significant point was its relatively small size, compared to the armies of its enemies. Secondly, it was an Army of unprecedented variety and flexibility, with training problems of corresponding difficulty. Third, it was an Army in which at least a year must separate a major training program from the battlefield. "I speak with careful consideration when I say that if we should halt this great training establishment which we have now built and timed according to the present timetable of the war, we should deal a heavier blow to our hopes of a complete final victory than by any loss which we are likely to sustain on the field of battle."

The Army must be raised; more than that, the nation must trust its leaders. It was possible of course that the Army and the Navy were proceeding in pigheaded blindness on the basis of wholly outdated concepts. Stimson could only rehearse the nature of wartime planning and give his solemn assurance that the figures for the size of the Army "have thus had the benefit of all the brains, accumulated research, and judgment which our governmental machinery provides for that purpose." Only time could prove whether the decisions made were wise, but all the advantages of study and experience lay with the administration and not its critics.

Another half-truth drawn from the concept of total war was the theory that the projected army would too greatly strain the nation's manpower resources. This theory in Stimson's view embodied one of the most pertinacious fallacies of all, and he jumped on it with both feet. For, however important the non-military aspects of the war might be, it was wholly illogical to support them at the expense of the Army until every other means of industrial mobilization had been exhausted. "Only those who believe that our industry and our farming and our general civilian activity are really keyed to an all-out war are entitled to make this argument. It is the duty of every citizen to examine into his own life, and his own community and see whether production in industry and on the farm cannot be increased enormously in efficiency; whether absenteeism, threatened strikes, general complacency, insistence on 'business as usual,' or even insistence on hoped-for standards of living, are not going a long way to prevent what could be accomplished by an all-out war effort."

To attack the size of the Army when the civilian economy was incompletely mobilized was absurd. "When you are driving a team of horses and one of them goes lame, you do not lame the other horse to equalize the team. You try to get two sound horses."

And then in his conclusion Stimson shifted from the defense of the Army to a note of personal challenge. "For myself, I have reached the conclusion that one of the reasons why industry and agriculture and the whole civilian population have not moved more rapidly towards an all-out effort is that we have relied almost entirely on voluntary co-operation. This voluntary co-operation would work with a large part of our population as soon as they clearly understood the need for it. But the effect of the recalcitrant or thoughtless few is so great upon the minds and efforts of others that I am convinced that the only way to accomplish the result which we must all reach, is through a General [National] Service Act. This has proved true in England and I believe it is now true here.

"The issue between the proponents of the Army program and its critics in my opinion largely narrows down to this difference: the leaders of the Army are trying, by shortening the war, to save the lives of thousands of young Americans—lives vital to the future of this country. The opponents of the Army program are trying to avoid present trouble—the inconveniences and relatively minor sacrifices which would be involved in a more thorough and drastic reorganization of our industrial and civilian life for the remaining period of this war."

This was Stimson's first public statement in favor of a principle to whose support a large proportion of his time was given in the following two years—without success.

2. NATIONAL SERVICE

Of all the shortages which complicated America's war effort, almost the last to appear was the shortage of manpower. At the beginning of the crisis, in 1940, there were more than

THE EFFORT FOR TOTAL MOBILIZATION

nine million unemployed, and even at the time of Pearl Harbor there were still four million men out of work. It thus happened that as the manpower problem gradually became pressing in 1942, it was approached by most administration leaders with partial and specific remedies not based on any general policy for the mobilization of the nation's human resources. Later, when the general theory of national service was advanced, it was faced by the existence of commissions, policies, and attitudes based on the theory of voluntary or piecemeal arrangements. In December, 1942, the President had given to Paul McNutt, head of the War Manpower Commission, executive authority in the field of manpower which was loosely described at the time as dictatorial. But in point of fact McNutt's authority was extremely limited, nor was his commission so organized as to exercise any broadly effective leadership. Although Stimson's relations with McNutt were always personally friendly, it would be too much to say that the War Department and the War Manpower Commission approved of each other's views of the manpower problem. The War Department believed in drastic action; the Manpower Commission was committed to guidance and cajolery. And in between the two was Selective Service, a prize for the control of which both contended. This particular battle was decided against Stimson by the President late in 1942 when the former was away for a short rest. Mr. Roosevelt took the sting out of his decision in the first Cabinet meeting after Stimson's return. "He saw me, welcomed me back, and said 'Harry, I've been robbing your henroost while you were away.' I was ready for him and snapped right back, 'I won't go away again.' " (Diary, December 11, 1942)

But the Manpower Commission, the War Department, and Selective Service might be shuffled and reshuffled as often as the President chose, without changing the basic situation, for there was no law providing for genuine executive direction of the mobilization of civilian labor. Unlike Great Britain, Russia, and all the British dominions, the United States possessed no law in the area of civilian manpower matching its Selective Service Act for raising an army and a navy by compulsion. In other words, unlike her allies and enemies, she had no legislation which compelled a man to work for his country in the arsenals and factories and other activities which equipped and supplied American soldiers.

National service legislation was urged early in 1942 by such men as Grenville Clark; in July of that year a subcommittee of the War Manpower Commission, under Stimson's devoted assistant Goldthwaite Dorr, recommended such legislation in a comprehensive and compelling report; but the Dorr report was opposed by other elements of the administration, and the introduction of a national service bill in February, 1943, was left to Senator Warren Austin and Representative James Wadsworth, two men who as Republicans were wholly outside the administration and whose nonpartisan interest in the war effort was beyond challenge. Stimson promptly gave his support in principle to the proposals they had advanced, but in the absence of official backing from the White House the War Department refrained from active advocacy. Meanwhile, throughout 1943, Stimson continued to urge on the President the need for such legislation, pointing out that without active presidential support there was no possibility of its enactment. Mr. Roosevelt, alive as always to the political difficulties involved, and hopeful that his toothless War Manpower Commission might prove adequate to the emergency, held back; most of his administration, and particularly those members of it connected with labor and progressive circles, strongly supported his decision.

In December, 1943, the country was shaken by the imminent threat of a national railroad strike. Similar threatened tie-ups in coal and steel had already produced a strong wave of feeling against small groups who appeared to put their private interests above the wartime interests of the nation, and it seems certain that Mr. Roosevelt was himself deeply stirred by these events. Feeling that strikes and threatened strikes were merely surface evidence of the incompletely warlike attitude of the nation, Stimson joined with Secretary Knox and Admiral Land of the Maritime Commission in strongly urging that the President take the lead in advocating a National Service Act. Stimson further supported this appeal with a personal letter to "My dear Chief," pointing out that the President owed it to himself not to leave the nation in any doubt as to his support of a complete war effort.

As far as Stimson ever knew, the President's annual message of January 11, 1944, was prepared by him without the advice and consultation of either the advocates or the opponents of national service legislation, and Stimson was as surprised as he was delighted to find that in this message the President came out strongly and persuasively in favor of such an act, describing it as the only truly democratic method of organizing American manpower. Fortified by this pronouncement, the advocates of national service began a vigorous campaign for the enactment of a revised Austin-Wadsworth Bill. On January 19, 1944, Stimson appeared before the Senate Committee on Military Affairs as the first administration spokesman for this measure. The line of argument he there developed fairly depicts his general approach to the problem.

After stressing that 1944, as a year of extraordinary military operations, must also be a year of all-out production and unity at home, he pointed out the existence of labor unrest in some areas and labor shortages in others. Such a situation at home could hardly be viewed with understanding or approval by the men in the armed forces. "The evident remedy is for the nation to make clear in no uncertain terms the equality of obligation of its citizens. . . . The men in war production are not essentially different from the men who are proving themselves heroes in the South Pacific and on the Italian peninsula. They can be more accurately defined as the victims of the failure of the nation to develop a sense of responsibility in this gravest of all wars. . . . We must . . . bring home to each of these men the fact that his individual work is just as patriotic and important to the Government as any other cog in the great machine of victory. . . . The purpose of a National Service Law is to get at this basic evil which produces the irresponsibility out of which stem strikes, threats of strikes, excessive turnovers, absenteeism, and the other manifestations of irresponsibility with which we are now plagued. It is aimed to extend the principles of democracy and justice more evenly throughout our population. There is no difference between the patriotic obligations resting upon these two classes of men which I have described. Certainly the nation has no less right to require a man to make weapons than it has to require another man to fight with those weapons. Both processes should be so designed and carried out as to serve the interest of the country in winning the war. In a democracy they should also be so designed and executed as to serve the principles of justice between its citizens."

This was admittedly a principle new to the United States. Stimson rehearsed the historic reasons which had made such a move unnecessary in previous wars, pointing out that World War II was the first in which the nation had come anywhere near to a full mobilization. The dependence of the armed forces on the entire economy was obvious, and it was equally obvious that millions of civilian workers were not efficiently meshed into the war effort. An extremely heavy labor turnover in some war industries and severe labor shortages in others were seriously affecting war production. To meet this situation a new approach was needed.

The basic purpose behind Stimson's advocacy of a National Service Act was the same as his purpose in almost all other wartime affairs. "I have been discussing the logic of national service as an orderly, efficient process by which a democracy can give all-out effort in war. But more important now, national service will be the means of hastening the end of *this* war. . . . Every month the war is prolonged will be measured in the lives of thousands of young men, in billions of dollars. The attrition in manpower and in our national wealth will be felt for generations if this conflict is prolonged. National service is the one weapon we have neglected to use. Posterity will never forgive us if we sacrifice our plain duty to a desire for creature comfort or for private gain." Then as head of the War Department he emphasized the critical importance of giving full support at home to the troops abroad. "It will be tragic indeed if the discontent and resentment felt by our gallant soldiers on the fighting fronts burns deeply and festers in their hearts. . . . The voices of these soldiers speak out very clearly today in demanding that all Americans accept the same liability which a soldier must accept for service to country. . . . To me it appears to be the plain duty of the

Congress to give our troops this all-out necessary backing. It is time for all pledges to be redeemed in acts. . . . I remind this committee now of the solemn statement with which our Congress concluded its declaration of war against Japan and against Germany on December 11, 1941: 'to bring the conflict to a successful termination, all the resources of the country are hereby pledged by the Congress of the United States.' I ask no more than that you examine this proposed legislation in the light of that statement."

Stimson's support of the Austin-Wadsworth Bill was followed by similar statements from other leaders of the service departments. To these men their case seemed irrefutable, and they drew great hope for success from the fact that public opinion polls showed better than 70 per cent of the people to be in favor of their position. Yet the Austin-Wadsworth Bill was never even reported from committee, and a second great effort in 1945 produced a heavily diluted measure which was finally beaten by the Senate in April, one month before the end of the European war.

The idea of national service, for all its logic and its popular support, was roundly defeated by a combination of forces unlike any other in the war years. The first and most important factor in this combination was the violent opposition expressed by the leaders of organized labor. With complete unanimity, labor leaders denounced the President's proposal of January, 1944, and their opposition continued unabated throughout the war. Yet it was impossible for Stimson to believe that in the light of the British experience American union leaders were wholly honest in their claims that national service meant "slave labor." Stimson, like other advocates of national service, repeatedly emphasized that there was no intention of indicting labor as a whole. It was merely a matter of providing obviously needed leadership and direction in making full use of the nation's labor force. Nor did he believe that national service would operate against the rights of labor. "A National Service Act will not cause the evils which have been feared by its opponents. The man or woman who wants to do his or her part to win the war as quickly as possible has nothing to fear from a National Service Act. The act does not impair the rights of the worker in respect to wage scales, hours of labor, seniority rights, membership in unions, or other basic interests of the civilian workers. Wherever justified by considerations of family or health, deferment from service would be granted by the local Selective Service Board. I would not advocate any National Service Act which would not protect such elemental rights to the fullest. National Service Acts have been enacted by the great English-speaking democracies which are now fighting this war with us, namely Great Britain, Canada, Australia, New Zealand. With them the legislation has worked so successfully that the exercise of sanctions has become rare; the existence of the national service organization and the morale which it creates having proved that the people of a country want to do their duty when it is clearly pointed out to them by their government."[3]

But the leaders of American labor were not persuaded, and they were joined in opposition by spokesmen of industry in the National Association of Manufacturers, the Chamber of Commerce, and by industrial advisers within the Government itself. Both labor and management preferred the anarchy of a voluntary system to the imagined perils of Government direction.

Nor were matters made easier by division within the administration itself. The coolness of labor was reflected among many members of Congress who were ordinarily among the President's most ardent supporters, and in the War Manpower Commission, which should logically have been the principal proponent of national service legislation, there was deep-seated opposition not only to the general principle but to the specific form of the Austin-Wadsworth Bill, which would have by-passed McNutt's widely unpopular organization. Further, since only the leaders of the service departments and the Maritime Commission were explicitly on record in favor of the bill, there was a natural tendency to argue that national service was a militaristic proposal. How far this was from the truth, at least in Stimson's case, may be suggested by the fact that he constantly insisted that the director of any national service program must be a man commanding the support of labor and

[3] Statement at Senate hearing, January 19, 1944.

civilian groups; the only name which appears in his notes as a suggestion for this post is that of Henry A. Wallace. But the bulk of Mr. Roosevelt's New Deal supporters did not share the President's view of national service, and their opposition, though quiet, was consistent and strong.

In the face of this opposition the President himself did not until 1945 conduct any vigorous campaign for the legislation he had so eloquently advocated, and in one sense there was a justification for this reluctance which extended beyond a mere question of political prudence. In his message of January, 1944, Mr. Roosevelt had coupled his demand for national service legislation with requests for broader taxes and other powers of wartime control, and he had insisted that the message be considered as a whole. In the absence of congressional support for these other aspects of his program, he adhered through 1944 to his original pronouncement that it would be unfair to press for specific controls over manpower alone. Although Stimson could not share these conclusions, since manpower legislation was a matter of special importance from the standpoint of the War Department, he nevertheless agreed that the failure to obtain a National Service Act was essentially similar to the congressional failure in passing adequate tax legislation. Both were reflections of the national refusal to fight an all-out war.

Under different circumstances of timing, and with a different relationship between the executive and the legislative branches, a National Service Act, a strong tax program, and other measures adequately enforcing the austerity of effective war-making might perhaps have been passed even early in the war, but of this Stimson could not judge. National service was basically a matter not in his jurisdiction; he was drawn into it only by the pressure of events and by the default of those administration leaders directly responsible for the nation's manpower. Although the war was won without it, he was certain that an earlier, stronger policy would have brought a quicker and cheaper victory. And he was certain too that if for any reason the war had been prolonged, the absence of a National Service Act would have had most serious consequences. Stimson believed that in this field, as in many others, the American people were better judges than their representatives in Washington.

3. LABOR AND THE WAR

Through the early months of his service in Washington, Stimson had found his relations with labor leaders gratifyingly cordial. The question of labor relations was one on which he found the Roosevelt administration somewhat "tender," but fortunately Sidney Hillman, labor member of the National Defense Advisory Commission, was a man of breadth and character, and Stimson was quickly able to establish with him an enduring relationship of mutual confidence. Through Hillman he was able in the summer of 1940 to reverse a previous administration decision and shift the War Department's arsenals from a forty- to a forty-eight-hour week. The result of the longer hours, and higher wages, was increased morale and a 30-per-cent increase in production. Hillman was also cooperative in insuring approval of War Department arrangements for the movement of Jamaican laborers to Panama for work on the canal defenses. Both the increase of hours and the importation of labor were sensitive subjects in labor circles, and Hillman's assistance was proof of his stature.

Stimson's own view of the position of labor in the national crisis he expressed in a speech to the American Federation of Labor in convention assembled at New Orleans, on November 18, 1940. No group, he pointed out, was more directly concerned with the Nazi menace than labor. British labor was demonstrating that no group was more determined to defend its liberties. He expected a similar response from American labor, and thus far there was every evidence that his expectations were correct. In the coming struggle, labor, like everyone else, would have to make sacrifices; no responsible man could promise "business as usual." He *could* promise that "the practice and procedure of collective bargaining through freely chosen and independent unions will not be sacrificed." Within this policy the War Department was confident that all particular problems could be worked out.

These general views Stimson maintained throughout the

war. There were strikes and threats of strikes which did not meet his concept of the proper obligations of labor in a national emergency, and some of them involved energetic remedial action by the War Department; and some few labor leaders, with the administration's favorite enemy John L. Lewis in the van, behaved with outrageous irresponsibility. But on balance he thought that the response of organized labor was as patriotic as that of the rest of the nation.

Stimson always insisted that strikes affecting military production must be prevented. It followed that the rights of labor must be protected and equitable conditions of work and pay insured by the Government, for the strike is the one compelling weapon of the worker. But there must be no strikes in defiance of the Government's awards and decisions. A good example of the kind of action Stimson approved in dealing with such strikes occurred in June, 1941, when there was a strike at the North American Aviation plant, in Inglewood, California. The prompt and decisive handling of this affair was a matter on which Stimson looked back with great pride, the more so because it was an action of a united Government, in which the President and Sidney Hillman were quite as firm as Stimson and his assistants.

The North American plant was in 1941 one of the most important and successful producers of military aircraft. In defiance of an agreement to mediate, a strike was instigated by men whom all competent observers believed to be Communists. The Government reacted quickly, taking over the plant and bringing in troops to insure the undisturbed return to work of those who wished to respond to the President's appeal. Stimson himself ordered that Army patrols should protect the homes of returning workers, which had been threatened by the strike leaders. With the President's explicit approval, Stimson co-operated with General Hershey in the issuance of a directive to all local draft boards instructing them to cancel the draft deferments of those who engaged in such strikes. It is illustrative of the crosscurrents within the administration that one of the President's administrative assistants later publicly announced that Hershey's statement had been issued without Presidential authority. The strike quickly collapsed.

The North American strike was only one of a number on the west coast in early 1941 which the Government believed to be Communist-led. The party line at the time was of course that the imperialist Roosevelt was warmongering to hide the fatal weaknesses of his so-called New Deal. Whatever their other failings, the Communists were quite skillful in concentrating their operations in plants of major military importance; the issue sharply presented by the North American affair was whether the Government was strong enough to overcome such activities on the part of men whose primary allegiance was to a foreign (and at the time not friendly) power. The distinction between Communists and others in the labor movement was to Stimson one of vital importance. "I am drawing the line sharply between legitimate labor controversies and subversive action by men who have ulterior motives against our defense," he wrote in June 11, 1941; the same line was being drawn by the President, and by the Justice Department under Jackson. The issue was not decisively settled, because within two weeks of the end of the North American strike it vanished in the sharpest reversal on record of the Communist party line. The Nazi invasion of Russia thus had the incidental effect of postponing indefinitely a reckoning between the American Government and American Communists which would otherwise probably have occurred in the summer of 1941.

The use of the Army to break strikes is not pleasant; neither soldiers nor citizens like to see the armed forces employed against Americans. That it was necessary several times during the war Stimson regretted, but this was the result of a situation beyond his control or responsibility. His own duty was to protect the reputation of the Army, and he therefore insisted that in each case, when the Army was called in, it must have an opportunity for careful planning and energetic action. The outbreak of violence in such cases is usually the result of faulty preparation or imperfect leadership; in the record of the Army in its ventures into domestic conflict during the years 1940 to 1945 Stimson found another proof that the United

States Army deserved its reputation for versatility and tactful firmness. The decision to use troops of course never rested with the War Department, and in the case of the Montgomery-Ward strike Stimson strongly opposed the President's decision, for he was unable to see a connection between the war effort and a retail storekeeper, however intransigent.

In critical labor cases throughout the war Stimson found that he and the President were in broad agreement. On the other hand, Mr. Roosevelt's cautious approach to the general problem did not correspond with Stimson's thinking at all. He did not sympathize with the administration's unwillingness to take a flat stand against stoppages affecting war production. Here again Stimson believed that Mr. Roosevelt missed an opportunity for aggressive leadership; he could not believe that American labor was any different from other sections of the country, or that intransigent labor leaders should be solicitously treated by the administration. Labor's no-strike pledge was in the main loyally kept, but Stimson saw this loyalty as one reason the more for dealing sternly with those who chose to break the pledge. And there came a time, in 1943 and 1944, when Mr. Roosevelt's conciliatory methods in dealing with labor troubles became in Stimson's view a serious obstacle to all-out mobilization. Many a man in Congress—leaving aside the few who are always against labor—was reluctant to pass such drastic measures as a National Service Act or a stronger tax bill when the administration seemed to be unwilling to use its full existing strength to control irresponsible labor leaders.

4. THE ARMY AND WAR PRODUCTION—A NOTE ON ADMINISTRATION

We have seen that an important segment of the manpower problem as Stimson saw it was the relationship between the Army and civilian agencies of the Government; in the field of war production this relationship was the central difficulty. After Pearl Harbor there was never any doubt about the determination of the whole country to produce for war as it had never produced for peace, but disagreements on ways and means involved Stimson against his will in the resulting squabbles.

The question of organization for war production had faced the President since 1940, and by January, 1942, it was clear that the evolution from NDAC to OPM to SPAB was incomplete. As the President considered his next step Stimson wrote him a letter on January 7 which summarized his own broad view of the problem. In essence, two things were needed: First, there must be a reorganization giving adequate authority to a single man; this reorganization must not destroy the natural and traditional procurement functions of the Army and the Navy, but it must provide clear and sufficient authority for co-ordination at the top. Second, the President must find the right man for the job—and to Stimson this meant a man with real and demonstrated talent in production, or at least with a proved capacity for dealing with production executives. The post, furthermore, was of such importance that the President "should not move until you are dead sure of your man."

Mr. Roosevelt, on January 16, established the War Production Board with Donald M. Nelson as chairman. Both the form of the new organization and the man selected were satisfactory to the Secretary of War; Nelson had a good reputation, and he was now to have the priceless advantage of possessing genuine authority. Stimson, like most other members of SPAB, was a member of the new board, but his powers were merely advisory, and in the main he left his seat to Patterson. He was glad that the great abilities of William Knudsen were not lost in the shuffle; Knudsen moved to the War Department and for the rest of the war the Army had the assistance of his remarkable understanding of industrial management. His appointment as lieutenant general was a Presidential gesture which neither Stimson nor Knudsen considered very helpful but by sheer personal quality Knudsen gave distinction to his uniform and rank.

The War Production Board continued in operation throughout the war. During this period there occurred several sharp disagreements between WPB and the War Department; these matters were only of tangential importance in Stimson's life, since the procurement and production problems of the War

Department remained in the capable hands of Patterson. But there was current in the discussion of these widely publicized disagreements one misunderstanding which Stimson considered extremely dangerous. At the time he made no public comment on the question, adhering to his general view that it is never useful to indulge in public debate over intragovernmental problems, but his feelings on the matter were and remained strong.

Much of the comment on disagreement between the War Production Board and the military, both at this time and later, was based on the assumption that the underlying issue was a contest between civilians and the military for the control of the national economy. This view seemed to Stimson palpably preposterous. He was fully aware that in Patterson and Somervell he had two strong-minded associates, both of them fired by the single-minded purpose of meeting the Army's needs. But to assume that it was War Department doctrine that the Army should run the country's economy was arrant nonsense; this assumption, however, seemed to be accepted as gospel by a small group of men in WPB who were on cordial and communicative terms with the press, and who seem also to have converted Mr. Nelson. This was a conspicuous example of the sort of twisted thinking that Stimson met time after time among administration officials whose minds were fixed in the rigid grooves of self-styled "liberalism." These men had an ingrained distrust of military leaders which led them always to look for sinister militaristic motives in every Army action. That some irritation should be caused by the driving energy of General Somervell was not surprising, but there was no need to denounce the War Department—or Somervell himself—as "militaristic." Stimson and Patterson were themselves civilians, and they remained the chief officers of the War Department; what they wanted for the Army was not control, but supplies, and at no time did they believe that war production could be organized under other than civilian control.

The real issues between the Army and WPB were quite different. There was a difference of emotional value; there were men in WPB who felt that the Army failed to understand the needs of the civilian economy and men in the War Department who felt that WPB was not sufficiently aware of the needs of war. There was also an issue of administrative policy, centering on the desire of the service departments to supervise their own procurement. That these operations should in turn be supervised and co-ordinated by WPB was quite proper, and clearly there was room for disagreement on the exact manner in which this dual interest should be adjusted, but there was here no question of "militarism," and a compromise plan approved by Stimson in November, 1942, provided a clear basis for co-operation. All plans, however, depended on the quality of the head of WPB, and for his great task Nelson lacked the necessary stature as a man and talent as an administrator, or so Stimson was forced to believe. And he found an excellent proof that strong and able men were unfrightened by "militarism" in the relationship between the War Department and the War Shipping Administration, whose able deputy chief for operations was Lewis W. Douglas. Douglas had his troubles with overzealous Army officers, but by dealing openly with the War Department's civilian heads he was able to resolve his difficulties.

At first it was Stimson's hope that Nelson could be bolstered by the appointment of strong assistants, and he joined in the negotiations which brought Charles E. Wilson and Ferdinand Eberstadt into WPB in September, 1942. Although both men eventually broke with Nelson, they served with conspicuous skill while they lasted. In February, 1943, when Nelson proved unable to drive so spirited a team, Stimson and other administration leaders joined in asking the President to replace him with Bernard Baruch. No action was taken, however, until eighteen months later when in young Julius Krug the President found a man who was able to take over the WPB and run it without constant friction.

The history of war production showed the President's administrative technique at every stage. Having tinkered for nearly two years with boards and commissions he finally gave real power to the wrong man. Then when that man got into trouble, the President coasted along; he neither fully backed Mr. Nelson nor fired him. Stimson believed that it was Mr.

Roosevelt's irritated but indecisive tolerance of men lacking strength of character that lay behind many wartime administrative difficulties. Disagreements with men like Hull and Morgenthau were painful, but in these cases Stimson always knew where he stood; disagreements with men who backed and filled were extremely irritating.

In March, 1943, after several months of friction in the Government, Stimson took time out to register a summary complaint to his diary. After acquitting Mr. Roosevelt of the charge of playing politics with the war effort, he continued:

"But the President is the poorest administrator I have ever worked under in respect to the orderly procedure and routine of his performance. He is not a good chooser of men and he does not know how to use them in co-ordination.

"When I last held the post of Secretary of War under Mr. Taft, who was a very good administrator, there were only nine Cabinet officers or ten persons at the Cabinet table including the President. Barring the Interstate Commerce Commission and perhaps one or two other minor quasi-independent commissions, every administrative function headed up in one of the nine Cabinet officers and went to the President through the departmental head. Mr. Taft dealt with his departments through his Cabinet and that gave you a sense of responsibility and security that could not otherwise be obtained. Today the President has constituted an almost innumerable number of new administrative posts, putting at the head of them a lot of inexperienced men appointed largely for personal grounds and who report on their duties directly to the President and have constant and easy access to him. The result is that there are a lot of young men in Washington ambitious to increase the work of their agencies and having better access to the President than his Cabinet officers have. The lines of delimitation between these different agencies themselves and between them and the Departments [are] very nebulous. The inevitable result is that the Washington atmosphere is full of acrimonious disputes over matters of jurisdiction. In my own case, a very large percentage of my time and strength, particularly of recent months, has been taken up in trying to smooth out and settle the differences which have been thus created." (Diary, March 28, 1943)

Whatever his weaknesses as an administrator, however, the President had a firm understanding of the facts of war. His underlings might wish to give antitrust suits precedence over war production, but the President was not persuaded. Publicity-seeking officials might wish to turn a military trial of saboteurs into a public spectacle, in spite of the fact that these same officials had informed the War Department that much of the evidence would be valuable to the enemy; the President stood firm. In some of these matters, and notably in his impatience with irresponsible sections of the press, Mr. Roosevelt was indeed more vigorous than his Secretary of War.

5. PUBLIC RELATIONS

Stimson's relations with the press in World War II were easier than ever before in his public career. Although the War Department was a conspicuous target for criticism, its Secretary had learned many lessons in thickness of skin when he was Secretary of State, and only once in his last five years in Washington was he seriously annoyed by any personal attack. A national news magazine in 1941 portrayed him as unable to stay awake in conferences, and his lust for combat briefly stirred him to thoughts of a libel suit, but his friends calmed him in the same way that he later calmed subordinates. Life was too short for such irritations; in 1943, writing to a leading Republican who wanted confirmation or denial of a story by Drew Pearson, Stimson remarked that "I do not have the time to read the output of Drew Pearson and Company. Fortunately the work of running the Army keeps me so entirely occupied that I am spared these irritations which seem to be inherent in the American version of a free press." Except in the case of particularly vicious or sensational charges it was his policy not to try to catch up with irresponsible attacks. Nevertheless commentators (with a few conspicuous exceptions) remained a pet abomination; their lofty omniscience was a severe trial to a man who had always felt more sympathy with the actor than with the critic.

The central problem of the Army's public relations was to get and keep the confidence of the people. Basically, of course, the way to win this confidence was to earn it in action; no skill in public relations would offset failure in the Army's mission, while in a successful Army all problems of public relations would become minor. This principle came naturally to Stimson, whose eagerness for appealing to the public had always been limited by a rigid sense of what was fitting in a public servant.

The only enduring report on the Army furthermore would be that rendered to the people by the millions of citizen soldiers; in 1943 Stimson remarked to a friendly group of critics seeking improvement in the Army's public relations that "In general . . . our liaison agents to interpret the Army to the people of the United States are the five million young men who are in the Army and who can act as missionaries to their parents and families and who are doing so very successfully." (Diary, February 25, 1943) He saw nothing to be gained, and much to be lost, in flamboyant self-advertisement of the type that occasionally occurred in other parts of the armed forces and in the younger branches of the Army itself, and he sometimes became impatient with the irrepressible enthusiasms of the Air Forces. Especially while the Army remained largely untried there was no call for boastfulness; throughout the war Stimson avoided predictions of success and tried to guide himself by the counsel of the Old Testament: "Let not him that girdeth on his harness boast himself as he that putteth it off."[4]

The major difficulty in the Army's press relations was the necessity for military secrecy. While it was easy to agree in principle that nothing useful to the enemy should be made public, it was not always easy to determine in practice where the line should be drawn. Especially in the early months of the war there were many who felt that the War Department was unnecessarily niggardly in its release of information. But with both Archibald MacLeish and Elmer Davis, the two government officials who were successively concerned with this problem, Stimson found himself able to establish cordial relations, and although they did not always agree with his judgment, he

[4] I Kings 20:11, quoted to press conference, August 13, 1942.

found them open to persuasion. Stimson himself occasionally thought the professional rulings of his military advisers a trifle stern. Beyond a certain limit secrecy became self-defeating; especially in the case of units in combat the morale value of extensive and specific publicity seemed to outweigh any loss likely to result from telling the enemy about units he had probably already identified.

But criticism from within the Government was frequently caused by an incomplete appreciation of the problem. The War Department, for example, maintained a strict control over all information about Americans in Japanese hands and Japanese in American hands, not because it feared to tell the people the whole story, but rather because material incautiously made public might well give the Japanese authorities an excuse to suspend the exchange of prisoners or to cut off the supply of Red Cross packages to those remaining in their hands. Nor was it through any kindly feeling toward Francisco Franco that Stimson eliminated scenes accurately describing the Spanish dictator from an official War Department film in January, 1943; it was rather that early 1943 seemed a singularly poor time for official disparagement of a man whose armies lay on the flank of the whole North African enterprise.

The real fear of those who mistrusted the War Department's information policy was that material might be suppressed merely because it was unfavorable to the Army. There were certainly some instances of this kind of suppression in the war, but most of them occurred in areas far from Washington, and such suppression was no part of Stimson's or Marshall's policy. Stimson himself repeatedly described Army reverses in blunt and definite language for what they were, and he consistently approved release of photographs and motion pictures graphically portraying the horror of battle. Everything that would bring the war closer to those at home he thoroughly supported. Indeed, in his eagerness to see the American people fully aware of the war he sometimes found in military reverses a stimulation that was lacking in reports of success. Thus the battle of the Bulge, in December, 1944, and January, 1945, had a favorable effect on American determination, as Stimson saw it, while conversely the later rapid advances of General Patton so nourished public optimism that Stimson wrote to Patton in mock protest against his sabotage of the home front.

When suppression of news did occur in overseas theaters there was ordinarily much more involved than mere face-saving. Probably the most sensational such case in the war was the slapping by General Patton of two psychoneurotic soldiers under hospital treatment in Sicily. General Eisenhower had made a gentleman's agreement with the press in his theater not to report this affair; he had severely reproved Patton and had exacted an apology to the troops; he now wished to pre-serve the usefulness of a great combat leader. But Mr. Drew Pearson spilled the beans. In the ensuing hullabaloo Stimson firmly supported Eisenhower, meanwhile dispatching a per-sonal letter to Patton in which he clearly expressed his dis-appointment that so brilliant an officer should so far have offended against his own traditions. The incident was not a pretty one, but Stimson fully agreed with Eisenhower's view that Patton's services must not be lost. When a further outburst from Patton again embarrassed Eisenhower in the spring of 1944, Stimson wrote another and much stronger letter to this "problem child," but once more he supported Eisenhower's courageous acceptance of such annoyances and his refusal to relieve Patton. Perhaps no decision of the war was more triumphantly vindicated by events than this one; in the sum-mer of 1944 Patton became almost overnight the idol of many of the same newspapers and politicians who had most loudly demanded his removal in 1943.

Although criticism in such cases as the Patton affair was sharp, and although he was never able to satisfy certain sec-tions of the press and some of the members of Congress that the War Department was not holding out on them, Stimson found that as the war progressed mutual understanding grad-ually developed. He considered it most regrettable that only in exceptional cases did congressional committees prove re-liable guardians of secret information, for it would clearly have been well for the Army and Congress to understand each other better than they did. This weakness, like others in the Government, seemed to him deeply rooted in the mechanics and traditions of his ancient enemy, "Congressional Government." Whenever it proved possible to narrow the gap between legislators and administrators, the results were helpful to both parties. In 1943 the War and Navy Departments initiated a series of confidential meetings with Congress; whether because these meetings satisfied the ordinary human eagerness for "inside information" or because they truly served, as Stimson hoped, to give Congressmen a better understanding of the war, they certainly produced an improved relationship.

Both during the war and later Stimson regretted that he had not been able to do more of this sort of work himself. It was one of the disadvantages of his age that in conserving his strength he was forced to limit his own public activity as an interpreter of the Army. If he could have seen more of Congressmen and other Washington leaders, he could perhaps have prevented or limited some of the public misunderstandings and governmental squabbling that occurred. In general it seemed to him true throughout the war that the closer a civilian came to the Army, the more likely he was to give it his broad approval.

What he asked of critics, whether members of the Government or not, was that they start with some sympathy for the Army's problems and that their remarks be designed to help the War Department do a better job. When the rubber "czar" sneered at "Army and Navy loafers" he may have been referring to genuine weaknesses, but his approach was hardly helpful. In contrast, when James F. Byrnes quietly suggested that each agency of the Government investigate its own procurement work, the resulting Army report by General Frank McCoy was extremely useful. Stimson believed that the shrewd and skillful work done by Byrnes in his Office of War Mobilization was of vital importance in the operation of Mr. Roosevelt's fantastically complex administrative mechanism.

In his own press conferences Stimson tried to present at weekly intervals a balanced review of the war as he saw it. The factual material for these reports was written for him in the Bureau of Public Relations over which Major General Alexander Surles presided with great good sense throughout the war, executing without complaint a task which must have been distasteful to a soldier who had been in line for a corps command; Surles was much more than a "public relations man." His sound judgment and military knowledge were of frequent assistance to the Secretary of War in much broader fields. In his weekly summaries Stimson frequently added more personal comments, generally designed to set recent events in their broad focus. Against both optimism and undue gloom he waged a continuous battle, drawing from both victory and its absence the same lesson: there was much still to be done. Occasionally, at the year's end or at the close of a campaign, he would allow himself to point with pride at the work of the Army. Regularly he turned aside all questions relating to intragovernmental squabbles, until newsmen learned to ask them with hopeless and amused foreknowledge that they would get no answer. As the men who covered the Pentagon became old acquaintances, the atmosphere of the press conferences became more amiable than anything he had known in the past, and in his last press conference, on September 19, 1945, he spoke in a tone that was as sincere as it was unusual in him when he said, "In taking leave of you, I should like to tell you how greatly I have valued our association. In the midst of a war, there are many tensions. Tempers are apt to grow short. For my part, I feel that our differences have been unimportant during the five years I have been the subject of your scrutiny.

"You have always seemed to me to be carrying out your duty to the public with a high regard for the ethics of your profession and the safety of the Nation. . . . I should like to take this occasion to offer you my sincere thanks for the quality and understanding of your service and to give you my best wishes for your future success."

Throughout the war a heavy majority of the people remained satisfied that they were being adequately informed by the Government. Certainly there was never a war or an army more completely reported, and in the enormously difficult task of bridging the gulf fixed between soldier and civilian the press and the radio did distinguished work.

It was bridging this gulf—as far as it was possible to do so —that seemed to Stimson throughout the war to be the central task of war reporters and Army spokesmen. Evident and solid national unity seemed to him the greatest single moral force with which to crack the enemy's will to resist, and, finding himself constantly inspired by his own direct contacts with the troops, he regularly sought to give a similar directness of contact to other civilians. In public relations as in other matters where the Army touched on civilian life, it was his object so to spread the spirit he found in the armed forces that it might become the spirit of the nation as a whole. And while the failure to enact a national service law remained as proof that this unity of attitude was never fully achieved, it would not be fair to end this chapter on any note of failure. Taken as a whole the effort of Americans at home was more than sufficient, and if many sources of strength remained unused, Stimson was inclined to place the responsibility for waste more on the Government than on the people. His own greatest fear had been that in the different standards set for citizens and soldiers there might be bred a lasting bitterness between those who fought and those who stayed at home. But whether because so many at home made great and earnest efforts, or because so many in uniform "never had it so good," or because the citizen soldiers were always more civilian than military, no such cleavage seemed to develop in the early postwar years.

CHAPTER XX

The Army and the Navy

SO FAR as the United States was concerned the Second
World War was an amphibious war. "No enemy forces
reached our mainland, and five million American soldiers
were required to be transported across various oceans in order
to get at their enemies. Troop transport and assault landings
are traditionally the most difficult and dangerous of all military operations. The American Navy, co-operating in some
cases with the British Navy and the two national air forces,
furnished the cover and protection for such transport and
landings. It rendered this service with brilliant success. Practically no losses of men occurred in the transocean voyages,
and remarkably few which could have been prevented by
naval action occurred on the landings." (Memorandum,
August 15, 1947)

As this quotation shows, Stimson thoroughly appreciated
the help the Army received from the Navy. He had traveled
as a soldier across waters infested by hostile submarines, and
he knew from anxious study the extraordinary difficulty of
landing attacks. Further, though he was not directly concerned
with the purely naval campaigns of the American fleet, he was
of course an admirer of the courage and skill with which the
Navy wrote into military history the names of the Coral Sea,
Midway, Guadalcanal, Leyte Gulf, and many other fleet
actions.

This much said, we must proceed in this chapter to a discussion of Army-Navy relationships in which the less pleasant
side of the story will be emphasized. In this field as in others,
Stimson as Secretary of War was called in when there was
friction and not when there was peace.

1. STIMSON AND THE ADMIRALS

The Army and the Navy fought the war together. After
Pearl Harbor they fought in most areas under unified command. They fought well together, and they reached a level of
co-operation and mutual trust unknown in earlier wars. But
the fact remained that they were two separate services.

"Their leaders were not only separate but filled, ever since
their cadet service at West Point and Annapolis, with a spirit
of rivalry which reached into many phases of their lives. Not
only had there been allowed between the two forces active
competition for new personnel and equipment but even in
sport the annual football game between the two academies had
during the war reached a peak of rivalry where it became a
national problem where and how the game should be located
and managed." (Memorandum August 15, 1947)

When Stimson wrote that the problem of the Army-Navy
football game was a national issue, he did not exaggerate. He
had himself made it a subject of Cabinet discussion in 1943.

"At Cabinet meeting this afternoon I swung into a new
line. Drew Pearson had had a recent article describing the
present meetings of the Cabinet and their futility and how
the Secretaries of War and Navy no longer tell the Cabinet
anything but preserve that for private meetings with the President. Today when the President reached me in turn and asked
the usual conventional question of whether I had anything, I
said 'Yes, Mr. President, I have something of very grave importance.' I then in humorous oratorical fashion presented
the charges that had been made that the Cabinet was decadent
and that the Secretaries of War and Navy had felt unable to
discuss their matters before the lady and gentlemen sitting in
front of them and that in consequence of these serious charges
I had gone through my files and picked out a matter which
was of very serious importance to bring before the Cabinet.
I then narrated how I had written a letter to the Secretary of
the Navy, copy of which I had sent the President, asking that
the Academies at Annapolis and West Point should take the
lead in sacrifice in public opinion and give up their annual
football game; that I had received a reply from the Secretary

of the Navy to the effect that football was of such 'inspirational' value to the young men of the Academy that he did not feel able to give it up. I pointed out that these letters had lain unanswered on the President's desk ever since April 20th and I asked whether there were any matters of equal importance that had claimed his attention during this time. By that time I had the Cabinet in a roar of laughter. To my amusement, however, they took the subject of athletic sports up from my lead and debated it for over an hour and a quarter with such seriousness and diversity of opinion that the President suggested that he would appoint a committee to determine it. We all turned on him and said that this was a matter of such importance that he must decide it himself. This he was evidently afraid to do but he finally said he would give it very serious consideration and let us know later. But it was the first gleam of really vigorous and widely dispersed fun that we had had in the Cabinet for many months." (Diary, May 21, 1943)

The disagreement over the Army-Navy game was fit material for a joke, but it was nevertheless symbolic of a problem which was one of the most serious that Stimson faced. The Army and the Navy were called on in the Second World War to act with a co-operation and a mutual trust for which they had never been properly trained, and it required all the wisdom and self-restraint of which both sides were capable to achieve the astonishing success that was in general attained.

Although Army-Navy co-operation was close to Stimson's heart, the Army was closer still, and his wartime view of the relationship between the services cannot be taken as wholly dispassionate. Like everyone else involved, he occasionally lost his patience with the opposite service; still he always did so in private, and one Army Reserve officer who indulged in public squabbling with an admiral found himself summarily silenced by order of the Secretary of War. Stimson went out of his way to show his personal gratitude to naval officers who had served with distinction and good will in combined operations under Army command; cordial relations were conspicuously the rule in the European war, and he personally decorated both Admiral Hewitt, of Africa and the Mediterranean, and Admiral Kirk, of Normandy, with the Army's Distinguished Service Medal.

Stimson and his civilian staff maintained intimate and friendly contact with their colleagues of the Navy Department. Frank Knox was a man of robust integrity, without any trace of pettiness. He and Stimson became close friends whose mutual respect was not shaken by their occasional disagreement. A similar if somewhat more cautious friendship seemed to exist among most of the senior generals and flag officers. But on many issues friendship gave way to interest.

Differences between the Army and the Navy were frequent. Many of them were simply the inevitable clashes between two agencies of strong will; there were similar disagreements between the Ground Forces and the Air Forces, and between smaller subdivisions of the War Department. But some of the Army-Navy troubles, in Stimson's view, grew mainly from the peculiar psychology of the Navy Department, which frequently seemed to retire from the realm of logic into a dim religious world in which Neptune was God, Mahan his prophet, and the United States Navy the only true Church. The high priests of this Church were a group of men to whom Stimson always referred as "the Admirals." These gentlemen were to him both anonymous and continuous; he had met them in 1930 in discussions of the London Naval Treaty; in 1940 and afterwards he found them still active and still uncontrolled by either their Secretary or the President. This was not Knox's fault, or the President's, as Stimson saw it. It was simply that the Navy Department had never had an Elihu Root. "The Admirals" had never been given their comeuppance.

A striking illustration of this general situation was the Navy's refusal to share the Pentagon Building. Such a sharing was originally suggested by Admiral King; it was enthusiastically taken up by Marshall and Stimson, supported by the President and Knox, and finally blocked by resistance in the Navy Department. Since the suggestion was made at a time (October, 1942) when it would have provided a badly needed public demonstration of genuine Army-Navy solidarity, this naval obstinacy seemed particularly irresponsible. "The Admirals" wanted more of the Pentagon than the Army offered. Yet the Army offered space in the new building for as large a proportion of the Navy in Washington as it would keep for the Army itself. When it became apparent that the bright hope of October was to be smothered in November, Stimson noted in his diary (November 19) that "the Bureau admirals are holding Knox up and he is as helpless as a child in their hands. As a result, it seems as if this really important improvement of having the Navy come in to our building and share it with us in such a way as to assist united command will break down simply from the crusty selfishness of some Bureau officers . . ." and he continued with his central criticism of the Navy: "The Navy presents a situation very much like that which confronted Elihu Root [in the Army] in the first part of the century. The Navy has never had the benefit of the changes which Root made in the Army and which has removed from the Army the bureaucratic service officers who used to dominate the Department and defy the Secretary of War and the Commander in Chief of the Army." The Navy in World War II had in Knox, Forrestal, and King three strong men at its head; they accomplished much in moving their Department forward. But in Stimson's mind it was no discourtesy to remark of them that not one was another Elihu Root.

Other disagreements with the Navy revolved around somewhat different issues. The question of the Negro struck against strong Navy prejudice, and so did the ending of volunteer enlistments. General MacArthur was a constant bone of contention; Stimson was bound to admit that the extraordinary brilliance of that officer was not always matched by his tact, but the Navy's astonishing bitterness against him seemed childish. Another interservice difference was on the question of five-star rank. The whole idea of a new grade above that of general or admiral seemed absurd to Stimson and Marshall, who inclined to believe that a good officer would not need it, while a bad officer should not have it. But the Navy disagreed and eventually had its own way, even to taking half the new ranks while providing only a third of the armed forces.

But the bare rehearsal of all these disagreements is hardly

helpful. What seemed important to Stimson, in retrospect, was to look behind the disagreements toward their causes, in an effort to prevent or minimize their future occurrence. The best way to do it is to study one particular disagreement in some detail. And the one with which Stimson was most deeply concerned was the prolonged struggle over antisubmarine warfare.

2. LESSONS OF ANTISUBMARINE WAR

In the first sixteen months of American participation in the war, from December, 1941, through March, 1943, German submarines destroyed 7,000,000 tons of Allied shipping, a large majority in areas of American responsibility. The submarine was the only weapon with which the Germans could take aggressive advantage of American weakness, and they used it energetically. The complete history of the American defense against this attack will not here be told; the battle was a naval responsibility. But a combination of circumstances brought Stimson into closer contact with antisubmarine warfare than with any other single campaign of the war, and the story of his experience is instructive.

The battle of the Atlantic, whoever might be in charge of it, was a matter of vital interest to the War Department and its Secretary. The basic strategic purpose of Stimson and the General Staff, as we have seen, was to move American air and ground forces against the Germans as quickly and strongly as possible. Ship losses on the scale of those in 1942 and early 1943 were destructive of this purpose. However great the accomplishments of the shipbuilders, continued sinkings meant losses of both bottoms and equipment which seriously limited the effective deployment of American striking forces in Europe. Though submarine success might hurt naval pride, it was the Army which more seriously felt the pinch.

If its effect on the Army's grand strategy had been his only connection with the submarine, Stimson might have confined himself to proddings and complaints, but it happened that one branch of the Army was directly concerned with antisubmarine warfare, and the weapon which gave that branch new and vastly increased effectiveness was one in which his interest was personal and intense. The Army Air Forces, by ancient agreement, retained in 1941 and 1942 the general responsibility for all shore-based air operations, although late in 1941 General Marshall had granted a naval request to share in the use of long-range landplanes. And the development of radar, in particular of microwave, ten-centimeter air-borne radar, provided for aircraft a weapon of search at sea which in Stimson's view revolutionized the essential contest of submarine warfare, changing it from a battle between unseen U-boats and surface vessels into a battle between frequently surfaced submarines and far-ranging planes with superhuman powers of vision. For a long time this view was not shared by the naval officers directly responsible for antisubmarine operations, and in the resulting conflict many of the complexities of Army-Navy relations were clearly illustrated.

Stimson's interest in radar dated back to 1940. In that period, during the battle of Britain, the primary military use of the electronic eye was the detection of enemy aircraft from ground radar stations. Air-borne radar was a later development, the tactical importance of which was first brought home to him during his study of the defenses of Panama in early 1942. From the use of radar by aircraft to detect approaching enemy surface vessels it was an easy step to proceed to the idea of radar as an air-borne antisubmarine weapon, for submarines (until the annoying invention of the Schnorchel pipe in 1944) had to spend a substantial part of their lives on the surface.

This advance in Stimson's thinking roughly matched the development of radar sets suitable for this type of work. In the spring of 1942 ten pre-production sets of ten-centimeter radar were installed in Army bombers, B-18's with no other combat value, and in antisubmarine operations off the Atlantic coast these aircraft immediately demonstrated their power, catching their first submarine on April 1. (The first Army sinking confirmed in postwar analysis occurred on July 7.)

Stimson at once began to push for increased emphasis on this new weapon. He lectured the President and Secretary Knox; after having himself flown out over the Atlantic to observe the new radar set in action, he ordered Marshall and Arnold, on April 23, to follow his example. He put Lovett to work to make sure that radar production was at its maximum speed, and he ordered a reorganization of Army antisubmarine training along lines worked out by his radar consultant, Dr. Edward L. Bowles.

Under the combined pressure of air operations and increased escort protection, German submarines soon withdrew from the Atlantic coast, shifting their attack first to the Gulf of Mexico and then to the southeastern Caribbean. Meanwhile there came into the open a serious disagreement with the Navy over the tactics and control of antisubmarine aircraft.

For the War Department, the model of antisubmarine air operations was to be found in the work of the British Coastal Command, a division of the Royal Air Force which was charged with the primary responsibility for all British-controlled shore-based antisubmarine air operations. Coastal Command had been set up in early 1941 and had been increasingly successful in destroying submarines. Although it was under the "operational control" of the British Admiralty, it operated with a very high degree of autonomy, exercising direct and complete control over all its subordinate groups and wings. In the commands on each coast of the British Isles, air and naval officers operated as partners and friends in combined headquarters, but there was no attempt by the local Navy commander to guide and control the operations of the air. Thus autonomously organized, with no restrictions on its tactical doctrine, Coastal Command had developed and applied with striking success the theory of the antisubmarine offensive. Granting the essential function of the convoy, this theory assigned to aircraft the primary mission of searching out and killing submarines *wherever* they might be, and although it regularly responded to Admiralty requests for convoy cover in critical areas, Coastal Command devoted the weight of its effort to a direct offensive on U-boats.

The American setup in 1942, with all units, sea and air, Army and Navy, under naval command, was entirely different. It was the conviction of the Navy, forcefully expressed by Admiral King, that "escort is not just *one* way of handling the submarine menace; it is the *only* way that gives any promise of success."[1] It followed that the appropriate function of aircraft was to provide additional convoy cover, supplementing the basically important labors of surface vessels. The Navy, furthermore, was not persuaded that aircraft were effective submarine killers. As late as June, 1942, Secretary Knox, apparently unconverted by Stimson's missionary work, was reported in the New York *Times* as telling Congressmen that no airplane had ever sunk a submarine; Knox corrected himself when questioned on this statement, but that he could make it at all was indicative of the blue-water attitude. (The postwar records show that at the time Knox reportedly made this statement two of the four kills of all United States forces against German submarines had been made by Navy planes.)

Finally, the Navy wholly differed from the Army in its view of the command and control of aircraft. Instead of permitting the concentration of Army aircraft under the direction of a single air officer, it insisted on assigning planes to the command of individual sea frontier commanders, thus effectively preventing the concentrated use of air power against the points particularly threatened by U-boats. Although Stimson pressed on Knox in July, 1942, the desirability of centralized control of both air and naval operations, his proposal was rejected; the Navy preferred to place its trust in making all areas independently strong, unconcerned by the waste of force and delay in action which in the Army view this solution necessarily involved. The result of this decision soon appeared in the statistics of the antisubmarine battle. In November and December, 1942, over thirty merchant vessels were sunk by U-boats in the Caribbean area and none in the Gulf and Atlantic coast areas; during this period the Navy's own experts estimated that ten German submarines, on the average, were working in the Caribbean area and only one in the Atlantic and Gulf areas combined. Yet during the same two months Army and Navy aircraft flew 45,000 hours on patrol in the almost unattacked northern areas, and only 9,000 hours in the

[1] Letter from King to Marshall, June 21, 1942. This letter is available in full in Samuel E. Morison, *The Battle of the Atlantic*, Little, Brown, 1947, p. 310.

beleaguered Caribbean. In the entire month of December no aircraft in the northern areas made any contact with a submarine. And the shift of U-boats from the Gulf and Atlantic coasts had already been evident in September, two months earlier. With all allowance for the logistic difficulties of a shift in air strength to meet the U-boat move, Army officials contended that this sort of situation clearly demonstrated the need for integrated control over the relatively flexible air arm; sea frontier commanders were not likely to part with their aircraft, once allocated, nor could they be expected to visualize the "big picture."

Throughout 1942 Stimson continued to urge upon the Navy the advantages of a truly co-ordinated antisubmarine command and an aggressive attitude toward the submarine. The Army in the autumn of 1942 expanded its originally experimental organization into the Anti-Submarine Air Command, but this Command remained much less effective than Stimson had hoped; its aircraft under Navy direction continued to be assigned mainly to defensive operations. Not all of the difficulty in organizing the Army antisubmarine forces came from the Navy, by any means. If the Navy was enamored in singleminded fashion of convoy and escort, the Army Air Forces were at least equally devoted to the concept of strategic air power, and for many months their antisubmarine command remained a good deal of a stepchild.

In March, 1943, the whole problem was reopened in a big way. During the first three weeks of that month U-boats operating mainly in the North Atlantic southeast of Greenland, in an area not yet covered by air search, sank over three-quarters of a million tons of shipping. The President sent a sharp note of inquiry to Marshall and King as to the air dispositions planned to meet this threat. The War Department, fortified by a comprehensive and extremely able report prepared by Bowles, began a final effort to win for Army aircraft the autonomy and full naval co-operation needed for a prosecution of offensive operations.

This effort failed. Stimson suggested to Knox the establishment of an autonomous, offensive air task force for antisubmarine work; the suggestion was rejected. Then Marshall urged in the Joint Chiefs of Staff the creation of a new over-all anti-submarine command embracing all air and surface units, and responsible like a theater command directly to the Joint Chiefs. King rejected this solution, but he indicated his awareness of the problem by creating instead the Tenth Fleet, under his direct command, to co-ordinate all antisubmarine operations in all the sea frontiers. Then Arnold urged the appointment of an Army air officer to co-ordinate all shore-based air operations under this Tenth Fleet; King did not immediately reject this proposal, but in detailed negotiations it became apparent that the difference between the Navy and the Air Forces on the meaning of "operational control" was irreconcilable. The Air Forces, strongly supported by Stimson and Marshall, believed that antisubmarine air operations *must* be co-ordinated and directed by an aggressive air commander like Air Marshal Slessor of the British Coastal Command, subject only to the most general guidance of his naval superior. Admiral King believed this concept to be wholly mistaken and insisted that air operations must be directly controlled in each area by the local naval commander. The impasse was complete, and finally, in June, General Marshall reached the conclusion that there was no future for the Army concept so long as the Navy retained final control of antisubmarine operations. In return for certain concessions in other fields of conflict, he turned over to the Navy, with Stimson's approval, the entire responsibility for antisubmarine air activity. The Army squadrons assigned to this mission were gradually withdrawn, and in November, 1943, two months later than it had at first promised, the Navy assumed full responsibility for the work. Stimson shared the disappointment of his British friends Churchill and Slessor that so much training should be so arbitrarily discarded, but he agreed with Marshall that it was no use to fight a battle in which grudging naval concessions would be no concessions at all, since full co-operation was the necessary condition of success.

Meanwhile the crisis of the submarine war had passed; Allied air power, partly shore based and partly carrier based, had closed the North Atlantic gap in the spring, and had done such damage to the U-boat "wolf packs" that by June they had withdrawn almost entirely from the North Atlantic convoy route. After that time the submarine was reduced, in Admiral King's words, "from menace to problem."

In 1947, assessing the questions involved in this prolonged and mutually unsatisfactory conflict between the Army and the Navy, Stimson found himself convinced that on the tactical issues the Army was proved right and the Navy wrong. The record of Allied antisubmarine activity in all areas where the Germans operated clearly demonstrated the effectiveness of aggressively employed air power. From 1942 onward—and it was only in 1942 that air-borne radar began to be extensively used—aircraft operating at sea destroyed more German submarines than did surface vessels, and more than five-sixths of the submarines destroyed from the air were killed by shore-based aircraft. Moreover, the vast majority of these shore-based kills were accomplished by aircraft flying under the control of Slessor's Coastal Command in accordance with the principles of air autonomy and aggressive search so long and vainly urged by Stimson on the American Navy. The early Navy notion that convoy escort was the *only* way of fighting the submarine was in Stimson's view completely exploded by the brilliant operations of the Navy's own hunter-killer groups in 1943 and afterwards, not to mention the shore-based campaigns of Coastal Command first in the Bay of Biscay and later in Norwegian waters.

But the issue of tactics was not the most important matter to be reviewed. Far more important lessons were apparent to Stimson in the contest over antisubmarine warfare. The first was the importance of listening closely to the scientists. Scientific contributions to antisubmarine warfare were enormous, and they extended far beyond the merely technical. Scientists like Bowles and Bush proved themselves to be capable of sound strategic comment and of constructive proposals for the tactical control and use of antisubmarine weapons. They were far wiser than either naval or air officers who had become wedded to a limited strategic concept.

The second lesson of the antisubmarine campaign was the critical importance of the doctrine of command responsibility. Much of the continuing failure of both the Army and the

Navy in antisubmarine matters rose out of the absence of any central and clear-cut command. At least until 1943 the Navy Department was not organized as was the British Admiralty, with a vigorous and independent group of senior officers conducting antisubmarine warfare as a continuous campaign. There was no officer who could be held responsible for that mission and only that one; antisubmarine warfare, both in the Navy Department and in the Army's high command, was everyone's business and no one's. And if General Arnold's officers were thinking mainly of strategic air power, Admiral King's were primarily concerned with the Pacific. With rare exceptions, antisubmarine warfare received only the partial attention of the first-rate officers, while actual operations were left to commanders not always chosen from the top drawer. Comparing this arrangement with the method applied in Africa and Europe and the different theaters of the Pacific, Stimson concluded that it provided the proof, in failure, of the wisdom that set up the other theaters under single, strong, full-time commanders.

A third important lesson was that the Joint Chiefs of Staff was an imperfect instrument of top-level decision. Certainly it represented a vast improvement over anything that had existed before, and on the whole it was astonishingly successful, but it remained incapable of enforcing a decision against the will of any one of its members. It was an exact counterpart in military terms of the Security Council later established by the United Nations; any officer, in a minority of one, could employ a rigorous insistence on unanimity as a means of defending the interests of his own service. Quite aside from the question of which service was right as to antisubmarine tactics, there was no justification for a situation in which the Army and the Navy worked at cross-purposes for more than a year, each appearing to the other as an ignorant, presumptuous, interfering bungler. And if Marshall had been as narrow a man as some previous Army Chiefs of Staff, the impasse might have continued throughout the war; the right of the Army to operate antisubmarine aircraft was one on which he could have stood his ground forever. Only the President was in a position to settle disagreements by a definite and final

ruling, and Mr. Roosevelt's general position was that disagreements should be adjusted without forcing him to act as
judge. This seemed to Stimson a sensible attitude, since the
President could hardly be expected to take time for a thorough study of dozens of differences, large and small. He remained as a court of last appeal, and fear of his displeasure
frequently forced compromise agreement in the Joint Chiefs
of Staff. But the absence of any constantly operating and truly
decisive authority placed a heavy obligation of self-restraint
on the Joint Chiefs, and the whole system might well have
broken down completely if all its members, and Marshall
particularly, had not been determined that it should reach
and enforce decisions at least on points of primary importance.
Stimson was appalled at the thought of what might have happened among the Joint Chiefs if Marshall had been replaced
by any officer, however able, whose interests and attitudes
were limited by a service viewpoint.

The fourth—and most important—feature of the antisubmarine affair was that it provided an almost perfect example
of the destructive effect of the traditional mutual mistrust of
the two services. Though the focus of the discussion was a
question of tactics, it was surrounded by all sorts of interservice recriminations. It was unfortunate that the Army side of
the question should have been mainly an Air Forces operation,
for the Navy and the Air Forces had a mutual grudge of over
twenty years' standing—the Navy feared that the Air Forces
wished to gain control of all naval aviation, while the Air
Forces saw in the Navy's rising interest in land-based planes
a clear invasion of their prescriptive rights. The Air Forces
considered the Navy a backward service with no proper understanding of air power; the Navy considered the Air Forces a
loud-mouthed and ignorant branch which had not even mastered its own element. Thus it happened that many an incident
which friendly commanders could have used as a signpost to
improvement became instead a source of added bitterness. Although in many cases local and junior officers of both services
established extremely friendly relations, what too often came
to Army and Navy headquarters in Washington were emotionally embroidered reports of the incompetence of the other

service. The simple fact of being under the Navy was no fun for the airmen, whose autonomy in action was their most jealously guarded principle of combat, and that the Air Forces should be sinking submarines at all was to some naval officers an affront. What should have been simply a question of tactics thus became at all echelons a question of feelings, and on neither side was much attention given to the vital task of see· ing the other man's point of view.

This matter of attitude seemed to Stimson the fundamental issue in the Army-Navy relationship. On the whole the war marked a new high point in mutual good feeling. Especially in their great joint ventures in the complex art of amphibious warfare the Army and the Navy learned to respect and like each other; a similar if less intense good feeling developed among the men in Washington who were of necessity thrown together in planning and supplying these vast overseas undertakings. But a strong residue of mutual disapproval remained. Stimson himself was not exempt. On October 20, 1942, at a meeting with Knox and Hull, "After I had expatiated on the fruits of the bombers, . . . Knox . . . rather unnecessarily put in the remark that the Navy didn't think much of high-altitude bombing anyhow. I then rose in my wrath and tore him to pieces. In fact the debate was so hot I could see Hull pulling his legs in under his chair and generally gathering himself into a fighting position lest he be hit by the flying fragments!" The two Secretaries attacked each other's sore points, trading unpleasant opinions about bombers, MacArthur, Guadalcanal, and logistics. "But finally we wound up with a laugh and the smoke blew away." Though Stimson was by long training and predilection an Army man, Knox had no such background as a naval advocate; this mutual jealousy was the daily and insistent atmosphere of the separate Departments, and it sank imperceptibly into the minds of the most balanced of men.

In the first two years of the war Stimson strongly opposed the holding of public Army-Navy football games in large cities, on the grounds that such a major spectacle would eat up gasoline and other supplies better employed in warmaking. In 1944 he somewhat changed his tune, and although the main reason for this change was simply that a year of victories had somewhat relaxed his insistence on austerity, there was a further thought in his mind. "The President wanted my advice as to whether or not he should shift the Army and Navy football game to New York. That comes a week from next Saturday. For two years we have been having semiprivate football games at the homes of the two Academies . . . but now the pressure is for having it a public one. The fact that the Army has a very good football team this year and has a darned good chance of beating the Navy makes me a little more lenient towards it than I was before." (Diary, November 13, 1944) The game was held in New York, and the Army won, 23-7.

3. UNIFICATION AND THE FUTURE

The war was fought successfully without any important revision of the separated status of the two services from which all these troubles grew. The Joint Chiefs of Staff and a number of other boards and committees were bridges across the gap. Sometimes in the operating theaters these bridges became so numerous and solid that the gap almost disappeared—and then incautiously someone would assume that it did not exist and learn his mistake from a new outburst of feeling. To Stimson and others thinking of the future it seemed evident that the primary objective of the postwar period in military affairs must be to end this division of feeling.

The difficulty of attaining such an objective became brutally clear in the spring of 1944, when a Select Committee of the House of Representatives began hearings on the controversial issue of "unification" of the armed forces. Stimson, like most of his War Department colleagues, believed that the consolidation of the armed forces into a single department would be enormously helpful in reducing friction and duplication of effort. He saw it as a means of eliminating the waste of time and money involved in the necessarily cumbersome method of "co-operation," and as a way of insuring action when and if "co-operation" ceased to exist. But knowing that his friends "the well-known Admirals" were strongly opposed to unification, he was at first reluctant to let his Department be involved in public discussion of an issue on which feelings would surely run high. Only the surprising discovery that Knox strongly favored a single unified department overcame this objection. Then just as the Army had completed a detailed statement of its position before the committee, Frank Knox died. His views were not shared by his successor, James V. Forrestal, who without directly opposing unification argued strongly against jumping at conclusions. Agreement between the Secretaries no longer existing, it was at once apparent that the hearings might become a free-for-all in which nothing but bitterness would be produced. Although Stimson and Forrestal agreed entirely that such a result must be avoided if possible, it was too late to stop the hearings; Stimson duly testified, with caution and restraint, but in its later stages the discussion before the House committee painfully foreshadowed the remarkable shrillness of tone that for a time dominated the debate when it was resumed in 1946.

But at last, in 1947, there was introduced in Congress a unification bill which had the firm support of both the Army and the Navy. This successful reconciliation of divergent views Stimson considered a triumph for all concerned and particularly for President Truman, and in a long letter to Senator Chan Gurney he joined the battle for the bill's passage. This letter presents in full Stimson's views on unification.

First he discussed the basic need as met by the new bill.

". . . I consider this measure to be one of the most important peacetime forward steps ever proposed in our military history. . . .

". . . Like many things which have been carefully worked out, the proposed measure is essentially quite simple. It creates a new 'National Defense Establishment,' within which the Army, the Navy, and the Air Force are to be included. For that Department it establishes a Secretary, and the functions and powers of this new official are the heart of the bill. 'Under the direction of the President, he shall establish policies and programs for the National Defense Establishment and for the departments and agencies therein; he shall exercise direction, authority, and control over such departments and agencies.' And he is to supervise and control as a co-ordinated whole the budgeted expenditures of the armed forces—in this respect as in others the bill presents a striking parallel with the notable legislative reorganization achieved last year by the Congress.

"The Secretary of National Defense is provided with the necessary military and civilian assistants; he becomes Chairman of a War Council; he is given authority over the Joint Chiefs of Staff, which splendid engine of military skill and thinking is continued with its present general functions; he is given a Munitions Board and a Research and Development Board which will serve him as flexible instruments for the exercise of two critically important functions. . . .

"It is my considered opinion that the new Secretary of National Defense will have it in his power to integrate our armed forces as they have never been integrated before. In World War II we accomplished great things by co-operation between two separate Departments, but from that experience we learned that co-operation is not enough. I will not rehearse the unhappy list of duplications, or the instances of friction and disagreement which then hampered our work. But I would emphasize that each succeeding emergency in the last fifty years has made heavier demands on our armed services. The element of economy in our use of armed force might well be critical in any future contest. It came nearer to being critical towards the end of this last war than I had dreamed likely during the years preceding the war. I do not mean economy in dollar terms (though in the long run we should greatly gain in that respect too under this bill), but rather that strategic economy which exerts maximum force with limited national resources. Without increased unity we cannot get that kind of economy; we will continue instead to operate with the wasteful opulence that has characterized much of our work in the past. This new bill provides the framework for the increased unity we need."

Then he turned to the fears of its opponents.

"The Secretary of National Defense will be a powerful officer. That is entirely proper. He cannot successfully exercise his functions without adequate and flexible power. But it should be observed that he is given no powers which do not already belong to the President as Commander in Chief. What this bill does is to delegate to a recognized officer of the Government a part of the authority over the military establishment which in the end always belongs to the President. If it were possible today for any President to give his full attention to military affairs, this step would not be necessary. But we all know that the President even now is much overworked, and that he cannot permit himself to become entirely preoccupied by his duties as Commander in Chief. .... Under this bill the President as Chief Executive retains his basic powers unchanged; he is provided with a suitable officer for the proper exercise of these powers; that officer remains under his entire control. This appears to me to be a wholly proper and natural step, entirely in keeping with our best administrative tradition.

"At the same time I see nothing in this bill that justifies any fear that tested and invaluable instruments of war like naval aviation—or specifically Army aviation for that matter—will be lightly and carelessly discarded. . . .

"In connection with this matter of specific fears and controversies, I can only repeat what I said to the Select Committee of the Congress three years ago: 'I would like to stress, as a major point, the importance of considering this organization of the armed forces from the standpoint of fundamentals rather than details. If the basic plan of centralization can be determined upon, hundreds of vexing problems will fall into proper perspective. They will lose much of their controversial aspect and be decided as matters of specific planning rather than of primary policy.'"

And finally he pointed out the fortunate circumstances in which the bill was presented and emphasized their importance, drawing on his own experience for illustrations.

"Not only is the bill a good one, but the time is ripe and the winds are fair for launching such a great reform. Political action is always in large measure a matter of time and circumstance, and in this case the time and circumstance seem so conspicuously right that I should like to emphasize them in detail." He recalled the painful atmosphere which had dominated the discussion in 1944 and again in 1946, remarking that "it began to appear that discussion of unification was serving merely to drive the services farther apart."

"With great wisdom and judgment, the President withdrew the matter from immediate consideration and referred it to the War and Navy Departments for thorough study, insisting that divergences be reconciled. As study and discussion proceeded ... it became possible to reduce areas of disagreement until the great common objective again dominated, and, as I understand it, the present bill has the hearty endorsement of the responsible officers, civilian and military, of both of our present service departments.

"This fact is in itself of critical significance, as I think I can show by referring to a bit of War Department history with which I am personally familiar. When Elihu Root established the General Staff, integrating—unifying, if you please—the high command of the Army, he was faced by very decided military opposition from men in high administrative posts; but with the support of the top men of the Army and a majority of the Congress, he carried his work through successfully. Ten years later when the whole concept of the General Staff was violently challenged by an able administrative soldier of the old school, General Leonard Wood (as Chief of Staff) and I (as Secretary of War), as a team, were successful in defending the Root reforms. . . . When the civilians and the soldiers are in cordial and sympathetic agreement, each conscious of his proper function and his proper relation to the other, there are few limits to the advances that can be made. . . .

"With this sort of agreement and harmony existing, only one additional element is required to give life and meaning to the bill if enacted. That is, of course, the leadership and support of the President, now to be exerted in the first instance through his Secretary of National Defense. The Root reforms depended on the firm backing of Presidents McKinley and Theodore Roosevelt; in our battle to preserve them General Wood and I should have lost without the courageous and understanding help of President Taft; the extraordinary wartime co-operation of the Army and Navy in the recent world struggle depended in the end on the vision and courage of

President Franklin Roosevelt. Without understanding and firmness at the White House, no progress can be made in military organization. Most fortunately we have as President a man who has fully demonstrated his grasp of the problem this new reform is designed to solve, and who has been himself a leader in securing agreement within the services. We may be certain that President Truman will search out for service as our first Secretary of National Defense the best man he can find for the job, and when he has found that man he will give him strong and intelligent support."

Though it did not pass the congressional gantlet without some amendment, the Unification Bill was finally enacted in July, 1947, and James Forrestal, to Stimson's personal satisfaction, became on the following September 19 the country's first Secretary of Defense. The Army, the Navy and the Air Forces were thus at once separated and combined in a new organization for whose future Stimson had the highest hopes. The new act was not perfect, but it was an excellent first step. That it provided the framework for a better high command was certain. What was still more important, it provided a setting wherein, under firm and sympathetic leadership, the bitterness and misunderstanding of the past might be ended. Under a single leader, the Army, the Navy, and the Air Forces could now learn, and be taught, to live together. The great gains of World War II might thus be consolidated, while a repetition of its occasional failures could be prevented, and Stimson earnestly hoped that the time would quickly come when the struggles discussed in this chapter, both serious and comic, would find no echo of recognition among the soldiers, sailors, and airmen of the United States.

CHAPTER XXI

The Army and the Grand Alliance

WORLD WAR II was the first major experience of the United States in the political complexities of coalition warfare. In 1917 and 1918 the vast strength of America remained mainly potential. There was great importance in Pershing's stand for a united American Army, and there were lessons for naval officers in the relation between Sims and the British Admiralty, but neither of these experiences was adequate preparation for the extraordinary variety of problems presented to the Washington government in the years after Pearl Harbor—problems created by the simple fact that among all the nations fighting against the Axis the United States possessed incomparably the largest amount of flexible military and economic strength. The military power of the U.S.S.R. was necessarily committed almost wholly to the vast eastern front; the persistent and skillful effort of the British was by 1941 pinned down in major part to northwest Europe and Africa. Only the Americans had a free hand.

To Stimson the record achieved by his country in the resolution of the problems thus created seemed on the whole magnificent. The greatest single set of decisions were those leading to the Normandy landing, already discussed in an earlier chapter. But the OVERLORD decision was in the main one of military strategy, although in securing its adoption there was much political negotiation. Several other problems presented more clearly the ticklish interrelation of military and political aspects which is so difficult for the ordinary democratic statesman to grasp and act upon. The great flair here shown by Franklin Roosevelt seemed to Stimson a blessing of Providence upon the American people; by 1940 the President had already shown his deep comprehension of the menace of Nazism, but only under the test of actual war was his talent as a war leader revealed.

His success was triumphant, and it was substantially his own. In this chapter we shall deal with certain problems with which for one reason or another Stimson came into direct contact; in these cases he at times held views widely differing from those of the President—and indeed feared that the President was acting unwisely. But it would be wholly wrong to take these differences as illustrative of any basic difference over the political strategy of the war. In the main he was a loyal and sometimes surprised admirer of the force and skill with which Mr. Roosevelt—almost by himself, for this was his nature—laid out his course and led his countrymen along it.

The central political decision of World War II was that it must be fought in an alliance as close as possible with Great Britain and Soviet Russia. Not once during the war was this decision questioned or any modification of it seriously considered by Stimson or by any man whose views he knew among the leaders of the administration. The three nations, in American eyes, formed the indispensable team for victory over Germany. Together, with or without welcome and helpful accessions of strength from smaller nations, they could not lose. Apart, or at cross-purposes, or with any one of them defeated, they could hardly win. It was thus the constant purpose of the American Government to do all that would achieve and cherish a cordial unity of action—and so to reinforce its two great allies, from the vast American reservoir of material wealth, that each would press on with increasing power to a final combined victory.

There was of course a marked distinction in the degree of genuine understanding aimed at and achieved by Americans in dealing with their two major allies. Stimson's own contacts with the British and the Russians were illustrative of the distinction. With the British, from the first, he established the kind of close and wholly confident connection that he had maintained ten years before with Ramsay MacDonald. The vehemence and heat with which he fought against British opposition to the Channel invasion was understandable only in the light of his complete confidence that between such fast friends there could be no final falling out. Stimson argued with Mr. Churchill more bluntly than he ever did with Mr. Roosevelt; he could cut loose at the Englishman as he never felt free to do with his chief. And he talked with English officers as easily as with his own Army leaders—sometimes to get their advice and sometimes to give them his, in fairly vigorous terms.

The Russian question was different. Stimson's direct contact with Russian matters was very slight until near the end of the war. In the earlier years, when the main American object was simply to help the Russians, his role was inconsiderable. In diplomatic negotiations he had no part; in Lend-Lease transactions he sometimes found himself the advocate of the Army's needs against those of the Russians; this was the necessary result of his duty to equip the Army, and implied no disagreement whatever with the policy of aid to Russia. Of course Russian visitors came to his office; ordinarily these were merely formal calls, but occasionally Stimson had a chance to put in a word—as in the following discussion of July 29, 1941: "At 11:18 I saw the Soviet Ambassador, Mr. Oumansky, a rather slick and unscrupulous gentleman I have been told, who used to belong to the OGPU—the secret police of Russia—and had had a rather brutal record. He came to pay his respects but, as I knew he would, brought in at the end a request for arms. He told me how important the battle in Russia was, and what great service the Russians were doing for the rest of the world. I told him I had no doubt that was so but I said, 'Mr. Ambassador, I have no eyes to see the things that you tell me. You have taken away my eyes and until I get my eyes back, I cannot take the responsibility of recommending giving away our weapons.' He said, 'You mean your Attaché should be allowed to go to the front?' I said, 'I mean just that.' That gave him a poser. . . ."

Such posers were more verbal than practical, however. Whatever the American annoyance at Russian secretiveness, it was not United States policy to squabble over details, and Oumansky and his successors got more than they gave. With this policy of one-sided generosity Stimson had little to do, but during the first years its objectionable features were quite obscured by the supreme importance of saving the Russians from defeat.

The real questions of American policy toward Russia went much deeper than such trivia. The great present goal was to help the Russians kill Germans. As they continued to fight effectively long beyond the most optimistic early estimates of most American intelligence officers, and as gradually a narrow but significant bridge of co-operation was constructed, it became clear that in their own strange way the Russians were magnificent allies. They fought as they promised, and they made no separate peace.

In 1943 and 1944 Stimson's concern for a proper second front led him to a certain sympathy with Russian suspicion of Western motives; not to open promptly a strong western front in France, he felt, would be to leave the real fighting to Russia. During the discussions at Washington in May, 1943, Stimson told the President "that the argument on the other side reminded me of the story of Lincoln with regard to General Franz Sigel who Lincoln said was a pretty poor general who, although he couldn't skin the deer could at least hold a leg. [Those who oppose invasion] are trying to arrange this matter so that Britain and America hold the leg for Stalin to skin the deer and I think that will be dangerous business for us at the end of the war. Stalin won't have much of an opinion of people who have done that and we will not be able to share much of the postwar world with him." (Diary, May 17, 1943)

But this fear was not realized; the alliance held together with each partner bearing a full load, and it was only in early 1945 that a cloud began to appear on the Russian horizon, as Stimson saw it. Nothing that happened in this later period seemed to him to bear against the wisdom and foresight of Mr. Roosevelt's decision to behave with complete friendliness and good will toward the Russians while the Allies were at war.

Thus on the central political issue of the war—alliance with Britain and Russia—Stimson was a wholehearted supporter

of the President, without having any major part in the
execution of policy. His principal activity in the field of
wartime international policy, beyond the question of the
Channel invasion, fell in three lesser fields into which he was
brought by his Army responsibilities and by his special
interest: China, France, and military government in Europe.
In none of these cases did he have a continuous or determinant
part, but his experience in each was illustrative of his own
attitudes and of some of the difficulties faced by a necessarily
inexperienced and unnecessarily personalized administration.

1. STILWELL AND CHINA

In Anglo-American grand strategy the war against Germany
came first. Second came the great "triphibious" movement
across the Pacific toward the Japanese island empire. The
China-Burma-India theater was a poor third. Yet in its strategic and political significance this part of the world was of enormous importance; in a situation of extraordinary complexity it
constantly offered the possibility of striking military and
political success, at a remarkably low cost. For nearly three
years Stimson and Marshall were leaders in an effort to
achieve this success, and although their greatest hopes were
not realized, the effort was not wholly barren, and in both
its achievements and its failures it was extremely instructive.

Strategically, the object of American policy in this area
was to keep China in the war, and so to strengthen her that
she might exact a constantly growing price from the Japanese
invader. The reinforcement of China depended on the maintenance of a line of supply through Burma, if necessary by
air, if possible by land. But Burma was a part of the British
Empire, and it was especially important to the British as the
last buffer between India and Japanese aggression. There
were thus three major Allied Nations whose respective interests came to a common point in Burma, and although all
three were presumably agreed on the vital necessity of winning the Japanese war, only the United States, of the three,
framed its policy in that area with military victory as its single
object. And it was the peculiar difficulty of the American

policy that it was dependent upon a British base and Chinese manpower. The situation was still further complicated by the traditional mutual distaste of the British and the Chinese, to both of whom any failure of the other was a source of racial satisfaction.

Long before Pearl Harbor the American Government established in Chungking a military mission. With American entry into the war, and the beginning of a Japanese campaign against Burma, it became evident that the American interest required in this theater a military representative of pre-eminent quality. Because of his intense interest in the Chinese situation, Stimson played a conspicuous part in the selection of this representative, and of few things was he more proud than of his share in the eventual choice of General Joseph W. Stilwell.

Stilwell's name was not the first suggested. The post was indeed offered, in January, 1942, to one of the Army's most senior generals. But after getting into a row with General Marshall, the officer under consideration submitted a memorandum of requirements which indicated a predominant interest in his own and not the national advantage. The response of the Secretary of War was definite.

"He had brought me a paper which he had drawn in which he virtually took the position that he did not think the role in China which I had offered him was big enough for his capabilities. The paper said a good deal more than that but that was what it boiled down to. I told him how much disappointed I was at the attitude that he had taken; that I myself had planned out the position which he was to take and that it seemed to me that it would lead to most important work for his country; that its sphere depended a good deal on his own abilities but that I had had confidence that he would be able to seize the opportunity to expand the importance of the place into a very important sphere. I showed him that he would have had the full support not only of myself but of Marshall and the General Staff. I told him I could not help contrasting the position he was taking with what I considered my own duty when I was offered a position in the Far East which I did not desire and which I felt constrained to accept even in the nonemergent times of peace, because my government had selected me for it. I then closed the interview." (Diary, January 13, 1942)

Although the general took it all back the next day and said "he would do anything I wanted him to do," his mistake was not one which Stimson could readily forgive. The job in China and Burma would require a man who believed in it. And fortunately on the same evening Stimson found such a man.

"In the evening on my request General Stilwell came to see me. . . . Marshall had suggested that I had better see him with a view to China, and I had a long talk with him over the fire in my library about the Chinese situation. I was very favorably impressed with him. He is a very quick-witted and alert-minded man. He knows China thoroughly and for more than two years campaigned with the Chinese armies against Japan in 1937-8-9. In half an hour he gave me a better first-hand picture of the valor of the Chinese armies than I had ever received before. Of this valor he had a very high opinion. He said that practically the whole success of my Chinese proposition would depend on whether or not Chiang Kai-shek would, as Soong has promised, give command of any of his troops to an American. This he has always refused hitherto. With that permission Stilwell said that the possibilities of the Chinese proposition were unbounded and he was very enthusiastic about it. . . . So I went to bed with a rather relieved feeling that I had discovered a man who will be very useful." (Diary, January 14, 1942)

After checking his opinion with General Frank McCoy and of course with Marshall, Stimson determined that Stilwell was the man for China and cleared his appointment with the President. Within three weeks Stilwell was on his way to what Stimson later judged as the most difficult task assigned to any American in the entire war.

Stimson and Marshall did what they could to get Stilwell off to a good start. In negotiations with Chiang Kai-shek it was agreed that Stilwell should be Chiang's Chief of Staff, and the harmony of feeling and purpose which appeared to result from this agreement was heartening to the War Department's leaders in a time largely barren of encouragement.

On February 3, 1942, Stimson went before the House Foreign Affairs Committee in executive session to speak in favor of a 500-million-dollar loan to China. It was a time for advocacy, and the advocacy came easily to Stimson, for the Chinese venture was one in which he deeply believed.

"I worked pretty carefully over what I should say to the committee and it went off, I think, better than almost any hearing I have ever had in Congress. I outlined the difficult situation we were in in the southwestern Pacific, outnumbered in the air and sea and on the ground, and with immensely long lines of communication. I pointed out China's strategic position towards that area, including Indo-China, Thailand, Malaya, and Burma. I gave them a picture of the fighting character of the Chinese troops as it had been given me by General Stilwell. I told of China's unique relations with us and her unique attitude and confidence towards our government as demonstrated in many ways as I had observed it in the Philippines. I described the onslaught which was now being made by the Japanese to pull down Chiang Kai-shek upon whose character and influence rested the Chinese defense, and then I told what we were doing recently in our negotiations with Chiang and how he had promised to make our nominee chief of his staff. I told them that, while nobody could prophesy events in war, this represented to me a unique opportunity to play for the highest stakes for the Far East and that the success or failure of the war might depend upon this act; and in the light of the billions we had spent for less favorable opportunities, I thought that if America refused to take this chance, she would not deserve to win the war. The committee listened attentively throughout and, when I closed, there was a dead silence. No one asked me a question. The chairman turned to me and said that the committee was paying me the highest compliment it could pay, not even asking a single question on my report." (Diary, February 3, 1942)

If this statement had eloquence—and the response from those present indicated that it did—it was because this was a subject on which Stimson felt very strongly. The great tradition of American friendship with the people of China was one in which his personal part had not been small, and, as he faced the challenge of the Japanese warmakers, he saw that tradition as a basis from which a great military triumph might be created—and of course in such a triumph the tradition itself would be still further strengthened for service to both nations and the world after victory. Nothing that happened in the war was more disheartening to him than the gradual shrinking of these hopes.

This book is unfortunately not the place for a detailed study of the history of the China-Burma-India Theater. To Stimson that history unfolded principally as the saga of Joe Stilwell, fighting heroically against overwhelming odds. Stilwell's central military objective was to strengthen the Chinese armies and bring their force to bear on the Japanese in Asia. His enemies were of four kinds—Japanese, Chinese, British, and American.

The Japanese took Burma in early 1942, cutting off the only land route to China. The recapture of northern Burma thus became to Stilwell the goal of first priority. Without a road into China for the shipment of arms and supplies, the vast potential strength of the Chinese armies could never be developed into reality. But the recapture of Burma was not a primary goal of the Chinese and the British.

The Chinese Government of Generalissimo Chiang Kai-shek defies any brief analysis. Of its firm opposition to the Japanese there was never any doubt, and the administration in Washington was fully sensitive to the extraordinary sufferings which the Chinese had endured in five years of war before 1942. But even Stimson, who had studied as Secretary of State the twisted and personalized operations of Chinese nationalist politics, was astonished at the number of obstacles placed by Chinese leaders in the path of General Stilwell. Some of the obstacles were those typical of all personal government; others were rooted in the complexities of Kuomintang policy.

Stilwell, commanding Chinese troops in the first Burma campaign, found that his Chinese subordinates constantly received tactical instructions from the distant autocrat in Chungking, and Chiang's tactical skill was in Stilwell's view almost nonexistent. After the retreat from Burma, when he turned his energies to the creation of an effective Chinese force, Stilwell found his work constantly delayed or blocked by Chiang's inability to understand the meaning of modern training. Even after Stilwell had made a success of his training center for Chinese troops in Ramgahr, India, he found the Chinese still slow to co-operate in extending the new training methods to China proper. The entire Chinese war establishment was riddled with graft and personal power politics; these factors limited what Chiang could do if he would, and his intense preoccupation with the perpetuation of his own power was a still further limitation. To Stilwell the Chinese war ministry was "medieval" and the adjective was accurately used; balancing and rebalancing the semi-subordinate warlords, blind to the meaning of training and supply, innocent of any concern for its enlisted soldiers, squeezing and squeezed in the worst Chinese tradition, the war ministry, and Chiang Kai-shek too, adopted the attitude that China had already done her part. They passed their days and nights in pleading for clouds of airplanes and swarms of tanks, constantly insisting to the Western world that 'America must help her faithful ally.' But they would not help themselves.

The position and purpose of the British were very different, but their effect on Stilwell's work was much the same. The initial failure of British forces in Malaya and Burma was a shocking blow to the prestige of the Empire; the repair of this damaged prestige at once became a primary objective of British policy. But unfortunately the British were not agreed among themselves as to the best means for attaining this objective; few of them shared the conviction of such officers as Major-General Orde C. Wingate that the way to serve the British interest was to show first-class fighting quality against the Japanese, and do it quickly. The caution and defeatism which had led to the original debacle were never fully dissipated; even so gallant and dashing an officer as Lord Mountbatten, dispatched by Mr. Churchill with the specific purpose of putting in "some new punch to it" (Diary on conversation with Churchill, May 22, 1943), was not able to reverse this attitude entirely. Nor did the British agree with Stilwell on the importance of reopening the Burma Road, which after all led to a China they mistrusted, and not to Singapore. Stilwell's persistent faith in the potentialities of the Chinese soldier was not shared by most Englishmen in India.

But to Stimson the most trying of all Stilwell's problems was the constant undercutting to which he was subjected by Americans. Although the degree of their difficulty had not been correctly estimated, the British and Chinese obstacles to his mission had been foreseen when Stilwell was first sent out. Stimson could not share the disillusioned rancor of many Americans who faced these problems for the first time and reached hasty conclusions about the wickedness of their allies. The Chinese in China and the British in India were dealing with a situation whose complexity was far beyond anything in American experience, and while Stimson believed that both groups were false to their own interests in much of their opposition to Stilwell, he was prepared to face their failures without bitterness. Toward the Americans who hampered Stilwell he was less charitable.

American opposition to Stilwell was partly tactical and partly personal. Tactically, opposition came mainly from the Air Forces, whose commander in China was Major General Claire Chennault. It was the view of Chennault and his many American supporters that Stilwell's insistence on a first priority for the Burma campaign was not correct. They argued that the bulk of the supplies carried by air across the Hump into China should be used not for Stilwell's ground-force training center in Yunnan but rather for the operations of Chennault's Fourteenth Air Force. To Stilwell, Marshall, and Stimson this view appeared wholly wrong. They feared that much activity from unprotected air bases would merely stimulate a heavy Japanese land campaign against Chennault's airfields. But this possibility did not disturb the airmen; Chennault even argued that his aircraft would be able to repel any such attack. In spite of all opposition Chennault's view was approved by the Washington Conference of May, 1943. Stilwell himself was called to the conference to state his case, but his advocacy was unsuccessful. His build-up of Chinese land forces was once more delayed, this time by the decision of Franklin Roosevelt.

Tactical disagreements are inevitable in war. Stimson was to find his dire prophecies fully confirmed in the Japanese attack of 1944, which overran seven of the principal bases of the Fourteenth Air Force, but the tactical mistake of the Washington Conference was a minor matter compared to the political errors and personal activities which came before and after it.

More than any other American theater commander in the war, Stilwell required the constant and vigorous political support of his own government, and less than any other commander did he get it. Engaged as he was in a great effort to make China strong almost against her will, he was bound to find himself frequently in the disagreeable position of telling unpleasant truths to an autocrat. Americans like Chennault and some of his political-minded associates, on the other hand, were in the position of advocating tactics which suited the politics and strategic concepts of the Generalissimo; Chiang was happy to accept serenely the view that American air power would defeat the Japanese. Still other Americans, preoccupied with the intense poverty and economic weakness of China, tended to think largely in terms of loans and civilian supplies, and this too was a language which the Generalissimo understood and approved. What to Stimson seemed unforgivable was that many of these Americans allowed their differences with Stilwell over tactics or purpose so to weight their loyalty that they joined in and even encouraged the efforts of Chiang Kai-shek to undermine Stilwell's authority and weaken his support from Washington. And to Stimson it was not surprising, although terribly disappointing, that all this intrigue was in the end effective in the mind of President Roosevelt, although in defense of Stilwell General Marshall acted with even more than his usual wisdom and energy.

Stilwell, unfortunately, never really "made his number" with the President. Although Mr. Roosevelt was by no means blind to the weaknesses of the Chinese Government, he was unschooled in the details on which Stilwell's tactical and political position was founded, and he was tied by personal sympathy to the support of Chennault. For his information on China he often depended on "personal representatives" who were usually easy dupes of the wonderfully charming circle around the throne at Chungking. He thus never gave to Stilwell the freedom of action and automatic backing which he so courageously accorded to his commanders in other theaters. Stilwell to him remained a somewhat testy, if obviously loyal, soldier who had some strange attraction for the War Department. It seemed doubtful to Stimson whether the President ever realized how much his own personal emissaries and his willingness to hear attacks on Stilwell contributed to the latter's difficulties. The only "emissary" to China throughout the war whose work seemed to Stimson truly helpful was Somervell, who happened on the scene in October, 1943, during one of Chiang's most violent outbreaks against Stilwell. With the aid of Mme. Chiang and some of her remarkable family Somervell pulled the Generalissimo round. Most of the other visitors, sometimes in ignorance, sometimes on the basis of definite personal instructions from a President playing by ear, only made matters worse. Stilwell thus never was able to speak as the voice of the United States war effort in Asia; he was only one side of it.

The last act in Stilwell's mission was played in October, 1944. By that time Stilwell had fully justified his insistence on a Burma campaign by his brilliant advance in north Burma, culminating in the capture of Myitkyina—this was one of the great and insufficiently noticed military epics of the war. But none of this satisfied Chiang, who had grown to hate Stilwell—even as Stilwell had grown to hate him.

On October 3 Stimson summarized the matter as he saw it: "After the daily conference with the Operations and Intelligence Staff, the morning was spent in preparing myself for my luncheon with the President; also in discussing with General Marshall the crisis in China. This last is rapidly growing more and more serious. The Japanese are advancing and have already made it necessary for us to evacuate two of our advance bases for our airplanes. By this they have already pushed us out of range of some of our important targets in

Japan. The Chinese Government of Chiang Kai-shek is getting more and more difficult to deal with. Not only has he failed to back Stilwell up but he has now again requested that we relieve him. Marshall and the Staff had prepared a sharp rejoinder for the President to send declining to do so, but the President has declined so far to send it. Stilwell has been the one successful element of the three forces that have been supposed to co-operate in Burma. The British dragged their feet, and Mountbatten last spring almost as soon as he got there sent us word that he wanted to have the campaign go over until after the monsoon. If we had accepted that, we would not yet have begun. On the other hand, Chiang Kai-shek has several times interfered with the Yunnan forces of Chinese whom he had promised to send and did send as far as the Salween River. In between these two hesitating and halting forces, Stilwell with his three American-trained Chinese divisions coming down the Ledo Road, and Wingate and Merrill with their air troops and raiders flying in to help, have brought victory out of hesitation and defeat. The British, stung by their example, have at last thrown the Japanese out of Imphal and our troops are well down near the Irrawaddy River. Stilwell has taken Myitkyina, and north Burma is virtually free of the Japanese. This campaign in all the difficulties of the monsoon has been a triumphant vindication of Stilwell's courage and sagacity. He had been pecked at from both sides, carped at by the British from India, and hamstrung at every moment by Chiang Kai-shek. Now the Japanese in China, stung by these defeats in Burma, have called their main forces into action in China and are closing in against the regular Chinese armies. If Chiang Kai-shek had supported Stilwell, we should have had a well-trained nucleus of these Chinese troops to meet them. As it is, they are still impotent Chinese, untrained and badly led. Incidentally, this result on both sides has shown the wisdom of Stilwell's diagnosis a year and a half or two years ago when he insisted that we must have ground bases and ground troops in China, well trained, to defeat just such an attack of Japanese; and on the other hand, at the same time Chennault was insisting that he could beat and drive off the Japanese attack by the use of air alone. Chen-

nault has been given almost twice as much in the way of equipment over the Hump as he asked for and yet he is now failing
abjectly to stop the Japanese. On the other hand, Stilwell
fighting against all these obstacles, British incompetence and
sluggishness, Chinese disloyalty, and the lack of supplies over
the Hump line which Chennault's demands made necessary,
has provided the only success in the whole horizon. One of our
difficulties throughout has been the attitude of the President.
He has insisted on sending his own people there . . . and (except Pat Hurley whom we suggested to him) they have all
been disloyal to Stilwell and have all joined hands with his detractors. They have all joined in supporting Chennault's views
and insisting that he be given a chance to save China in the
air. Several times the President suggested that Stilwell should
be relieved. Marshall and I have fought for him steadily and
hard throughout. Now the issue is up again and the President
again is siding against Stilwell. Marshall today said that if
we had to remove Stilwell he would not allow another American general to be placed in the position of Chief of Staff and
Commander of the Chinese armies, for it was so evident that
no American would be loyally supported. I am inclined to go
farther. The amount of effort which we have put into the
'Over the Hump' airline has been bleeding us white in transport airplanes—it has consumed so many. Today we are hamstrung in Holland and the mouth of the Scheldt River for lack
of transport planes necessary to make new air-borne flights in
that neighborhood. The same lack is crippling us in northern
Italy. This effort over the mountains of Burma bids fair to
cost us an extra winter in the main theater of the war. And, in
spite of it all, we have been unable to save China from the
present Japanese attack owing to the failure to support Stilwell in training adequate Chinese ground forces to protect
Kunming."

All this was a summary of what Stimson was prepared to
say to the President. He never said it, for Mr. Roosevelt was
not well that day, and in a two-hour conference Stimson had
quite enough to do in discussing eight other matters, of which
one was pressingly important. (See p. 580.) This seemed an
illustration in specific terms of the losses incurred through

Mr. Roosevelt's constant effort to keep all the threads in his own hands. One man simply could not do it all, and Franklin Roosevelt killed himself trying.

And by this time, too, the President's relation to Stilwell was water under the bridge. Chiang Kai-shek was prepared to insist on Stilwell's recall as a point of personal privilege, and to this position there could now be no answer. Mr. Roosevelt indeed felt more kindly to Stilwell at this time than he had ever felt previously, but it was too late. Greater than any single man or policy was the basic necessity for maintaining the wartime alliance with China, and it no longer seemed possible to keep both Stilwell and friendship with Chiang. Two weeks later Stilwell was recalled by Marshall and his great talents were put to other uses, first as chief of the Army Ground Forces, and then as commanding general of Mac-Arthur's Tenth Army. Stimson surrendered for good his bright hopes for a real rejuvenation of the Chinese forces. China became to him a definitely limited commitment; in the later operations of General Wedemeyer he had no important part.

In assessing the Stimson-Marshall-Stilwell policy, it was not easy for Stimson to be dispassionate. It seemed clear that if Chinese and British leaders had shared the American view, the result could only have been to the advantage of all three nations. Had Chiang Kai-shek permitted Stilwell to carry out his training program on the scale and in the manner that Stilwell originally planned, he must surely have found himself, at the end of the war, with a vastly stronger army, of whose military reputation there could have been no doubt. Such support for Stilwell would have required a vigorous purge of the incompetent and the dishonest in Chiang's military entourage, but there were able young officers to take the place of those removed. It would also have required a shift in Chiang's whole attitude, which remained throughout the war what Stilwell had described in 1942 as that of an ignorant, suspicious, feudal autocrat with a profound but misconceived devotion to the integrity of China and to himself as her savior. But his failure to make this shift was stupid, for the strength of nationalist China could be measured in direct proportion to her escape from a corrupted feudalism.

As for the British, there was no real profit for them in a policy of constant delay and inaction, as many Englishmen clearly understood. Stimson would have liked to see his friend Churchill as theater commander in India; that rugged old champion of empire would hardly have countenanced the passive and Fabian attitudes that hung like a pall over his subordinates in the Far East. Mr. Churchill might not have shared Stimson's view that it was blind folly for the British to act as if China, Burma, and India had not changed since 1800, but he would never have permitted the imperial tradition to be tarnished by a stolid insistence that action was impossible.

Washington's failure to support Stilwell was to Stimson a clear example of badly co-ordinated policy, but he was forced to admit that for that failure Stilwell's own vigorous distaste for diplomacy was partly responsible.

Stilwell's mission was to train Chinese and fight Japan. For this function he was equipped as was no other general in any Allied army. On the other hand, he was no diplomat. It seemed to Stimson unsound to assume that "Vinegar Joe's" bluntness was the cause of his differences with Chiang and Chennault and the British; the differences were deeper than manners. Yet Stilwell could have done much to moderate feeling against him if he had possessed the endless patience and self-control of Marshall. And if he had been a careful and persuasive advocate, rather than a brilliant soldier with a passionate but inarticulate loyalty to his job, he would perhaps not have failed at Washington in May, 1943, in his greatest single chance to win the President's personal backing. But this was asking a great deal, and if Stimson had any regret about his support of Stilwell it was that his own work in explaining and defending the general to the President was not good enough.

And if, in the larger sense, Stilwell's mission was a failure, there were yet in it many redeeming points of success. China under Chiang *did* stay in the war; Stilwell *did* prove that Chinese troops well trained and led could match the valor of soldiers anywhere; he *did* clear the Ledo Road to China (rightly renamed the Stilwell Road); most of all, he left to the American Army a matchless record of devotion to duty and professional skill.

To Stimson the relief of Stilwell was a "terribly sad ending" to a great effort. His admiration and personal affection for Stilwell had constantly increased through nearly three years. Knowing the Secretary's personal interest in his mission, Stilwell had written to Stimson a series of letters (some of them in longhand) which gave the full measure of the man— his insight and understanding of the Orient, his imaginative grasp of warmaking, his modesty, and what General Marshall called his "amazing vigor." This was a man who could refer to his extraordinary retreat from Burma in 1942 with a single laconic sentence, "I then picked up my headquarters group and brought them out." This man's personal vision created a new army almost in spite of its own government, in the face of the skepticism and obstructionism of most Englishmen and many Americans; yet to him jungle fighting was "a heavenly relief" from planning and politics. Certainly, whatever else it was, Stilwell's record in Asia was the record of a great American soldier. On February 10, 1945, Stimson decorated Stilwell with the Legion of Merit and an oak-leaf cluster to the Distinguished Service Medal. "I was particularly happy to lay this encomium on Stilwell's hard and terrific work in Burma and in China and so I read the two citations myself and made a few comments to Stilwell which I think he appreciated. I said that I thought he had had the toughest job of any of our generals and that I had never conveyed one of these medals with such pleasure as I had in doing this."

2. FRANCE—DEFEAT, DARLAN, DE GAULLE, AND DELIVERANCE

The fall of France, in June, 1940, was to Stimson the most shocking single event of the war, and during the five years that followed, dealing with French affairs as they stood after this catastrophe, he was constantly aware of the essentially tragic character of the whole experience of a great and proud nation in defeat. Very little of his connection with the French in this period was wholly pleasant; in almost every problem there stood forth a painful choice of evils.

France after the armistice in 1940 became at once a battle-ground of wills, centering around the Vichy government of Marshal Pétain. The names and actions of the Frenchmen who were most conspicuous at Vichy were profoundly disappointing to Stimson. The apparent treachery of Pierre Laval astonished and deeply pained him—this was not what he would have expected from the practical and direct young Frenchman he had known nine years before. The position of Pétain he viewed with more sympathy; whatever his errors of policy and whatever his failings from simple senility, Pétain in Stimson's view was an honest servant of France. But Pétain became in 1940 the center of a two-year contest for the remaining strength of France; in this contest the whole effort of the American Government was to prevent France from joining the New Order, with the major specific objectives of blocking German expansion into French North Africa and German capture of the French Fleet.

With this policy Stimson wholly agreed. It was a policy in which he had no active part, but as he understood it Mr. Roosevelt and Hull, through Ambassador Leahy and others, were exerting all of their political and diplomatic skill to strengthen Pétain's will to resist German demands, while at the same time they were encouraging separate French agencies of defense in North Africa.

In the autumn of 1942, in preparation for the North African invasion, the American Government undertook a most complicated diplomatic and secret-service negotiation designed to produce a friendly French reception to the invaders. After pursuing a course so complex that Stimson, a highly interested observer, was never fully aware of all its ins and outs, this operation reached a quite unexpected climax three days after the landings, in the so-called "Darlan deal," which became one of the most violently controversial decisions of the war.

Stimson's view of the Darlan affair was throughout absolutely definite and clear, and in his view the outburst of criticism directed against it by his countrymen was a disturbing illustration of the political ignorance—and the ideological naïveté—of many kind-hearted Americans. That Darlan had an unsavory record Stimson fully understood. But the important fact in November, 1942, was that Darlan—and only Darlan—was able to issue an effective cease-fire order and to swing to the side of the invading armies the armed forces and the civil administration of French North Africa. In a vast and precarious military enterprise, squeamishness about the source of such considerable help was in Stimson's view absurd.

The number and quality of those who disagreed was astonishing, and Stimson promptly found it necessary to undertake an energetic campaign in support of General Eisenhower's decision. On November 16, at McCloy's suggestion, he argued the case at Woodley to a small group of doubtful administration leaders. "I gave them all a little talk, pointing out first the hazardous nature of our operation in North Africa and the perilous condition in which our troops would have been in case there had been any delay caused by the obstruction of the French, to say nothing of the loss of lives unnecessarily on both the American and the French sides. . . . I read them the telegram of Eisenhower in full, setting out admirably the reasons for the performance.[1] I pointed out to them that this was a temporary military arrangement, that the Army could not make foreign policy. . . . Finally after grunts and groans . . . I think I sent them home reconciled." (Diary, November 16, 1942) That same evening, hearing that Wendell Willkie was about to attack the agreement, Stimson telephoned to Willkie and did what he could to dissuade him; that a man of Willkie's stature should attack Eisenhower's stand seemed to Stimson very dangerous. "I . . . told him flatly that, if he criticized the Darlan agreement at this juncture, he would run the risk of jeopardizing the success of the United States Army in North Africa and would be rendering its task very much more difficult." Willkie reluctantly withheld his attack for the time being, expressing himself forcefully, however, a little later when the immediate crisis had passed.

With the firm support of the President, the Darlan agreement was maintained, and until his assassination in December

---

[1] This message is paraphrased in full in William L. Langer, *Our Vichy Gamble,* Knopf, 1947, pp. 357-360.

Admiral Darlan remained a very useful military support to General Eisenhower. Stimson was so placed as to see the importance of this military support more clearly than most Americans, and it was with real regret that he learned of Darlan's death. Whatever his sins, the Admiral in his last months did effective service in helping to fight the war.

Yet in looking back it can hardly be denied that Darlan's death was in some ways a relief to United States policy. Darlan had been taken up purely as a military expedient; there was no easy way of letting him down when he had served his purpose. His continued existence as the French leader in North Africa would almost surely have been a powerful embarrassment to the United States during the liberation of France; for his crime of collaboration with the Germans there could be no forgiveness by the French people, no matter what his achievements in Africa, or what the explanation he might give to Allied leaders.

But even this future embarrassment of a living Darlan would have been a light price for his services in Africa, as Stimson saw it. The North African venture was not a massive riskless attack by skilled and overwhelming forces; it was a daring and imaginative improvisation undertaken with full knowledge of its great risks and with high hopes for surprising success. The cutting of risks and the increase of hopes which came from Darlan's adherence might well have been the margin of success, and success for American arms in their first great venture against the Nazis was a military gain whose meaning could hardly be overestimated. And Darlan after all could never have become a Frankenstein's monster; even before his death the march of events had shifted the balance of bargaining strength to his disadvantage, and he was learning that he held his power only on sufferance. If he had lived, he would have been an embarrassment but not a danger.

No one in the American Government understood the Darlan affair more thoroughly than Franklin Roosevelt. On the night of his conversation with Willkie, Stimson telephoned the President to tell what he had done. "He was very nice about it; said he was glad I had done it, and told me of a Balkan quotation which he had found which had rather aptly fitted the present situation. It was somewhat to the effect that, if the devil offered to help you over a bridge, it was just as well to let him do so but not to continue to walk with him on the other side." (Diary, November 16, 1942) Later Stimson "thought up . . . a new analogy for the Darlan case, namely the story in the Bible of Joshua sending the spies to Jericho and their making a pact with Rahab the harlot which was ratified by Joshua, and I told the President of this analogy and he roared with delight over it." (Diary, December 11, 1942) It was in his warmhearted and unhesitating support of his soldiers on such trying issues as this one that Mr. Roosevelt earned the particular affection of his Secretary of War.

The death of Darlan led to a brief interregnum under General Henri Giraud, an officer whose chivalrous devotion to France was only matched by his lack of political skill. Giraud was soon succeeded in North Africa by General Charles de Gaulle, the man who had been first to raise the standard of French resistance in 1940. Increasingly, through 1943 and 1944, De Gaulle's Committee of National Liberation became the center of French anti-Nazi leadership, and its constantly growing stature among Frenchmen inside and outside France presented a serious problem to the American Government. In discussions of this problem Stimson, who had been a firm supporter of the President's Vichy policy and Eisenhower's Darlan decision, gradually found himself in the unexpected position, in some questions, of supporting De Gaulle against President Roosevelt and Secretary Hull.

During the winter of 1943-1944, as plans proceeded for the Normandy invasion, it became necessary to determine American policy toward liberated France, and it also became highly important to develop effective contact with the French resistance movement. The critical aspect of both of these questions was their relationship to De Gaulle's French Committee. To what degree should the Committee be recognized as the government of freed areas of France, and what part should it have in Allied dealings with the Resistance? To these questions there could be no easy answer, but Stimson was disappointed by the degree of feeling which seemed to enter into the thinking of Mr. Roosevelt and Mr. Hull, both of whom had been sorely tried, over a long period, by the personal peculiarities of the Free French leader.

Not that Stimson found De Gaulle personally charming. Since 1940 the General had consistently behaved with an arrogance and touchiness that were not pleasant to any of the Anglo-Americans. His abrupt seizure of St. Pierre and Miquelon in December, 1941, had been a typical example of his natural intransigence. In North Africa his behavior had been consistently annoying, and it was apparent that he had inextricably confused the cause of France with the cause of General de Gaulle as a latter-day Joan of Arc. To Secretary Hull, whose sensitive pride had been deeply aroused by unjustified and violent attacks on American policy toward Vichy, the very mention of De Gaulle was enough to produce an outburst of skillful Tennessee denunciation, and to the President, De Gaulle was a narrow-minded French zealot with too much ambition for his own good and some rather dubious views on democracy. The validity of these opinions Stimson did not deny.

A further factor in the President's mistrust of De Gaulle was Mr. Roosevelt's strong aversion, on principle, to any prejudgment by the United States on the government to be established in liberated France. This, he insisted, was a problem for Frenchmen, and he did not propose to confer the advantages of American recognition on any group whose position was unconfirmed by the French people. And with this position too Stimson agreed.

But admitting that De Gaulle was a difficult man to deal with, and admitting that the French Committee must not be recognized as the government of France until after it had been clearly approved by the French people, Stimson was nevertheless convinced of the military importance of effective working relations with De Gaulle and his supporters. In early January, 1944, Eisenhower emphasized to Stimson his view that closer dealings with the Committee would be a great contribution to the success of his forthcoming operations; Eisenhower was also hopeful that the Committee might be outgrowing some of its bad habits in dealing with Anglo-

Americans. On January 14, 1944, Stimson and McCloy went to see Secretary Hull and reported Eisenhower's views. Stimson there said that in his opinion the time had come for a change of heart toward De Gaulle. "I pointed out that for the past six weeks . . . ever since we received that telegram from the President when he was at Cairo [see p. 560], we were absolutely prevented from discussing with the Committee two important things—first, to get in touch through them with the Resistance, that is, the underground organization in France from which we hope to be able to get assistance. We want to get into communication with them from the very moment of the attack so that we will find friends on the shore waiting for us, so to speak. Secondly, we will also need to have their assistance when we are setting up the first regular organizations of government in the districts through which our Army will be operating and through which its lines of communication will run. I pointed out that time was running very short." Hull was not unsympathetic to Stimson's position. He strongly opposed the broader proposal of McCloy that the Committee should receive general recognition as the *de facto* government of the whole of France as soon as part of France was liberated. On the narrower questions Hull agreed that Stimson and McCloy should take their ideas to the President.

Mr. Roosevelt proved a tough customer. He deeply mistrusted De Gaulle and the French Committee, and his first draft of a directive to Eisenhower severely limited the Supreme Commander's authority to deal with the French Committee. All that Stimson was able to do is indicated by the following diary note: "The President granted me an interview . . . and I . . . put up to him my revised draft of his own draft of a directive to Eisenhower in respect to the French Committee. This was a ticklish matter which I, after much reflection, decided to handle lightly and personally. I told him I had committed the great sin of attempting to revise one of his papers; that I had tried not to change the aim of his paper but merely to put it in a form which I thought would go down more easily with the French Committee and also not to lay too much burden of detail on Eisenhower. He was very nice about it. He said his paper was only a draft and he had dictated it in a hurry. We went over my draft together, I pointing out the changes. He said he thought that was all right and that he would approve the paper though he wanted to look it over more carefully that evening. I told him that I had shown it to Stettinius [then Under Secretary of State] and that Stettinius had approved it, at which he expressed his approval." (Diary, March 3, 1944)

Mr. Roosevelt finally approved this draft, which permitted Eisenhower some freedom in treating with De Gaulle and his followers on military matters. But it was not enough. In June, 1944, there was a further demand on the President for more friendly treatment of De Gaulle.

The situation in this later negotiation was remarkably complex. On the one hand, the British Cabinet, led by Foreign Secretary Eden, were pressing for outright recognition of De Gaulle, to which both Secretary Hull and the President were sternly opposed. In the absence of agreement among his superiors, Eisenhower was seriously embarrassed in his choice of a policy. Meanwhile, De Gaulle, with his usual instinct for the wrong move, had outraged all and sundry by a denunciation just after D-day of the Allied military currency. As the French Committee had previously acquiesced in the issuance of this currency, De Gaulle's attack seemed particularly irresponsible. "It's as bad as if he were trying to steal our ammunition on the battlefield or turn our guns against us." (Diary, June 11, 1944)

This move did not improve the atmosphere in which Washington now reconsidered the issue of recognition. Stimson himself was extremely angry and for several days discarded his former stand in favor of increased cordiality to De Gaulle. But on June 14 he found himself back in his old position: De Gaulle was bad, but not to deal with him was worse. The diary record of his work and thinking on that day provides a full summary of the situation as he saw it:

"During the day I had been thinking carefully of the situation and I came to the conclusion that the President and the State Department were dealing a good deal in unrealities. Their policy is based upon giving the French people an opportunity to choose their own government by democratic methods

which in substance means by a free election. That is the formula devised by the State Department for solving the various
problems that come up in the different countries which have
been enslaved, after we succeed in freeing them. But it is a
very different thing to announce a formula on the one side and
to put it into effect on the other. Very few countries outside
the English-speaking countries know by experience what a
fair election is. . . . I found this out some years ago in my
experience in Tacna Arica and Nicaragua. . . .

"America cannot supervise the elections of a great country
like France. Consequently we must eventually leave the execution of the State Department formula to the French themselves
and I am deeply concerned lest in insisting upon this formula
we get dragged into a situation where we ourselves will assume
the responsibility in part or more for its execution according
to Anglo-Saxon ideals. That would result in terrific dangers
and would be likely to permanently alienate the friendship of
France and the United States. Consequently I have been
brought to the conclusion that all we can do is to insist upon
a pledge of free elections from De Gaulle and his party, who
apparently are the only available representatives of the French
people at the present time, and that we should devote the rest
of our time to winning the war instead of quarreling with
De Gaulle's efforts to gradually inch himself forward into a
position where he and his Committee will be the Provisional
Government of France pending such an election. In other
words, no matter what we do, if he tries to use his preferred
position to win further rewards from the French people at the
election, we really cannot stop it and it is better not to run the
risk of bickerings now which will serve not only to divide us
from De Gaulle but will divide us from the British who more
and more are supporting De Gaulle. It is this latter situation,
namely the cleft between us and the British, which most alarms
me. We have been unable thus far to agree with them upon a
directive to Eisenhower as to his conduct in setting up French
authority in the operations of France which he is liberating.
He is the General not of the United States but of the two allied
governments, and he is in a dreadful position when those two

governments differ and get deadlocked on such an important question.

"This morning a telegram came through from Marshall, King, and Arnold voicing in serious language Eisenhower's embarrassment and earnestly recommending that we and the British get together, but as yet nothing has been done to solve that deadlock. . . . On his part De Gaulle is doing his best to exploit this division and to rouse up feeling against us, which has serious danger. He has even denounced the provisional currency which we are introducing for temporary use in France until she establishes a government with new currency. This is a dangerous blow at our advancing troops. . . .

"Personally I have great distrust of De Gaulle and I think that the President's position is theoretically and logically correct, but as I said in the beginning, it is not realistic. The present situation I have come to believe requires for its solution an immediate reconciliation between the British and American Governments even if we provisionally recognize De Gaulle.

"Well, McCloy and I talked this over when I got back from my ride and he fully agrees with the position which I have just stated. In fact he has all along been anxious to recognize De Gaulle provisionally in order to bring to the aid of our war effort the uprisings of the Resistants with whom De Gaulle is in close touch. McCloy and I worked the thing out and I jotted down a memorandum for a talk with the President.

"But first I called up Hull and sought to make him see the difficulties of the situation. I read him the telegram above mentioned. . . . He didn't think it could be done unless the military forces did it. I pointed out to him that it was a political question into which the military forces could not be asked to enter, but I got nowhere. I had wanted to build up a foundation on which to approach the President with the consent of the State Department behind me. I failed.

"At nine o'clock I got a telephone connection with the White House and talked with the President. He had already received the telegram from Marshall, King, and Arnold but gave it scant attention. He was adamant in his refusal to depart from his position taken in the directive, that is now waiting in London, and considered it would be a departure from moral standards to do so. I patiently went over the different steps above enumerated in a talk which lasted on the telephone for nearly an hour, but I made very little advance. I pointed out the impossibility of actually supervising French elections and he fully agreed. But he believes that De Gaulle will crumple and that the British supporters of De Gaulle will be confounded by the progress of events. This is contrary to everything that I hear. I think De Gaulle is daily gaining strength as the invasion goes on and that is to be expected. He has become the symbol of deliverance to the French people. The President thinks that other parties will spring up as the liberation goes on and that De Gaulle will become a very little figure. He said that he already knew of some such parties. . . .

"Our conversation, while it was clear and the issue plainly stated on both sides, was perfectly friendly and . . . the President not only took no offense at my persistence but apparently wished himself to argue the matter out because he kept the conversation going even when I gave him several opportunities to stop."

This was almost Stimson's last effort on the recognition of De Gaulle, for from this time forward events pressed Mr. Roosevelt more effectively than his Secretary of War was able to do. De Gaulle himself calmed down considerably in the following weeks and carried through a visit to the United States without any particular outrages. During this visit his government was accorded "limited recognition." Still it was not until late August that Eisenhower finally received authority from the British and American Governments to deal with De Gaulle as the *de facto* authority in France, and not until October that the United States finally gave full diplomatic recognition to De Gaulle's French Provisional Government. Both of these moves were so grudging and late that relations between France and the United States were clouded for many months thereafter. What might have been a truly warm—and emotionally strong—relationship in the Lafayette tradition was on both sides marked by coolness.

It was hardly fair, in Stimson's view, to lay the major responsibility for this coolness on anyone but De Gaulle himself. A man of greater flexibility and judgment would surely have avoided the constant series of gratuitous obstructions and unilateral actions with which the general plagued American leaders, civil and military. On the other hand, Stimson could not believe that it was wise for the State Department to have so long a memory for such annoyances. Perhaps this was a counsel of perfection, but the disadvantage of Mr. Hull's—and Mr. Roosevelt's—feeling about De Gaulle was that it blinded them to the generally evident fact that De Gaulle *had* made himself the leader of all France. This was a miscalculation which cooler statesmanship might have avoided, and its result was that the American Government never had the advantages of a genuinely close relationship with the France of the liberation, although individual officers and diplomats on both sides did much to bring the two countries together in practical dealings.

The Vichy government, the Darlan episode, and dealings with De Gaulle were none of them hopeful signs to Stimson for the renaissance of France which he had anticipated as the first by-product of the great invasion. He had shared the aspirations of his old friend Herriot, who sent him by a neutral diplomat in 1942 his verbal assurance that the old France would rise again. But when a man he had trusted as he had Laval became "a mere Quisling," when Pétain, who had been a fine soldier, permitted in senility outrageous crimes against Frenchmen by Frenchmen, when French North Africa would join the Allies only on the word of a Darlan, when fighting France could find no greater leader than a man of twisted pride and out-of-date political ideas—then Stimson could say only that this was not the France that he had known.

Reluctant to judge—for who shall judge what peoples and their leaders do and feel under a defeat so shattering, and at such hands, as that of France in 1940?—Stimson could only trust that from her ruined cities and her damaged pride France might in time rebuild in strength and honor her own freedom and her self-respect. For seventy years, since his childhood days in the gardens of the Tuileries, he had been trained to love and honor France, and in 1945 and afterwards he was still hopeful that a new France would be reconstructed. The great achievements of the French Resistance were the best guerdon of such hopes. Frenchmen and Americans in the year after D-day had fought together with a common purpose, and in this fact, not in past differences—and still less in the envies of some Frenchmen or the ill-considered scorn of some Americans—he saw the true basis of enduring postwar Franco-American relations.

3. FDR AND MILITARY GOVERNMENT

World War II demonstrated with unprecedented clarity the close interconnection between military and civilian affairs; nowhere was this connection more evident than in military government. Yet no task undertaken by the Army produced more misunderstanding at high levels of the Government.

To the War Department and its Secretary the importance of adequate provision for government in the military theaters was obvious. It was a basic military principle, as General Marshall later wrote, that "Orderly civil administration must be maintained in support of military operations in liberated and occupied territories." It was obvious, furthermore, that such administration must at the beginning be under the control of the military commander, and even before Pearl Harbor the War Department began planning in anticipation of this sort of work. In May, 1942, the War Department established a school at Charlottesville, Virginia, for the training of military government officers. All these steps Stimson approved, but it was not until August, 1942, that a difference of opinion in the administration on the matter of military government brought the subject forcibly to his attention.

"Marshall and McCloy brought me news of a new tempest in a teapot raised by the jealous New Dealers around the throne, this time in respect to General Gullion. Gullion has started a school for the education of Army officers in their fiscal and economic duties in occupied territories, and this seems to have raised a storm among people who were anticipating such activities as an opportunity for themselves. As a result they made the most ridiculous attacks on Gullion and he is very much troubled. Apparently they have been to the President about it, so this brings the matter up to me. They accuse Gullion of being a Fascist and all other kinds of iniquity—a typical New Deal attack from the New Deal cherubs around the throne." (Diary, August 27, 1942)

Three months later this rumor of attack ripened into a sharp memorandum of inquiry from the President. Fortunately it proved easy to defend the Charlottesville school. Stimson was able to show the President that such preparation was absolutely essential, and Mr. Roosevelt was less easily frightened than the "cherubs." Stimson also found that he had a stanch ally in Secretary Hull, who agreed with his view that administration in foreign lands must initially be an Army responsibility, while Stimson in turn fully accepted the State Department's responsibility for the formulation of political policy. On the basis of this agreement in principle the two Departments were able to co-ordinate their work without major clashes.

But the trouble did not end there; indeed, this was only the beginning. The invasion of North Africa brought into the open latent differences between the White House and the War Department which were not wholly settled for more than a year; during part of that time Stimson found himself in the difficult position of acting without the real support of his chief. Luckily the President in the end was wholly converted, but at the beginning there was a significant divergence in principle.

The North African landings, in comparison with later Allied operations, were hastily improvised. Barely three months elapsed between the final decision to invade and the sailing of the invasion convoys. In this interval only sketchy preparation could be made for the handling of civil affairs after the landing, and no final decisions were reached as to organization and responsibility for such matters. As a result General Eisenhower was plagued in the early months of the operation by a series of problems that appeared to be of interest to nearly every Department of the American Government. As early as November 20, "The President opened up by a general scold of the Cabinet for trying to butt in and interfere with the civilian government of the occupied territories in North Africa. He said he addressed it to everybody except Frank Walker, the Postmaster . . . but I assume [perhaps rashly] that he did not mean either the Army or the Navy."

The scolding was not wholly effective. Nor was it sufficient merely to prevent conflicting agencies from interference in North Africa; what General Eisenhower needed was full authority and sufficient staff assistance, and from Casablanca, in January, Marshall cabled to Stimson that Eisenhower was getting neither. On his return Marshall recommended that McCloy be sent to help Eisenhower organize his civil affairs staff.

Stimson promptly recognized that the central difficulty in the situation was not in North Africa, and not in the War or State Department, nor even among the "cherubs." The central difficulty was in Mr. Roosevelt's way of handling things, and in a telephone conversation with Mr. Roosevelt on February 1 Stimson's worst fears were promptly confirmed. "He was very friendly but, as I expected, takes a different and thoroughly Rooseveltian view of what historic good administrative procedure has required in such a case as we have in North Africa. He wants to do it all himself. He says he did settle all the matters that were troubling Eisenhower when he was over there and that, if McCloy went over, there wouldn't be anything else to do; and as to Murphy he said that he was not there as a diplomat to report to Hull but as a special appointee of his own to handle special matters on which he reported to Roosevelt direct. This was a truly Rooseveltian position. I told him frankly over the telephone that it was bad administration and asked him what a Cabinet was for and what Departments were for except to have reports considered in that way, but I have small hopes of reforming him. The fault is Rooseveltian and deeply ingrained. Theodore Roosevelt had it to a certain extent but never anywhere nearly as much as this one. But I hammered out with him the proceedings that even in his opinion must be regarded as matters for the War Department. He admitted that in the handling of the railroads that were taken over and the lines of communication and the radios, such matters must be handled as military and as a part of the duties of the commanding general and be reported to the War Department. He says he wants to see me tomorrow or next day and at that [time] I shall have a real talk with him. It was hard to do it over the telephone. I think he realizes that he has transgressed the line of proper procedure in some matters, and I shall make him read my letter to get the historical viewpoint. I told him frankly that, if the process of whittling down the powers of the Secretary of War should continue, I would be in a very embarrassing position for I had no desire, in the words of Churchill, to go down in history as the person who consented to the liquidation of the great historic powers of my office."

The letter to which Stimson referred was one which he had prepared earlier the same day; it showed clearly how far his stand was from that of the President. To Mr. Roosevelt the whole concept of military government was both strange and somewhat abhorrent; to Stimson it was a natural and inevitable result of military operations in any area where there was not already a fully effective friendly government. Mr. Roosevelt argued that operations in World War II should be patterned on those of Pershing, but to Stimson the true parallel was rather with American experience in the Philippines, in Cuba, and in Puerto Rico, for there would be no full-fledged central government in France or any of the other countries in which the American Army was going to have to fight. To Stimson the lessons of history were clear, and the tradition of military government was an honorable one. So in this letter, after rehearsing the facts of past experience—and they were facts which he knew at firsthand, facts which revolved around names like Elihu Root, Leonard Wood, and Frank R. McCoy —he summarized his conclusions in a form which showed why he felt strongly in the matter. This whole field of activity to him was one of the great and proper functions of an American Secretary of War.

"From the foregoing the following facts stand out as the historical policy of the United States Government in cases of military invasion and government:

"1. The authority of the military governor in each case has stemmed out from the military power of the United States exercised by the President as Commander in Chief.

"2. In each case the military governor has been compelled to employ agents for the solution of civil administrative problems of government. In each case these agents have been in the first instance composed of Army officers although many of them have been men of high civilian experience; for example, Tasker Bliss who conducted the customs of Cuba with consummate skill and success; Gorgas and Walter Reed who constructed its sanitary system; and many others like them.

"3. These Army officers continued until they were replaced by competent local native administrators.

"4. The administrations thus set up have been so successful as to constitute a bright page of American history, free from scandal and, in such difficult communities as Cuba and the Philippines, have laid the foundation of permanent good relations between those countries and the United States.

"5. In each case the President has used the Secretary of War as the departmental officer who carried out this exercise of the President's military power; who organized the plans and systems under which the various governors general acted; and whose Department served as the medium of record and communication between the military governments and the President.

"This necessarily followed from the fact that the War Department from its connection with the military occupation and its possession of a highly trained staff of military officers was the normal, natural, and in fact only Department of the government capable of rendering this service. I believe this condition still exists today.

"6. There is ample opportunity in North Africa as there was in the second intervention of Cuba for the exercise of the functions of the American Department of State. But these functions are not administrative. . . ."

The theory set forth in this letter was one which was very dear to Stimson, but as he considered the nature of his problem in the White House, he decided that no such blunt approach would serve. Mr. Roosevelt was not going to be persuaded by a lot of Republican history, nor were arguments about administrative procedure likely to hold his attention. So on February 3, Stimson took a different line. Arming himself with examples of the existing confusion, he set out simply to get his camel's head McCloy into the President's tent of personal government. The contrast between the undelivered letter and the actual conversation is striking:

"The President was in fine form and I had one of the best and most friendly talks with him I have ever had. He was full of his trip, naturally, and interspersed our whole talk with stories and anecdotes. But I had carefully prepared what I wanted to say and held him pretty well to the line. I had abandoned entirely the idea of bringing up the formal legal argument which I had made in the letter written last Monday, having come to the conclusion that the main thing was to get McCloy over there on a friendly basis and then work out from that. And so my object was just to show the President, in answer to his inquiries over the telephone Monday night, that there was a real problem of disorder there in which McCloy could be of help and in which we ought to support Eisenhower. In this I was perfectly successful. He cordially accepted the idea; asked to have an appointment made with McCloy for him to see him personally and this was done as I came out.

"But it was amusing, though to some degree discouraging, to see how he clung to the idea of doing all this sort of work himself. In the first place he thought he had practically wiped up the situation by his visit there and there was not much left to be done in the way of organization. But in this I pulled him down by the facts that I had gathered, showing that poor Eisenhower's first attempts to do the work with his 'Civil Affairs Section' of his General Staff, which is the usual annex of Army commanders for such work, were not successful; then how he had created as a part of his Staff the North African Economic Board as a more efficient engine for it, but that this was still incomplete; and then I swamped the President by showing him that none of these activities had been reported through any regular channels to me; the great difficulty I had had in finding even what had been done, the delays which necessarily occurred and the importance therefore of having a routine for this business. I showed him how neither Marshall nor I nor anybody in the Department had known of the vital papers which he, the President, had signed while on his conference there until I had dug them up this morning, getting one of them from the French mission that was here in Washington, and had a French copy of what they claimed was a contract the President himself had signed. This quite put him at my mercy. I gave him a translation which they had made for me in the Pentagon Building and he went off into an amusing story of how he had signed at least a part of the covenants in the paper and he could not deny the rest. The paper covered such important matters as the change in the ratio of exchange between the Morocco franc and the dollar which Roosevelt had made. He recollected this all right and told me a good story about it. I retaliated by telling him I knew all about this one because Hull had told me it was an agreement 'signed over a drink' by the President, at which he laughed and virtually admitted that the other covenants in the paper might have been accomplished the same way."

The permission given for McCloy's trip was a long step ahead. McCloy had already become Stimson's principal agent for all problems of civil affairs and all questions that affected the State Department; it was he who carried the main burden of work in these matters from this point forward. Mr. Roosevelt continued to believe that the administrative direction should be a function of the State Department and so ordered in early February. But Stimson was certain that experience would justify him, and carefully maintaining mutual understanding with Mr. Hull, he established in the War Department a Civil Affairs Division which soon became the province of Major General John Hilldring. In May, McCloy became Chairman of a Combined Civil Affairs Committee operating under the Combined Chiefs of Staff. This committee later extended its work to include such vital politico-military problems as terms of surrender, and it served as an invaluable bridge between military and political leaders. From this time onward the significance of and necessity for co-ordinated military government was not seriously questioned. Events once more taught the President what Stimson had tried to teach him by advocacy. Before the invasion of Sicily Mr. Roosevelt made one more effort to insure the dominance of civilian agencies in civil administration, but the experience gained in this operation and in the early stages of the Italian campaign appears to have convinced him that for good or ill the armed forces must have the administrative responsibility in all military theaters. Two actions in November, 1943, showed Stimson how far the President had moved. First, on November 10 he wrote a letter to Stimson declaring that the War Department must assume the responsibility for civilian relief in all liberated areas during the first six months after their liberation. Second, from Cairo he cabled to Stimson his view that all arrangements for civil administration and dealings with the French people and their leaders must initially be purely military; his main purpose in this second order was to minimize political contact with De Gaulle and so avoid any implied recognition of the Frenchman's status, but the cable was also proof that he had finally recognized the value and the inevitability of military government. That Mr. Roosevelt continued to be cautious in permitting the military to deal with the French (see p. 546) was to Stimson a minor matter compared with his conversion to sound principles of administration.[2] During the remainder of the war the Army was given a constantly increasing measure of the President's confidence in its work in civil affairs, and under McCloy and Hilldring the War Department organization became more and more effective in co-ordinating and administering a responsibility that in its eventual size and scope far exceeded anything that Stimson himself had anticipated. So clearly did the Army prove itself to be the proper agency for such work that more than two years after the end of the war, long after the military importance of the overseas theaters had been superseded by the dominance of economic and political problems, the War Department was still carrying on the administration of the American occupation in defeated countries. And this too Stimson held to be a proper assignment, notwithstanding the argument that the State Department

[2] The experience of Franklin Roosevelt in dealing with military government reminded Stimson very strongly of a similar lesson learned forty years earlier by his cousin Theodore. It was T.R. who tried civilian engineers in Panama before he turned to the Army and selected Goethals, remarking, as Stimson heard the story, that "the great thing about an Army officer is that he does what you tell him to do." Discipline without brains was of little value, but both Roosevelts learned to their cost the uselessness in administration of brains without discipline.

should handle such matters. From his experience in both Departments he was wholly convinced that the State Department by its nature was unequipped for major administrative chores, while administration was the War Department's normal, constant business. The State Department must frame the policies, but it could not hope to equal the Army in the task of carrying them out.

4. A WORD FROM HINDSIGHT

After the war, considering such problems as those just discussed Stimson was reinforced in his wartime belief that Mr. Roosevelt's personal virtuosity in high politics carried with it certain disadvantages which might have been limited if the President had been willing to provide himself with a War Cabinet for the co-ordinated execution of his policies—a body which might have done in war diplomacy what the Joint Chiefs of Staff did in military strategy.

Problems like those of China and France were not merely diplomatic—the State Department could not and would not assume the whole labor of determining policy in areas where the military interest was so significant. Yet the military interest could not of itself be wholly determinant; it was not proper that such questions should be decided by the Joint Chiefs of Staff, as the members of that body well understood.

Mr. Roosevelt therefore could not rely on his regularly constituted advisers—military or diplomatic—for final recommendation and co-ordinated execution in problems of war diplomacy. Nor were his regular Cabinet meetings a suitable place for such discussion and decision; there were nearly twenty men in Cabinet meetings, and during the war they became a formality; to Stimson they were useful principally as a way of getting into the White House to have a word with the President in private after the meetings were over; a typical diary entry describes a Cabinet meeting toward the end of the war as "the same old two-and-sixpence, no earthly good." Mr. Roosevelt's own view of Cabinet meetings was not wholly different: "The Cabinet meeting this afternoon was brief. The President opened it by saying humorously that he had just told his family that he wanted a short Cabinet meeting and they had said, 'Well, you know how you can get it. You can just stop your own talking.' There was a smile around the table because of the truth of the statement. The Roosevelt Cabinets are really a solo performance by the President interspersed with some questions and very few debates. When the President told this story, Hull broke in in his dry way. 'Yes,' he said, 'I found that when I was asked by the President to come over to lunch for a conference, I used to have to get a little bite to eat first myself so that I could talk while he was eating.' This met with great applause." (Diary, May 1, 1942)

The proper solution, Stimson believed, would have been for Mr. Roosevelt to provide himself with a War Cabinet like that upon which Winston Churchill relied in Great Britain. Cabinet responsibility of course is not the same in the United States as in Great Britain, but Stimson felt that Mr. Roosevelt would have found it helpful to have some such body for the handling of his war policies in foreign lands. Such a body would have included his most trusted personal adviser, Harry Hopkins, and perhaps the Secretaries of State, Treasury, War, and Navy. Organized like the Joint Chiefs of Staff, with a secretariat of top quality and a continuing record of the policy decisions made or approved by the President, such a body might have avoided some at least of the difficulties discussed above, and others not unlike them in other areas. Stimson would never have desired that the President's personal initiative and extraordinary talent should be limited by red tape, but he felt sure that such a body would have been a reinforcement to Mr. Roosevelt's less evident abilities as a co-ordinator and executive. Unfortunately the whole idea was foreign to the President's nature; only reluctantly had he accepted the notion of such an organization even in the purely military field, and he never showed the least disposition to alter his methods in diplomacy. Stimson himself never recommended a War Cabinet to Mr. Roosevelt; he had no desire to appear to push himself forward. But others made such a recommendation, and the President was not impressed.

To be useful, such a body would have had to be the President's own creation. No attempt to co-ordinate action on any lower level could have much value so long as the central threads of policy were personally managed in the White House. Back in 1940, in an effort to fill a gap which he felt at once on his arrival in Washington—and which he had noticed from the other side of the fence when he was Secretary of State—Stimson had been the leading spirit in setting up regular weekly meetings of Hull, Knox, and himself. These meetings were wholly unofficial and personal. They served a useful purpose in keeping the three Secretaries informed of one another's major problems. But they had no connection with Mr. Roosevelt's final determinations of policy, and in 1942 and 1943 they became less and less valuable. Reorganized late in 1944, with McCloy as recorder and with formal agenda and conclusions, this Committee of Three became more useful; Stimson, Stettinius, and Forrestal were able to use it for the solution of some important points and they were able to establish at a lower level, for routine co-ordination, the extremely useful State, War and Navy Co-ordinating Committee. But the Committee of Three, in considering major problems, always remained more of a clearing-house than an executive committee.

Another embryonic War Cabinet had existed before Pearl Harbor—the War Council, which met at frequent intervals in the White House. This group included Hull, Stimson, and Knox in addition to the senior military officers. But when Mr. Roosevelt learned to like the Joint Chiefs of Staff, in 1942, he allowed himself to dispense with any general meetings on war policy.

Stimson's belief in this notion of a War Cabinet was based partly on hindsight, and he knew that he might seem to be elevating his personal feelings into a theory of government. He hoped this was not the case. He had served in too many Cabinets to expect that all decisions would match his advice, and it was not his disagreements with the President on details of policy that bothered him, as he looked back in 1947; it was rather that Mr. Roosevelt's policy was so often either unknown or not clear to those who had to execute it, and worse yet, in some cases it seemed self-contradictory. In the case of

China, for example, all those who worked so energetically at cross-purposes in Chungking undoubtedly regarded themselves as possessors of a mandate from Washington—and even from the White House.

In summary, then, Stimson's experience of the diplomacy of coalition warfare in World War II left him with this conclusion: Franklin Roosevelt as a wartime international leader proved himself as good as one man could be—but one man was not enough to keep track of so vast an undertaking.

CHAPTER XXII

The Beginnings of Peace

I. A SHIFT IN EMPHASIS

THE main object of war is peace, and we have now to study Stimson's part in the framing of American policy for the establishment of a lasting peace after World War II. Not only as Secretary of War but as a man who had been forced to learn in 1931 and afterwards the consequences of bad peacemaking, he was deeply interested in the problems of the postwar settlement.

But it should be remembered that peace was an objective which depended first of all on victory, and, by reason of his official position as well as his natural inclination, Stimson's work until the latter part of 1944 was almost wholly concerned with winning the war. In this respect his attitude was little different from that of the President and most of the administration. Even in diplomatic questions like those discussed in the last chapter, the major consideration was almost always the advancement of military victory.

Some critics of American policy have judged it astonishingly naïve in this single-minded concentration on victory. Stimson could not agree. The general objectives of American policy had been clearly and eloquently stated by Mr. Roosevelt first in the Atlantic Charter and later in his assertion of the Four Freedoms. It was further clear that American policy envisaged the development of the wartime United Nations into a peacetime organization of friendly nations. So long as wartime policy did not directly and violently contravene these general principles, it seemed to Stimson wholly proper that detailed action should be governed by the overriding requirement of victory, in the confidence that as victory was the great common immediate objective, action which advanced victory must in general promote good international relations.

It was only in the summer of 1944 that high officials outside the State Department began to give their close attention to postwar problems. The extraordinary success of the great invasion lifted from men's minds all fears and doubts about the basic strategy of victory; at the same time it created a pressing need for attention to new problems. The Normandy landing and the great Avranches break-through precipitated a situation in which victory was certain and apparently close, and as General Eisenhower's forces advanced toward the German border it became clear that the armies had outrun the policy makers. From this unsettled situation there developed in September the most violent single interdepartmental struggle of Stimson's career—the issue over the "Morgenthau plan" for the treatment of Germany. In order to set Stimson's part of this struggle in its proper focus, it will be useful to consider briefly his two most firmly held general views about the peace settlement.

His first and great commandment was the maintenance of friendship with Great Britain. Of itself, such friendship would not be sufficient to keep the peace—here Stimson differed somewhat from some who felt that an Anglo-American coalition could somehow assert its virtuous will throughout the world. But without the maintenance of close relationships with the British Stimson did not see how America could hope to be an effective member of world society. Division from the British would neutralize in mutual opposition two nations whose fundamental principles and purposes were so much alike that their opposition could only work to the disadvantage of both. Friendship with Great Britain had been cardinal in Stimson's policy as Secretary of State; in 1939 and 1940 his advocacy of "intervention" had been based on his belief in the fundamental unity of Anglo-American interests; it was a belief which he saw no reason to discard. Several times during the war he expressed forcibly to various groups of administration leaders "the conviction I am getting more strongly every day that our plan must be a plan to continue after the war the same controls as have saved us during the war, namely close association between the English-speaking countries." (Diary, May 11, 1943) This was a view which he found general among his colleagues; indeed much of his later disagreement with Mr. Roosevelt over the Morgenthau plan rose out of a misplaced Presidential eagerness to help the British.

Stimson's second great principle was that the essential basis of enduring peace must be economic, and here again his opinion was based on his own experience. The sermon preached by Keynes after Versailles had acquired deep and poignant meaning for Stimson when as Secretary of State he had wrestled with the results of that economically impossible treaty. Now he hoped for a settlement which would involve no burden of debts, no barriers to the internal trade of Central Europe, no politically independent and economically helpless group of "successor states." Evidence that these objectives were being ignored deeply disturbed him—when he learned of the pending three-power decision to restore an independent Austria his mind turned back to the financial collapse of Austria in 1931. "They haven't any grasp apparently of the underlying need of proper economic arrangements to make the peace stick. . . . If they restored Austria to her position in which she was left by the Versailles arrangement twenty-five years ago, why they would reduce her again to a non-self-sustaining state and they don't seem to have that thing in mind at all. Central Europe after the war has got to eat. She has got to be free from tariffs in order to eat." (Diary, October 28, 1943)

Although most of his time at meetings with Mr. Roosevelt in this period was devoted to more immediate questions like the OVERLORD command, he had a chance on December 18, 1943, to express his position briefly. "I got an occasion to tell him that I had seen proposals in regard to the division of Europe in case of victory and that I had only one general recommendation at present and that was not to divide Europe up into separate pieces which could not each of them feed itself on its own land." He went on to point out that in the case of Germany this policy must involve the retention of much German commerce and industry, for "unless this commerce was protected she could not probably feed her population by agriculture."

Until late in 1944 Stimson's thinking on the peace did not develop much beyond the two principles outlined above. While he of course accepted the general notion of an international organization to replace and if possible improve on the League of Nations, he did not regard any such organization as a proper point of focus for the peacemaking; he entirely agreed with the President that the problem of the peace settlement was necessarily one to be solved by the major victorious powers, a position explicitly stated by three of them in the Moscow Declaration of November, 1943. The question of future relations with Soviet Russia was one about which until early 1945 he was cautiously optimistic.

2. THE MORGENTHAU PLAN

It was with this general attitude that Stimson returned from Normandy in July, 1944, to find the administration belatedly but vigorously engaged in the construction of a policy for the treatment of Germany. At the same time, in anticipation of the Dumbarton Oaks Conference, the outlines of a postwar organization were being sketched in the State Department. It was a very different atmosphere from the one he had left a month before, and he at once recognized that he must shift his attention. In his own Department, officers responsible for civil affairs reported that they were face to face with a situation—the forthcoming occupation of Germany—for which they had no orders; it was not even settled which part of Germany United States forces should occupy. On July 31, after hearing from Harry Hopkins about "the postwar problems," Stimson remarked, "I myself am thinking along those lines now, and . . . as a result of all these thoughts, I had Jack McCloy and Ed Stettinius in to dinner and we talked over the pending negotiations. . . . The most pressing thing is to get the President to decide on which part of Germany will be occupied by the American troops. He is hell-bent to occupy the northern portion. We all think that

that is a mistake—that it will only get us into a head-on collision with the British." (Diary, July 31, 1944)

During the first weeks of August Stimson was on vacation in New York, leaving McCloy to act for him in these matters. Returning to Washington he found that no progress had been made. On August 25 he lunched with the President, and gave him five good reasons for a decision to occupy southwestern Germany; "I was inclined to think that I had made an impression on him but of course it was impossible to say." Then, after some discussion of the general nature of the German problem, "I made my main point—that we were running into a lack of preparedness. Our troops were going into Germany and they had no instruction on these vital points. . . . I pointed out that the President himself couldn't do the necessary study to decide these various points and suggested that he ought to appoint a Cabinet Committee who could assimilate the work that was already being done by men on a lower level and prepare it for the President himself. He took that point and accepted it and then we went into Cabinet and at the very beginning of Cabinet he . . . said that he would appoint Secretaries Hull, Morgenthau, and myself as the members of that committee, with the Secretary of the Navy acting on it whenever a Navy matter was involved." To this list Mr. Roosevelt later added Harry Hopkins.

The first meeting of the Cabinet Committee was called on September 5. In the meantime Stimson found that there was a strong divergence of view in Washington, between those who were in favor of a firm but discriminating treatment of Germany, looking toward her eventual reconstruction as a prosperous and peaceful nation, and those who frankly desired a Carthaginian peace. The night before the committee meeting Stimson and McCloy dined with Morgenthau and his assistant, Harry White. "We had a pleasant dinner but we were all aware of the feeling that a sharp issue is sure to arise over the question of the treatment of Germany. Morgenthau is, not unnaturally, very bitter and . . . it became very apparent that he would plunge out for a treatment of Germany which I feel sure would be unwise." (Diary, September 4, 1944)

The Cabinet Committee meeting confirmed Stimson's worst

fears. "Hull brought up a draft of agenda for the meeting. . . . This paper was all right on its face down to the last section which contained some extreme propositions and principles, and as soon as we got into a discussion of these I, to my tremendous surprise, found that Hull was as bitter as Morgenthau against the Germans and was ready to jump all the principles that he had been laboring for in regard to trade for the past twelve years.[1] He and Morgenthau wished to wreck completely the immense Ruhr-Saar area of Germany and turn it into second-rate agricultural land regardless of all that that area meant not only to Germany but to the welfare of the entire European continent. Hopkins went with them so far as to wish to prevent the manufacture of steel in the area, a prohibition which would pretty well sabotage everything else. I found myself a minority of one and I labored vigorously but entirely ineffectively against my colleagues. In all the four years that I have been here I have not had such a difficult and unpleasant meeting although of course there were no personalities. We all knew each other too well for that. But we were irreconcilably divided. In the end it was decided that Hull would send in his memorandum to the President while we should each of us send a memorandum of views in respect to it." (Diary, September 5, 1944)

It is worth noting the general nature of the parts of Hull's paper on which the Cabinet Committee was unanimous. These paragraphs provided for the complete demilitarization of Germany, the dissolution of the Nazi party and all affiliated organizations, with energetic punishment of war criminals, the institution of extensive controls over communications and education, and the acceptance of the principle of reparations to other states, though not to the United States. It was only on the issue of the destruction of German industry that Stimson was violently opposed to his colleagues.

His basic position on this issue was stated in the memorandum sent later the same day to his three colleagues, and forwarded by Hull to the President. This memorandum must be quoted nearly in full:

---

[1] This later seemed to Stimson an overstatement of Hull's position; in any event the Secretary of State soon took a quite different view.

"I have considered the [State Department] paper entitled 'Suggested Recommendations on Treatment of Germany from the Cabinet Committee for the President.' . . .

"With the exception of the last paragraph I find myself in agreement with the principles stated therein and they are in conformity with the lines upon which we have been proceeding in the War Department in our directives to the Armed Forces.

"The last paragraph, however, is as follows:

" 'h. The primary objectives of our economic policy are (1) the standard of living of the German population shall be held down to subsistence levels; (2) German economic position of power in Europe must be eliminated; (3) German economic capacity must be converted in such manner that it will be so dependent upon imports and exports that Germany cannot by its own devices reconvert to war production.'

"While certain of these statements by themselves may possibly be susceptible of a construction with which I would not be at variance, the construction put upon them at the discussion this morning certainly reached positions to which I am utterly opposed. The position frankly taken by some of my colleagues was that the great industrial regions of Germany known as the Saar and the Ruhr with their very important deposits of coal and ore should be totally transformed into a nonindustrialized area of agricultural land.

"I cannot conceive of such a proposition being either possible or effective and I can see enormous general evils coming from an attempt to so treat it. During the past eighty years of European history this portion of Germany was one of the most important sources of the raw materials upon which the industrial and economic livelihood of Europe was based. Upon the production which came from the raw materials of this region during those years, the commerce of Europe was very largely predicated. Upon that production Germany became the largest source of supply to no less than ten European countries, viz: Russia, Norway, Sweden, Denmark, Holland, Switzerland, Italy, Austria-Hungary, Rumania, and Bulgaria; and the second largest source of supply to Great Britain, Belgium, and France. By the same commerce, which in large part arose from this production, Germany also became the best buyer or customer of Russia, Norway, Holland, Belgium, Switzerland, Italy, and Austria-Hungary; and the second best customer of Great Britain, Sweden, and Denmark. The production of these materials from this region could not be sealed up and obliterated, as was proposed this morning, without manifestly causing a great dislocation to the trade upon which Europe has lived. In Germany itself this commerce has built up since 1870 a population of approximately thirty million more people than were ever supported upon the agricultural soil of Germany alone. Undoubtedly a similar growth of population took place in the nations which indirectly participated in the commerce based upon this production.

"I cannot treat as realistic the suggestion that such an area in the present economic condition of the world can be turned into a nonproductive 'ghost territory' when it has become the center of one of the most industrialized continents in the world, populated by peoples of energy, vigor, and progressiveness.

"I can conceive of endeavoring to meet the misuse which Germany has recently made of this production by wise systems of control or trusteeship or even transfers of ownership to other nations. But I cannot conceive of turning such a gift of nature into a dust heap.

"War is destruction. This war more than any previous war has caused gigantic destruction. The need for the recuperative benefits of productivity is more evident now than ever before throughout the world. Not to speak of Germany at all or even her satellites, our allies in Europe will feel the need of the benefit of such productivity if it should be destroyed. Moreover, speed of reconstruction is of great importance, if we hope to avoid dangerous convulsions in Europe.

"We contemplate the transfer from Germany of ownership of East Prussia, Upper Silesia, Alsace and Lorraine (each of them except the first containing raw materials of importance) together with the imposition of general economic controls. We also are considering the wisdom of a possible partition of Germany into north and south sections, as well as the creation of an internationalized state in the Ruhr. With such precautions, or indeed with only some of them, it certainly should not be necessary for us to obliterate all industrial productivity in the Ruhr area, in order to preclude its future misuse.

"Nor can I agree that it should be one of our purposes to hold the German population 'to a subsistence level' if this means the edge of poverty. This would mean condemning the German people to a condition of servitude in which, no matter how hard or how effectively a man worked, he could not materially increase his economic condition in the world. Such a program would, I believe, create tension and resentments far outweighing any immediate advantage of security and would tend to obscure the guilt of the Nazis and the viciousness of their doctrines and their acts.

"By such economic mistakes I cannot but feel that you would also be poisoning the springs out of which we hope that the future peace of the world can be maintained. . . .

"My basic objection to the proposed methods of treating Germany which were discussed this morning was that in addition to a system of preventive and educative punishment they would add the dangerous weapon of complete economic oppression. Such methods, in my opinion, do not prevent war; they tend to breed war."

On September 6 the President held a meeting with the Cabinet Committee. Stimson and Morgenthau submitted their new memoranda. The President addressed most of his comments to Stimson, "reverting to his proposition . . . that Germany could live happily and peacefully on soup from soup kitchens," but he appeared not to accept Morgenthau's view that the Ruhr should be dismantled, arguing rather "that Great Britain was going to be in sore straits after the war and . . . that the products of the Ruhr might be used to furnish raw material for British steel industry. I said that I had no objection certainly to assisting Britain in every way that we could but that this was very different from obliterating the Ruhr. . . . There was quite an easing up in the attitude of Hull, and the President certainly was not following Morgenthau. . . . I wound up by using the analogy of Charles Lamb's dissertation on roast pig. I begged the President to remember that this was a most complicated economic question and all that I was urging upon him was that he should not burn down his house of the world for the purpose of getting a meal of roast pig. He apparently caught the point." (Diary, September 6, 1944)

Stimson came away with the feeling that he had made some progress. Secretary Morgenthau apparently shared this feeling, for he promptly requested a rehearing before the President. A new meeting was set for September 9. Meanwhile both Morgenthau and Stimson prepared new papers expanding their views. The new Morgenthau paper, submitted on September 9, asserted that it was a fallacy that Europe needed a strong industrial Germany, that the mines and mills of the Ruhr had indeed been a depressing competitor of Great Britain particularly, and "it contained a specious appeal to the President's expressed desire to help England by . . . the proposal that by sealing up the Ruhr we would give England the chance to jump into Germany's business of supplying Europe industrially and thus curing the alleged English depression in coal mining. It asserted that England had coal enough to supply its present output for five hundred years! This certainly is contrary to everything I have heard about the mines of Great Britain which have been constantly asserted to have been dug so deep as to become almost uneconomic." (Diary, September 9, 1944)

In Stimson's memorandum of the same date he summarized again the basic difference between his position and Morgenthau's. The latter had expressed in writing (in his paper of September 6) the proposals made orally before the Cabinet Committee. Speaking of the Ruhr "and surrounding industrial areas" to a total of over 30,000 square miles, Morgenthau had written: "This area should not only be stripped of all presently existing industries but so weakened and controlled that it cannot in the foreseeable future become an industrial area. . . . All industrial plants and equipment not destroyed by military action shall either be completely dismantled or removed from the area or completely destroyed, all equipment shall be removed from the mines and the mines shall be thoroughly wrecked." Stimson reiterated his unalterable opposition to any such program. It would breed war, not peace; it would arouse sympathy for Germany all over the world; it would destroy resources desperately needed for the reconstruction of Europe. Asking that no hasty decisions be made, he urged the President to accept for the time being a slightly revised version of Secretary Hull's original memorandum, leaving the controversial economic issue for future discussion.

Without making any decision on any of these papers, Mr. Roosevelt went to Quebec, where on September 11 the Octagon Conference with Mr. Churchill began. One of the principal issues on the agenda for this meeting was the German problem, and Stimson was not happy about the President's state of body and mind. "I have been much troubled by the President's physical condition. He was distinctly not himself Saturday [September 9]. He had a cold and seemed tired out. I rather fear for the effects of this hard conference upon him. I am particularly troubled . . . that he is going up there without any real preparation for the solution of the underlying and fundamental problem of how to treat Germany. So far as he had evidenced it in his talks with us, he has had absolutely no study or training in the very difficult problem which we have to decide, namely of how far we can introduce preventive measures to protect the world from Germany running amuck again and how far we must refrain from measures which will simply provoke the wrong reaction. I hope the British have brought better trained men with them than we are likely to have to meet them." (Diary, September 11, 1944)

The President seemed to Stimson to be further hampered by his obsession with the notion of a coming revolution in France. "I have argued the question with him already several times. He has been warned by Leahy that he may expect a revolution in France. . . . Although [Leahy] has had the advantage of being stationed in Vichy for several years, I don't think his advice is good. I think it is very doubtful whether there will be a revolution. But as I have pointed out to the President, the revolution can hardly possibly occur until Germany is conquered. Pending that time the danger of a common enemy, Germany, will keep the French factions together. Therefore by the time such a revolution can come, in all likelihood our forces will be in Germany and will have lines of communication not running across France. Therefore there is no reason why we should accept any call to occupy France. In fact it seems entirely farfetched that any of the Allies should occupy France. She has had many revolutions before now which she has been left to settle herself and that ought to be done now. But the President has worked himself up into an apprehension of this. . . . At that meeting on Saturday morning whenever any question came up as to our duties in Germany, he would say: 'I want somebody to be sure and keep a buttress between us and France'." (Diary, September 11, 1944)

His preoccupation with France seemed to be preventing the President, not only from making a decision on the zone of occupation, but even from any balanced consideration of the German problem as a whole. And although he finally accepted the southwestern zone at Quebec, he did not so quickly master the German question as a whole. As the Quebec Conference proceeded Stimson began to hear disturbing reports. On the thirteenth he learned that Morgenthau had been called to the conference; on the sixteenth he heard that the President and the Prime Minister had accepted the Morgenthau plan. But it was not until the twentieth, when Morgenthau had returned victorious to Washington, that he learned the whole story.

It appeared that the President had called Morgenthau to Quebec, where he had argued the case for his plan, that Morgenthau had found the British at first entirely opposed to him, that Mr. Churchill had been converted by the argument that the elimination of the Ruhr would create new markets for Great Britain, and that finally the President and the Prime Minister had initialed the following agreement:

"At a conference between the President and the Prime Minister upon the best measures to prevent renewed rearmament by Germany, it was felt that an essential feature was the future disposition of the Ruhr and the Saar.

"The ease with which the metallurgical, chemical, and

electric industries in Germany can be converted from peace to war has already been impressed upon us by bitter experience. It must also be remembered that the Germans have devastated a large portion of the industries of Russia and of other neighboring Allies, and it is only in accordance with justice that these injured countries should be entitled to remove the machinery they require in order to repair the losses they have suffered. The industries referred to in the Ruhr and in the Saar would therefore be necessarily put out of action and closed down. It was felt that the two districts should be put under some body under the world organization which would supervise the dismantling of these industries and make sure that they were not started up again by some subterfuge.

"This programme for eliminating the war-making industries in the Ruhr and in the Saar is looking forward to converting Germany into a country primarily agricultural and pastoral in its character.

"The Prime Minister and the President were in agreement upon this programme.

O.K.

F.D.R.

W.S.C.

15 9.

"September 16, 1944"

Morgenthau told this story "modestly and without rubbing it in, but it was the narration of a pretty heavy defeat for everything that we had fought for." The extraordinary document initialed by the two leaders marked a remarkable shift from another document signed by the same two men three years before. As McCloy pointed out to Stimson, it was the Atlantic Charter which had pronounced that the United States and the United Kingdom would "endeavor, with due respect for their existing obligation, to further the enjoyment by all States, great or small, victor or vanquished, of access, on equal terms, to the trade and to the raw materials of the world which are needed for their economic prosperity."

Fortunately for all concerned, the Quebec memorandum did not long remain official United States policy.

When he first heard of the President's decision, Stimson was about to sign a third memorandum to Mr. Roosevelt on the Morgenthau plan. Although it seemed a waste of time to submit a further paper when the decision was already made, he decided to keep the record straight. "It will undoubtedly irritate him for he dislikes opposition when he has made up his mind. But I have thought the thing over and decided to do it. I should not keep my self-respect if I did not." (Diary, September 17, 1944)

This third memorandum (drafted in large part by McCloy) pitched the argument on a higher level than anything that had before been written. The paper was designed to appeal from FDR., the hasty signer of ill-considered memoranda, to Franklin Roosevelt, the farsighted and greatly humanitarian President of the United States. Its critical paragraphs follow:

"The question is not whether we want Germans to suffer for their sins. Many of us would like to see them suffer the tortures they have inflicted on others. The only question is whether over the years a group of seventy million educated, efficient and imaginative people can be kept within bounds on such a low level of subsistence as the Treasury proposals contemplate. I do not believe that is humanly possible. A subordinate question is whether even if you could do this it is good for the rest of the world either economically or spiritually. Sound thinking teaches that . . . poverty in one part of the world usually induces poverty in other parts. Enforced poverty is even worse, for it destroys the spirit not only of the victim but debases the victor. It would be just such a crime as the Germans themselves hoped to perpetrate upon their victims—it would be a crime against civilization itself.

"This country since its very beginning has maintained the fundamental belief that all men, in the long run, have the right to be free human beings and to live in the pursuit of happiness. Under the Atlantic Charter victors and vanquished alike are entitled to freedom from economic want. But the proposed treatment of Germany would, if successful, deliberately deprive many millions of people of the right to freedom from want and freedom from fear. Other peoples all over the world would suspect the validity of our spiritual tenets and question the long-range effectiveness of our economic and political principles as applied to the vanquished.

"The proposals would mean a forcible revolution in all of the basic methods of life of a vast section of the population as well as a disruption of many accustomed geographical associations and communications. Such an operation would naturally and necessarily involve a chaotic upheaval in the people's lives which would inevitably be productive of the deepest resentment and bitterness towards the authorities which had imposed such revolutionary changes upon them. Physically, considering the fact that their present enlarged population has been developed and supported under an entirely different geography and economy, it would doubtless cause tremendous suffering involving virtual starvation and death for many, and migrations and changes for others. It would be very difficult, if not impossible, for them to understand any purpose or cause for such revolutionary changes other than mere vengeance of their enemies and this alone would strongly tend towards the most bitter reactions.

"I am prepared to accede to the argument that even if German resources were wiped off the map, the European economy would somehow readjust itself, perhaps with the help of Great Britain and this country. And the world would go on. The benefit to England by the suppression of German competition is greatly stressed in the Treasury memorandum. But this is an argument addressed to a shortsighted cupidity of the victors and the negation of all that Secretary Hull has been trying to accomplish since 1933. I am aware of England's need, but I do not and cannot believe that she wishes this kind of remedy. I feel certain that in her own interest she could not afford to follow this path. The total elimination of a competitor (who is always also a potential purchaser) is rarely a satisfactory solution of a commercial problem.

"The sum total of the drastic political and economic steps proposed by the Treasury is an open confession of the bankruptcy of hope for a reasonable economic and political settlement of the causes of war."

This paper was sent to Mr. Roosevelt at Hyde Park via Harry Hopkins. At the end of the week Stimson received word that the President had read it and would like to talk with him about it. "I hope this is a good symptom but I dare not be too sure." (Diary, September 23, 24, 1944) Then on Sunday the twenty-fourth, to Stimson's annoyance, but not surprise, a report of the Cabinet disagreement (but not including the documents) was published in the newspapers. Three days earlier a pro-Treasury version had been put out by Drew Pearson. The immediate press reaction was strongly in favor of Hull and Stimson (the Secretary of State had completely reversed his initial and tentative position); the bulk of the press strongly attacked Morgenthau, and the President too for reportedly backing him. On Wednesday the twenty-seventh Mr. Roosevelt telephoned to Stimson, who was at Highhold. "He . . . was evidently under the influence of the impact of criticism which has followed his decision to follow Morgenthau's advice. The papers have taken it up violently and almost unanimously against Morgenthau and the President himself, and the impact has been such that he had already evidently reached the conclusion that he had made a false step and was trying to work out of it. . . . He told me that he didn't really intend to try to make Germany a purely agricultural country but said that his underlying motive was the very confidential one that England was broke; that something must be done to give her more business to pull out of the depression after the war, and he evidently hoped that by something like the Morgenthau plan Britain might inherit Germany's Ruhr business. I had already treated that argument in one of my memoranda sent to the President while the controversy was on, so I said nothing further about it." The two men agreed to discuss the matter further on Stimson's return to Washington.

On October 3 Stimson had lunch with the President. Mr. Roosevelt was apparently very tired and unwell, but "he was very friendly, although in evident discomfort, and I put my propositions to him with all the friendliness and tact possible —and after all I feel a very real and deep friendship for him. So the program went through as follows:

". . . I reminded him that he had asked me to talk with him when we next met about our issue over the treatment of Germany. He grinned and looked naughty and said 'Henry Morgenthau pulled a boner' or an equivalent expression, and said that we really were not apart on that; that he had no intention of turning Germany into an agrarian state and that all he wanted was to save a portion of the proceeds of the Ruhr for use by Great Britain (which was 'broke') . . . leaving some of the products of the Ruhr for Germany. This he considered to be the only method of achieving a very desirable end which he could think of or which had been suggested. He got so affirmative to this effect that I warned him that the paper which Churchill had drawn and which he had initialed did contain the proposition of converting Germany 'into a country primarily agricultural and pastoral in its character,' and I read him the three sentences beginning with the one saying that 'the industries referred to in the Ruhr and in the Saar would therefore be necessarily put out of action and closed down' down to the last sentence saying that 'this programme for eliminating the warmaking industries in the Ruhr and in the Saar is looking forward to converting Germany into a country primarily agricultural and pastoral in its character.' He was frankly staggered by this and said he had no idea how he could have initialed this; that he had evidently done it without much thought.

"I told him that in my opinion the most serious danger of the situation was the getting abroad of the idea of vengeance instead of preventive punishment and that it was the language in the Treasury paper which had alarmed me on this subject. I told him that, knowing his liking for brevity and slogans, I had tried to think of a brief crystallization of the way I looked at it. I said I thought that our problem was analogous to the problem of an operation for cancer where it is necessary to cut deeply to get out the malignant tissue even at the expense of much sound tissue in the process, but not to the extent of cutting out any vital organs which by killing the patient would frustrate the benefit of the operation. I said in the same way that what we were after was preventive punishment, even educative punishment, but not vengeance. I told him that I had throughout had in mind his postwar leadership in which he would represent America. I said throughout the war his leadership had been on a high moral plane and he had fought for the highest moral objectives. Now during the postwar readjustment 'You must not poison this position,' which he and our country held, with anything like mere hatred or vengeance. In the course of the talk I told him of my personal friendship for Henry Morgenthau who had been so kind to me when I first came into the Cabinet and that I had shuddered when he took the leadership in such a campaign against Germany. . . ."

Stimson never discussed the "pastoral Germany" issue again with the President; it was clear that Mr. Roosevelt had never really intended to carry out the Morgenthau plan, and that the Quebec memorandum did not represent his matured opinions. Governmental discussions of policy toward Germany were resumed at a lower level, and McCloy carried the burden for the War Department.

But if Secretary Morgenthau's plan was discarded, the attitude which it represented remained, and continuous pressure was exerted throughout the winter before VE-day for a stern directive to General Eisenhower on the treatment of Germany. The eventual product of the debate was the directive known as J.C.S. 1067;[2] rereading this order two years later, Stimson found it a painfully negative document. Although it contained no orders for economic destruction, it certainly was not designed to make the rebuilding of Germany an easy task, and indeed it explicitly ordered the American military governor to "take no steps (a) looking toward the economic rehabilitation of Germany or (b) designed to maintain or strengthen the German economy"—with the exception that he might act to insure reparation payments and to prevent starvation or rebellion. Yet in the spring of 1945 J.C.S. 1067 seemed so much less punitive and destructive than earlier proposals that Stimson found its final draft "a fairly good paper." (Diary, March 29, 1945)

The question remained essentially one of attitude, and during the remaining months of his service Stimson constantly urged that there was no place for clumsy economic vengeance in American policy toward Germany. On May 16 he wrote at Mr. Truman's request a memorandum summarizing views already orally expressed to the new President. "Early pro-

[2] Published in Dept. of State *Bulletin*, Vol. XIII (1945) pp. 596-607.

posals for the treatment of Germany provided for keeping Germany near the margin of hunger as a means of punishment for past misdeeds. I have felt that this was a grave mistake. Punish her war criminals in full measure. Deprive her permanently of her weapons, her General Staff, and perhaps her entire army. Guard her governmental action until the Nazi-educated generation has passed from the stage—admittedly a long job. But do not deprive her of the means of building up ultimately a contented Germany interested in following non-militaristic methods of civilization. This must necessarily involve some industrialization, for Germany today has approximately thirty million excess population beyond what can be supported by agriculture alone. The eighty million Germans and Austrians in Central Europe today necessarily swing the balance of that continent. A solution must be found for their future peaceful existence and it is to the interest of the whole world that they should not be driven by stress of hardship into a nondemocratic and necessarily predatory habit of life." (Memorandum for the President, May 16, 1945)

In a further conversation with Mr. Truman on July 3, just before both men left for Potsdam, Stimson found that his views were fully shared by the White House. From this time forward American policy was more and more directed toward reconstruction of a denazified, demilitarized, but economically sound Germany. Unfortunately vestiges of the old attitude remained at lower levels. Still more unfortunately, the execution of American policy was necessarily dependent upon inter-Allied agreement, and in the two years that followed the Potsdam Conference of 1945 the difficulty of securing effective agreement became even more clear. The German question became part of a still larger and more complicated subject—American policy toward Soviet Russia.

NOTE: In 1948, when the issue over the Morgenthau plan had given way to a very different debate over the *control* and *use* of the resources of the Ruhr, it seemed important to remark that Stimson's position in 1944 and 1945 did not in any way commit him to support the reconstruction of Germany *as against* the reconstruction of France and other liberated countries. His general sympathies, indeed, ran in exactly the opposite direction. During his debate with Morgenthau and afterward he repeatedly made clear his belief that French claims upon Ruhr production deserved a most sympathetic hearing, and he believed too that France should share in the international control of the Ruhr. But he could not believe that the French interest, or any humane interest, would be served by a policy of deliberate destruction or by an attempt to make of Germany a land of permanent paupers.

3. THE CRIME OF AGGRESSIVE WAR

Concurrent with the struggle over the Morgenthau plan, and intertwined with it, was a debate over the proper treatment of the Nazi leaders. In this debate too Stimson was active, and because in his view the eventual result was a striking triumph for the cause of law and peace, his share in the matter deserves detailed attention.

One of the proposals in the Morgenthau memorandum of September 6 was that a list should be made of German archcriminals—men whose obvious guilt was generally recognized by the United Nations—and that upon capture and identification these men should be shot at once. Commenting on this proposal in his paper of September 9, Stimson wrote:

"The other fundamental point upon which I feel we differ is the matter of the trial and punishment of those Germans who are responsible for crimes and depredations. Under the plan proposed by Mr. Morgenthau, the so-called archcriminals shall be put to death by the military without provision for any trial and upon mere identification after apprehension. The method of dealing with these and other criminals requires careful thought and a well-defined procedure. Such procedure must embody, in my judgment, at least the rudimentary aspects of the Bill of Rights, namely, notification to the accused of the charge, the right to be heard and, within reasonable limits, to call witnesses in his defense. I do not mean to favor the institution of state trials or to introduce any cumbersome machinery but the very punishment of these men in a dignified manner consistent with the advance of civilization, will have all the greater effect upon posterity. Furthermore, it will afford the most effective way of making a record of the Nazi system of terrorism and of the effort of the Allies to terminate the system and prevent its recurrence.

"I am disposed to believe that at least as to the chief Nazi officials, we should participate in an international tribunal constituted to try them. They should be charged with offenses against the laws of the Rules of War in that they have committed wanton and unnecessary cruelties in connection with the prosecution of the war. This law of the Rules of War has been upheld by our own Supreme Court and will be the basis of judicial action against the Nazis.

"Even though these offenses have not been committed against our troops, I feel that our moral position is better if we take our share in their conviction. Other war criminals who have committed crimes in subjugated territory should be returned in accordance with the Moscow Declaration to those territories for trial by national military commissions having jurisdiction of the offense under the same Rules of War. I have great difficulty in finding any means whereby military commissions may try and convict those responsible for excesses committed within Germany both before and during the war which have no relation to the conduct of the war. I would be prepared to construe broadly what constituted a violation of the Rules of War but there is a certain field in which I fear that external courts cannot move. Such courts would be without jurisdiction in precisely the same way that any foreign court would be without jurisdiction to try those who were guilty of, or condoned, lynching in our own country."

The question of trial as against shooting was not decided at Quebec, but Stimson heard from McCloy reports that the President had there expressed himself as definitely in favor of execution without trial. It seemed probable that this was only a curbstone opinion, but it was deeply disturbing to the War Department, and Stimson and McCloy promptly set up a group of military lawyers to study in detail the possibilities for a trial. After a month of study these lawyers reported to the Secretary.

"Our meeting lasted for an hour and a half and was deeply interesting. These men had reached the conclusion that besides local tribunals to punish war crimes against the international Rules of War, we could for the same purpose establish an international tribunal if we wished it or mixed tribunals, the latter to prosecute criminals whose criminal activities had extended over several jurisdictions. . . . Colonel Bernays of the JAGD gave an interesting talk on the possibility of bringing charges against the whole scheme of Nazi totalitarian war, using for the promotion of its end methods of warfare which were in conflict with the established Rules of War. This was virtually upon the theory of a conspiracy and I then told them of my experience as United States Attorney in finding that only by [charging] conspiracy could we properly cope with the evils which arose under our complicated development of big business. In many respects the task which we have to cope with now in the development of the Nazi scheme of terrorism is much like the development of big business. It was a very interesting talk and carried my mind farther along the line which it has been following in connection with dealing with the German secret police and the forms of secret police itself among other nations." (Diary, October 24, 1944)

The concept of conspiracy became more and more, in Stimson's mind, the guide to a proper course in trying Nazi leaders. The advantages of showing the whole gigantic wickedness for what it was quite outweighed his initial distaste for a complex state trial, and he made his point not long after to the President. "I told him the story of the seventeen holes—the case which I tried against the American Sugar Refining Company. He was greatly interested in this and gave his very frank approval to my suggestion when I said that conspiracy with all of the actors brought in from the top to the bottom, or rather with representatives of all classes of actors brought in from top to bottom, would be the best way to try it and would give us a record and also a trial which would certainly persuade any onlooker of the evil of the Nazi system. In fact he was very nice about it." (Diary, November 21, 1944)

Meanwhile the War Department committee worked on, and in January its report was completed. In January, too, the President, shifting somewhat from his earlier view, appointed Judge Samuel Rosenman to study the question for him. Meeting with Rosenman, Joseph P. Davies, Attorney General Biddle, and others on January 18, "I was glad to find they were all in favor of legal action rather than political action against the head Nazis, and secondly, that in their study of the proper kind of legal action they were coming to the view

which I have held from the first[3] that we had better stage up
a big trial in which we can prove the whole Nazi conspiracy
to wage a totalitarian war of aggression violating in its progress all of the regular rules which limit needless cruelty and
destruction."

This was the tenor of the War Department's own recommendations, which Stimson signed "with great satisfaction"
on January 21. Two days before, he had argued his position
once more with Mr. Roosevelt, hoping to keep the President
from any hasty decision at the forthcoming Yalta Conference.
Stimson rehearsed to the President the views he shared with
his committee and with Judge Rosenman and the Attorney
General's office. He emphasized again the advantage of a trial
as against political action. Mr. Roosevelt "assented to what
I said but in the hurry of the situation I am not sure whether
it registered." (Diary, January 19, 1945)

The last view of Mr. Roosevelt Stimson never knew, for
when the final decision was taken in May another man was
President, but after these meetings and recommendations of
January there was never any serious question that the American Government favored a state trial. To Stimson's great surprise the principal opposition to legal proceedings came from
the British, who for a long time urged direct military execu-
tions instead. But with firm French and Russian support, the
American view prevailed, and in August, 1945, there was
signed at London a four-power agreement chartering the
International Tribunal which met at Nuremberg the following November. In the international negotiations which led to
the London Charter Stimson had no part, but he watched with
great admiration the work done for his country at London and
later at Nuremberg by Mr. Justice Jackson.

Both during and after the Nuremberg trial there was a
considerable debate in the United States and elsewhere over
its legality. To Stimson it was not merely legal but so clearly

---

[3] "From the first" is not quite accurate; as a matter of fact Stimson was skeptical
about the trying of war criminals on the charge of aggressive war when it was first
suggested to him by his law partner, William Chanler. He thought it "a little in
advance of international thought" (Memorandum to McCloy, November 28, 1944)
and it was only after further consideration that he became an ardent advocate of the
principle.

so that any other course would have been crassly illegal. From his retirement he wrote for *Foreign Affairs* a careful explanation of his view. The central argument of the article[4] represents so plainly his general attitude toward the international law of war that it is here quoted in part.

The principal complaint leveled against Nuremberg was that its charter dared to name aggressive war as a punishable crime. In Stimson's view this was its greatest glory, and to this point he addressed the bulk of his argument:

"The defendants at Nuremberg were leaders of the most highly organized and extensive wickedness in history. It was not a trick of law which brought them to the bar; it was the 'massed angered forces of common humanity.' . . .

"The Charter of the Tribunal recognizes three kinds of crime, all of which were charged in the indictment: crimes against peace, war crimes, and crimes against humanity. There was a fourth charge, of conspiracy to commit one or all of these crimes. To me personally this fourth charge is the most realistic of them all, for the Nazi crime is in the end indivisible. Each of the myriad transgressions was an interlocking part of the whole gigantic barbarity. But basically it is the first three that we must consider. The fourth is built on them.

"Of the three charges, only one has been seriously criticized. . . . The charge of crimes against peace . . . has been the chief target of most of the honest critics of Nuremberg. It is under this charge that a penalty has been asked, for the first time, against the individual leaders in a war of aggression. It is this that well-intentioned critics have called '*ex post facto* law'."

The charge of *ex post facto* law rested on the indubitable fact that the Nuremberg proceeding was unprecedented. But Stimson argued that the climate of opinion in which the Nazis launched their war of aggression was also unprecedented. In the years after the First World War the community of nations had repeatedly denounced aggression as criminal, most conspicuously in the Kellogg-Briand Pact of 1928. "In the judgment of the peoples of the world the once proud title of 'conqueror' was replaced by the criminal epithet 'aggressor'."

It was of course quite true, as critics of Nuremberg argued,

[4] "The Nuremberg Trial: Landmark in Law," *Foreign Affairs*, January, 1947.

that before 1945 there was little to indicate that the "peoples of the world" were prepared to accept the capture and conviction of such aggressors as a legal duty. "But it is vitally important to remember that a legal right is not lost merely because temporarily it is not used. . . . Our offense was thus that of the man who passed by on the other side. That we have finally recognized our negligence and named the criminals for what they are is a piece of righteousness too long delayed by fear."

Then Stimson came to the heart of the matter.

"We did not ask ourselves, in 1939 or 1940, or even in 1941, what punishment, if any, Hitler and his chief assistants deserved. We asked simply two questions: How do we avoid war, and how do we keep this wickedness from overwhelming us? These seemed larger questions to us than the guilt or innocence of individuals. In the end we found an answer to the second question, but none to the first. The crime of the Nazis, against *us*, lay in this very fact: that their making of aggressive war made peace here impossible. We have now seen again, in hard and deadly terms, what had been proved in 1917—that 'peace is indivisible.' The man who makes aggressive war at all makes war against mankind. That is an exact, not a rhetorical description of the crime of aggressive war.

"Thus the Second World War brought it home to us that our repugnance to aggressive war was incomplete without a judgment of its leaders. What we had called a crime demanded punishment; we must bring our law in balance with the universal moral judgment of mankind. The wickedness of aggression must be punished by a trial and judgment. This is what has been done at Nuremberg.

"Now this is a new judicial process, but it is not *ex post facto* law. It is the enforcement of a moral judgment which dates back a generation. It is a growth in the application of law that any student of our common law should recognize as natural and proper, for it is in just this manner that the common law grew up. There was, somewhere in our distant past, a first case of murder, a first case where the tribe replaced the victim's family as judge of the offender. The tribe had learned that the deliberate and malicious killing of any human being was, and must be treated as, an offense against the whole community. The analogy is exact. All case law grows by new decisions, and where those new decisions match the conscience of the community, they are law as truly as the law of murder. They do not become *ex post facto* law merely because until the first decision and punishment comes, a man's only warning that he offends is in the general sense and feeling of his fellow men.

"The charge of aggressive war is unsound, therefore, only if the community of nations did not believe in 1939 that aggressive war was an offense. Merely to make such a suggestion, however, is to discard it. Aggression is an offense, and we all know it; we have known it for a generation. It is an offense so deep and heinous that we cannot endure its repetition.

"The law made effective by the trial at Nuremberg is righteous law long overdue. It is in just such cases as this one that the law becomes more nearly what Mr. Justice Holmes called it: 'the witness and external deposit of our moral life.'

"With the judgment of Nuremberg we at last reach to the very core of international strife, and we set a penalty not merely for war crimes, but for the very act of war itself, except in self-defense."

This was to Stimson the great accomplishment of Nuremberg, and after devoting some attention to other lesser aspects of its achievement, he returned to the same point, from a slightly different angle, in his concluding paragraphs. Not merely was aggression now a crime, but in a sense it was the only important crime connected with war. For in World War II it had been shown that there is not much restraint or humanity left in modern warfare, once the bloody contest has begun.

"We as well as our enemies have contributed to the proof that the central moral problem is war and not its methods, and that a continuance of war will in all probability end with the destruction of our civilization.

"International law is still limited by international politics, and we must not pretend that either can live and grow without the other. But in the judgment of Nuremberg there is affirmed the central principle of peace—that the man who makes or plans to make aggressive war is a criminal. A standard has been raised to which Americans, at least, must repair; for it is only as this standard is accepted, supported, and enforced that we can move onward to a world of law and peace."

4. PLANNING FOR RECONSTRUCTION

The treatment of Germany and her leaders was important, but still more important was the general framework of American policy toward the postwar world. In this larger framework, as in the matter of Germany itself, Stimson's work was that of an adviser representing the War Department in the nation's councils; he had of course no authority and no responsibility in the larger task of advancing the American position among divergent Allied views. But the interest of the War Department and his own deep concern with foreign affairs combined to lead him during 1945 to the framing of a fairly comprehensive position on American policy. This position, constantly including as basic elements his long-standing insistence on friendship with Great Britain and recognition of economic reality, involved three additional general principles: America must participate in world affairs; America must be strong and secure; and America must get along with her wartime allies. Illustrations of his interpretation of each of these three principles were not lacking in 1944 and 1945.

As Secretary Hull again and again emphasized in his regular meetings with Stimson, the critical question of the postwar period was whether or not the United States would truly become a participating and effective member of the world community. Uncertain as the path to peace might be, it seemed clear that the decision of 1920 had led up a blind alley; the bankruptcy of isolationism was evident.

Upon the proper nature and extent of future American participation in world affairs there was less agreement. Stimson inclined to agree with Hull that here, as in the peace treaties, economics was central. America must so organize her trade and her foreign finance that the world might achieve the economic stability which had never been approached after 1918. In long-range terms, this meant a constant effort to expand American foreign trade, and especially American imports, by the kind of policy so valiantly begun by Mr. Hull twelve years before. When the Reciprocal Trade Agreements Act was extended in May, 1945, Stimson warmly congratulated President Truman. "I told him that I had always regarded these treaties as the fundamental basis for our postwar condition and that I thoroughly shared his views and was greatly relieved at the good size of the vote." (Diary, May 27, 1945)

Though proper long-range trade policy seemed the fundamental requirement, Stimson's thinking during the last year of the war was largely directed toward the more pressing immediate problems of reconstruction and rehabilitation. The relief operations directed by Army civil affairs officers in some areas and UNRRA officials in others he thoroughly approved in principle, but in looking ahead he believed the main difficulty to lie nearer home—in American unawareness of the scale of help required by the prostrated nations in war areas. In his approach to this difficulty Stimson found himself once again differing somewhat from other administration leaders.

Mr. Roosevelt and his advisers were thoroughly alive to the bitter need for American assistance existing in Allied countries, and particularly in the case of Great Britain they were determined that this help must be provided. British needs, eloquently explained by Prime Minister Churchill, were a major subject of discussion at Quebec in September, 1944, and Mr. Roosevelt returned to Washington determined to plan for and furnish further American assistance. But to Stimson's alarm he appeared to intend using the Lend-Lease Act for this purpose. Although possibly legal, such a course seemed to Stimson most unwise, and at the Cabinet meeting on October 13 he explained his position:

"I got involved enough to say that the only point that I thought came my way in that was that, as one of the members in the debate before the congressional committee for the original Lend-Lease, I was a witness of the representations made to Congress and that I knew perfectly well that Congress had made the lend-lease appropriations on the representations that it was in aid of an actual war effort to help an ally who was

actually fighting for us and not for the purpose of rehabilitat-
ing a nation which was not fighting or appropriations which
were not, in other words, an aid to our own war effort. I therefore thought that if we were going to go into making use of
lend-lease appropriations in the postwar period or when there
was no longer any connection between them and the actual
fighting of the recipient, we ought to consult Congress. I did
not at all oppose the purpose but I thought it would be very
dangerous to go ahead under the original authority which was
aimed at another objective." (Diary, October 13, 1944)

In the end no significant postwar assistance was given under
the alleged authority of Lend-Lease, but in Stimson's opinion
the discussions looking toward this goal had the unfortunate
effect of preventing adequate consideration of and preparation
for a more forthright and farsighted approach to the same
general goal. He would have preferred "a great act of statesmanship on the part of the President" (Diary, November 22,
1944) to close out the British lend-lease account, with its
enormous balance in favor of the Americans, followed by a
further act of statesmanship to provide help on a similar basis
after the war. Such a course would obviously have required
"a great effort of education," but it would have had the advantage of proceeding in an atmosphere of war, instead of in the
cooler and more cautious time of 1946, when a somewhat cold-
blooded British loan was with great difficulty passed through
Congress. But Stimson was forced to admit that in part this
was hindsight, for it was not until well after 1944 that he came
to a full appreciation of the desperate nature of the British
economic position.

That not only Britain but all of Europe would need large-
scale American help was wholly clear to Stimson by July,
1945, however, after he had seen, on his way to Potsdam, the
devastation left by the war. This was a challenge larger than
that of Germany, or even Great Britain—it involved the very
survival of Europe. In a memorandum submitted to the President on July 22 he summarized his view of American responsibility in the situation. In this paper he tied the German
question in with the problem of Europe as a whole.

"I am impressed with the great loss in economic values on

the Continent, but even more with the loss in widespread moral values which destruction and war conditions have caused in Europe.

"We have immediate interests in a return to stable conditions—the elimination of distress conditions to ease our problems of administration and the speed and success of our redeployment. But our long-range interests are far greater and much more significant.

"One hope for the future is the restoration of stable conditions in Europe, for only thus can concepts of individual liberty, free thought, and free speech be nurtured. Under famine, disease, and distress conditions, no territory or people will be concerned about concepts of free speech, individual liberty, and free political action. All the opposite concepts flourish in such an atmosphere. If democratic interests are not given an opportunity to grow in western and middle Europe, there is little possibility they will ever be planted in Russian minds.

"I therefore urge ... that Germany shall be given an opportunity to live and work; that controls be exercised over the German people only in so far as our basic objectives absolutely require, and that the ethnological *and economic* groupings of Germany should be disturbed only where considerations make it inescapable. We cannot be misled by the thought that because many plants, at least on our side of the line, exist in relative integrity, that German economy can readily be restored. I am satisfied that it cannot be unless there is a flow of commerce, establishment of transportation systems, and stable currency. The Russian policy on booty in eastern Germany, if it is as I have heard it reported, is rather oriental. It is bound to force us to preserve the economy in western Germany in close co-operation with the British, so as to avoid conditions in our areas which, in the last analysis, neither British nor American public opinion would long tolerate.

"Secondly, I urge that a completely co-ordinated plan be adopted for the economic rehabilitation of Europe as a whole; that in doing this, all the economic benefits which the United States can bestow, such as war surplus disposal, Export-Import Bank credits, etc., be channeled through one man and one agency. Our means must be concentrated in one agency in order to use all our power to achieve our ends. Diverse policy and diverse methods of distribution lead to competition in bestowal of favors and interfere with the carrying out of the only effective and politically supportable program, namely, one of helping Europe to help herself.

"There are large food, fuel, and industrial sources in Europe, and, if all resources are marshaled, much can be done to achieve stability in Europe with the promptitude and in the degree necessary to preserve democratic governments. It does require a period of management in which I am convinced we have to take a part. I would recommend one United States agency as I have indicated, and I would feel that an Economic Council for Europe should be set up. The chairman should be an American, in whose hands, subject to the authority of the President and pursuant to the directions of the central United States agency just recommended, would be vested the disposition in Europe of all benefits flowing from the United States. Other members of the Council would consist of the representatives of other contributing powers who would be similarly authorized. They should act in close liaison with the Control Council for Germany, and their duties should be, over a limited period, to assist the governments of Europe *to help themselves* in the restoration of stable conditions."

In the two years that followed his submission of this memorandum Stimson saw no reason to alter the essentials of the recommendations it contained. The surface aspect of the situation changed as the immediate postwar period passed and American war assets on the spot were largely liquidated. But the need for American assistance continued—and his estimate of the quantity of assistance needed was if anything increased by the passage of time.

5. A STRONG AMERICA

The difficulty of achieving popular understanding of America's place in the modern world was a favorite subject for Stimson's meetings with Secretary Hull, and sometimes when they had exhausted their stock of epithets for isolationism, they would shift their fire through a wide arc and take aim at the "fuzzy-minded idealists." To both men the world in which the United States was called to participate was the real world, fully equipped with problems and difficulties, and not an abstraction waiting for Good Will to give it life in a New Age of Lasting Peace. To Stimson as Secretary of War it was especially disturbing to note that very often the people who talked most persuasively about American responsibility for peace were the ones who seemed least aware of any connection between this responsibility and the maintenance of American strength. His own view was entirely different; he could not conceive of an effective United States except as a nation equipped with the military establishment required for a leading power. Twice in 1945 there arose questions which drew from him clear statements of this position.

On June 15, 1945, Stimson appeared before the Committee on Postwar Military Policy of the House of Representatives to testify in favor of peacetime universal military training. The argument he there developed was his final judgment on a subject to which he had given thirty years of study. Much of his statement was of course devoted to the specific advantages of universal training as a method of maintaining effective national defense, and another large section was given over to an attack on the notion that military training would lead to militarism. He also explained in some detail the incidental advantages which he had found for himself in military service and which he believed were found by most men. But the core of the argument was in a few paragraphs in the beginning; here he connected military preparedness with the maintenance of peace.

"I believe that a necessary foundation on which to build the security of the United States is a system of universal military training. And in saying this I intend the broadest meaning of the term 'security.' I mean not merely protection against the physical invasion of our territory. I mean the security which goes with the strong and tested character of the citizenship of a nation, giving to that nation a leadership among the peoples of the world and a well-founded respect for it on their part which swells its power and influence. . . .

"In the first place, let me speak of universal military training as necessary for the physical protection of our country and its people. Never in my long life have we lived in a world where the very civilization of humanity has become so broken and unsettled; where the methods of war have become so brutal and so far-reaching in their peril as today; and where the respect of civilized man for those constitutional safeguards of government, not to say even the traditions of religious and humanitarian regard of one group of human beings for another, have become so shaken. . . .

". . . And no matter how dearly we may desire to preserve our way of life by peaceful persuasion alone, no matter how earnestly we may deplore the resort by other nations to aggressive force to gain their ends, these attitudes of peaceful persuasion can never be a substitute for the physical means of our own self-preservation—certainly not in such a world as that we now live in. No nation is fit to assume responsibility for others unless it is capable of being responsible for itself.

"Universal military training is the fundamental basis of such security. No matter how complicated the weapons of war may become, no matter how necessary to the nation's future security are programs for scientific research and industrial mobilization, the disciplined, trained, and patriotic citizenry of a nation remain the bricks of the foundation upon which the other methods and means of security rest.

"But in the second place, beyond and above any responsibility attending her own sovereignty, there now attaches to the United States as a great world power a further duty. In a short span of years we have seen our nation emerge as a leading power of the world. It is worse than idle to blink the responsibility which goes with this position. Already in almost every international emergency which arises, the eyes of the other nations turn to us for leadership. Our country's retention in the years to come of a stature befitting such a position will depend in my judgment upon her possession of the balanced elements of greatness which now support her responsible position in the family of nations. Particularly she must retain her capacity effectively to discharge her obligations under the world peace organizations which are now in process of being formed. The ideals which inspired the world plan now being framed in San Francisco must be supported and made to work by methods of known efficacy—by the use of force in the last analysis if necessary to prevent the depredations of an aggressor.

"Again I speak from personal experience. From my service as Secretary of State during a period of national isolationism and irresponsibility for world affairs, I realize only too well the futility of what the Chinese call 'spears of straw' and 'swords of ice' when the first steps of a new war are seen approaching. In this disordered world, for decades to come, the success of a program for peace will depend upon the maintenance of sufficient strength by those who are responsible for that peace. To advocate any Dumbarton plan and then to shear ourselves of the power to carry it out would be even worse than our refusal to join the attempt at world organization in 1919. Although the objectives of a program for collective peace are loftier and more idealistic than the mere defense of national sovereignty, they take root in the same soil of national self-interest. The goal of each peace-loving nation is still its individual security, a goal now sought to be attained through the collective security of all nations.

"Thus to meet our obligation of bearing our full share in preserving world peace, a part of America's present military readiness should be retained."

At the end of his statement, he was asked a question by the committee chairman, Congressman Woodrum, which brought out a still stronger statement. Would he comment "in regard to the suggestion that has been made, that for the United States now, while the San Francisco Convention is laboring in the cause of setting up a world organization, to take any step of this kind would be not only an evidence of our lack of faith in their efforts, but would be construed as an overt act by our present allies and other nations."

Stimson replied that "to know that we are taking such a precautionary and preventive step against war . . . would have just the opposite effect; . . . it would show that we were in earnest. . . . The people who for a long time have got to preserve the peace are the people who have brought about the peace by the victories in this war. The fact that those people keep their armor girded on will be the best deterrent in the world against any one aggressor in the future, and such an aggressor would know, at the same time, that we had shared in forming this new organization at San Francisco and we were prepared to defend it and to make it work. The worst thing we did to break the chance of peace after the last war, and to tempt willful nations toward aggression, was to keep out.

"We did two things: We kept out of all efforts to organize, and we dissolved all our armies and took no precautions against a future war.

"It was those two things which made America—in quite a large share, in my opinion—responsible for what came afterward."

6. BASES AND BIG POWERS

More complex, and perhaps more significant, than his feelings on military training was Stimson's attitude on the vexed issue of American policy toward certain Pacific islands won from Japan during the Pacific war. In what way, if any, should American authority for these islands be subjected to the new systems of trusteeship under the United Nations? During the first months of 1945 there developed within the Government a considerable debate over this question.

The State Department, in preparing for the San Francisco Conference, wished to formulate a general American policy toward areas of the kind which under the League of Nations had been "mandates"—areas in which colonial people not ready for self-government were governed by member nations accountable for their stewardship to the League. It was the hope of President Roosevelt that the mandate principle, exercised by the League only in a limited number of places, most of them territories formerly owned by Imperial Germany, might now be extended so far as possible to all colonial territories, *whether or not* these territories had been held by the enemy before the war.

Since most such territories were the legal property of other nations behind whose ownership rested all the national pride and self-interest associated with colonialism, it was evident that such a hope could hardly be effectively expressed by the United States unless she too were prepared to submit to the new principle. Accordingly it was planned that any islands retained by the United States in the Pacific should be held by her only in trusteeship from the United Nations.

In principle this proposal was unobjectionable, but to Stimson it seemed dangerously unrealistic; his own immediate object was to protect American interests in the Pacific islands, and he did not believe that any useful purpose was served by classing such islands with colonial areas containing large populations and considerable economic resources. "They [the Pacific islands] do not really belong in such a classification. Acquisition of them by the United States does not represent an attempt at colonization or exploitation. Instead it is merely the acquisition by the United States of the necessary bases for the defense of the security of the Pacific for the future world. To serve such a purpose they must belong to the United States with absolute power to rule and fortify them. They are not colonies; they are outposts, and their acquisition is appropriate under the general doctrine of self-defense by the power which guarantees the safety of that area of the world."[5] To Stimson this proposition seemed beyond debate; World War II had made wholly evident the fact that the United States must be the principal guarantor of the peace of the Pacific, and it had also demonstrated the outstanding strategic significance of the scores of small atolls held before 1941 by the Japanese in the western Pacific. After World War I, ignoring the warnings of Army and Navy leaders, the American Government had permitted the western Pacific islands to be mandated to Japan, on assurances that they would not be fortified. The folly of this decision was written in blood. An equal error had been committed in the Four-Power Treaty of 1921, under which the United States had agreed not to add to the fortifications of the Philippines, and Stimson was insistent that there should this time be no such mistake. He had not himself understood in 1921 the dangers of such agreements; like the men who made the agreements, he had placed his faith in the sanctity of treaties. But as he explained to the American dele-

[5] Memorandum for the Secretary of State, January 23, 1945.

gates to San Francisco, in a meeting on April 17, he had had to learn of these errors at firsthand. "I pointed out that as Governor in 1928 it had been my unhappy position to go over the plans for the defense of Corregidor and to realize that the brave men on that island were deliberately being left there to a glorious but hopeless defense of the island. . . . We . . . shackled ourselves and placed our reliance upon treaties which the Japanese promptly broke, and I earnestly begged them [the delegates] never again to repeat that error. I then told them how in 1941 I was in office again and in the position where I could see the errors which I had pointed out ripen into their inevitable disaster. I stood in Washington helpless to reinforce and defend the Philippines and had to simply watch their glorious but hopeless defense. I said that I believed that we could under proper conditions introduce the trustee system even into these bases, but it must give us full control and full strategic rights for the protection of them." So long as the United States retained its vital interest in the western Pacific, and so long as American strength was the principal safeguard against aggression in that area, that strength must not be hamstrung by unconsidered idealism. The policemen must be armed.

A curious aspect of the debate within the Government was that no one seemed to deny that American interests in the islands under discussion must be protected. President Roosevelt was "just as keen as anybody else to take the full power of arming them and using them to protect the peace and ourselves during any war that may come, and for that reason his people at San Francisco will be trying to form a definition of trusteeships or mandates which will permit that to be done." (Diary, March 18, 1945) The difficulty with this approach, as Stimson saw it, was that it camouflaged the realities of the situation. "The State Department proposals were meticulously building up a world organization which was to be the trustee and were proposing that we should turn over these bases to this trustee and then take back the management of them and try to make the powers of management big enough to give us the power which we now hold from our efforts in the war." (Diary, March 30, 1945) Such a procedure seemed to Stimson pointlessly roundabout. He would have preferred to state plainly that the defense of strategic islands was essential to the United States and a definite advantage to all Pacific powers. "With that attitude properly demonstrated I feel sure that we could have met with no objection to retaining enough bases to secure our position in the Pacific. My point was that we had always stood for freedom and peace in the Pacific and we had waged this war to throw out an aggressor and to restore peace and freedom and everybody knew it; that these bases had been stolen by the aggressor, who had used them to attack us and destroy our power; that we had fought this war with much cost of life and treasure to capture these bases and to free from the threat of aggression all of the peace-loving nations of the Pacific. We had actually thus saved from threat Australia and the Philippines and we were engaged in the process of doing it to the East Indies and to China; that if we had called attention to all of this and then said that we proposed to hold the bases which we now had gained in this painful struggle as a means and for the purpose of protecting freedom and peace in the Pacific, no one would have objected. In other words, we should have announced our possession with a declaration of trust in which all peace-loving nations were the beneficiaries." (Diary, March 30, 1945)

The intragovernmental differences on trusteeships were safely resolved before the San Francisco Conference. It was agreed that no particular territories should be discussed, and in return the War and Navy Departments agreed that it would be practicable to devise a trusteeship system which would provide for the maintenance of United States military and strategic rights in the Pacific and elsewhere. As finally signed, the United Nations Charter contained only a general framework for the handling of trust territories; specific agreements on specific areas were left for later negotiation. In 1947 an agreement was signed which adequately safeguarded the American interest.

The real issue in the trusteeship question was one of attitude; both sides in the Government wanted the same results. They differed about the way of getting it. This same difference persisted in the much larger question of securing a successful peace settlement. However attractive it might be to think in terms of a world organization, the real guarantee of peace could only come from agreement among the major powers, and such agreement would be much more readily achieved if attention were not diverted from it to blueprints which must remain without effect unless guaranteed by the three great nations. On January 23, in a memorandum to Secretary Stettinius, Stimson explained this view in some detail.

"1. The Moscow Conference of November 1, 1943, contemplated two organizations: (a) 'A General International Organization based on the principle of the sovereign equality of all peace-loving states and open to membership by all such states, large and small' etc. (b) An interim consultative organization of the four large powers for 'maintaining international peace and security pending the re-establishment of law and order and the inauguration of a system of general security.'

"2. This recognized the self-evident fact that these large powers who have won the war for law and justice will be obliged to maintain the security of the world which they have saved during the time necessary to establish a permanent organization of the whole world, and for that purpose they will have to consult and decide on many questions necessary to the security of the world and primarily their own safety in establishing that security. I have always thought that this interim organization should be formal, subject to rules of consultation similar to Article XI of the old League, and actively at work until the world had gotten stabilized enough to establish and turn loose the large world organization which includes the small nations.

"3. The job of the four big nations is principally to establish a guarantee of peace in the atmosphere of which the world organization can be set going.

"This will necessarily include the settlement of all territorial acquisitions in the shape of defense posts which each of these four powers may deem to be necessary for their own safety in carrying out such a guarantee of world peace.

"4. For substantially this purpose, at the end of the last war President Wilson proposed a joint covenant of guarantee by

Britain and America of the security of France as the pillar of western Europe. But the mistake was made of not securing that guarantee before the second step of creating the League of Nations whose safety was in large part to be dependent upon such a guarantee. As a result the League of Nations lacked a foundation of security which ultimately proved fatal to it.

"5. I think we are in danger of making a similar mistake by attempting to formulate the Dumbarton organization before we have discussed and ironed out the realities which may exist to enable the four powers to carry out their mission, and I was much interested to read Senator Vandenberg's recent speech [of January 10, 1945] in which he took practically the same ground.

"6. Any attempt to finally organize a Dumbarton organization will necessarily take place in an atmosphere of unreality until these preliminary foundations are established. The attitude of the numerous minor nations who have no real responsibility but plenty of vocal power and logical arguments will necessarily be different from that of the large powers who have to furnish the real security. . . ."

The memorandum continued with specific references to the trusteeship problem, and then with a passage pointing out that Russian ideas and interests must also be considered. "She will claim that, in the light of her bitter experience with Germany, her own self-defense as a guarantor of the peace of the world will depend on relations with buffer countries like Poland, Bulgaria, and Rumania, which will be quite different from complete independence on the part of those countries."

And then Stimson re-emphasized his main point.

"For all these reasons I think we should not put the cart before the horse. We should by thorough discussion between the three or four great powers endeavor to settle, so far as we can, an accord upon the general area of these fundamental problems. We should endeavor to secure a covenant of guarantee of peace or at least an understanding of the conditions upon which such a general undertaking of mutual guarantee could be based.

"If there is a general understanding reached among the larger powers I do not fear any lack of enthusiasm on the part of the lesser fry to follow through with the world organization whenever a general meeting may be called.

"The foregoing constitutes a consideration which I believe to be fundamental yet it is no more than the common prudence one would exercise in preparing for the success of any general assembly or meeting in business or political life."

This insistence on the vital importance of achieving big-power agreement before entrusting the peace to an infant organization remained throughout 1945 and even afterward a cardinal point in Stimson's attitude toward world affairs. He believed that in general it was shared by President Roosevelt, although perhaps the President was less fearful than Stimson of the effects of too early a start with the United Nations Organization. Certainly this principle lay behind the President's constant and devoted effort to establish enduring friendship with Soviet Russia. And equally certainly the main block to Stimson's policy, as to the world of the United Nations later, lay in the peculiar difficulty of dealing with the Russians.

7. THE EMERGENT RUSSIAN PROBLEM

During the war two facts became quite apparent to Stimson from the American Army's dealings with Russia. One was that the Russians were, consciously or unconsciously, bad-mannered and irritating beyond the normal degree of permissible international effrontery. Trustfulness and courtesy in whatever quantity seemed to inspire little if any reciprocity in official dealings, however merry the receptions, dinners, and vodka parties. The balance of effort was strikingly illustrated when President Roosevelt hastened his death by traveling to the Crimea in order to meet with Stalin, who reported himself forbidden by his doctor to make a long voyage.

The second evident fact about Soviet Russia was her strength. The colossal achievement of the Soviet armies and the skill and energy of the Russian leaders were perfectly apparent to men like Stimson and Marshall who had spent many anxious hours in contemplation of the awful task of beating Nazi Germany if the Russians should go under. A nation which could do what the Russians did, after suffering the losses and the devastation inflicted by the invader in the first eighteen months of his attack, was a nation of whose strength and heart there could be no serious question.

Neither of these two facts particularly disturbed Stimson, for he was used to international bad manners, and he saw no reason for the United States to be upset by the fact of Russian strength. Diplomatic reports of 1943 and early 1944 gave reason to hope that in the future as in the past Russians and Americans could pursue their respective policies without clashing. Stimson was not disposed to contest the Russian claim that there must be no anti-Russian states along the Soviet borders, and pending their disproof he chose to accept as hopeful signs the constant Soviet assertions that the independence and integrity of states like Poland were a fundamental principle of Russian foreign policy.

Only one aspect of Soviet Russia gave him any deep concern. This was the absence of individual political freedom. The historic danger of authoritarian government, not only to its own citizens but also in any major power to other peoples as well, was a subject with which he was painfully familiar, and in the iron dictatorship of Russia he saw the greatest single threat to an effective postwar settlement. Still more disturbing was evidence that the secret police followed the flag and operated wherever the Russian Army penetrated. "Averell Harriman [then United States Ambassador to Russia] came in this morning and . . . as I listened to his account about the way in which the Russians were trying to dominate the countries which they are 'liberating' and the use which they are making of secret police in the process, my mind was cleared up a good deal on the necessity of beginning a campaign of education on the problem of the secret police in the postwar world. It very evidently is a problem upon the proper solution of which the success of our relations with Russia ultimately will largely depend. Freedom cannot exist in countries where the government uses a secret police to dominate its citizens, and there is nothing to choose between the Gestapo which the Germans have used and the OGPU which the Russians have historically used. Stalin recently promised his people a constitution with a bill of rights like our own, but he has not yet put it into execution. It seems to me now that . . . getting him to carry out this promised reform, which will necessarily mean the abolition of the secret police, lies at the foundation of our success. Harriman says that it will be practically impossible to get the Russians to do it for themselves just at present but that we ought certainly to prevent them from introducing [the secret police] into the countries which they are now invading, particularly Hungary. Hungary has not a Slavic population and I do not believe would willingly accept the methods of the OGPU. We should not allow them to be driven by the Russians into doing it. . . . The two agencies by which liberty and freedom have been destroyed in nations which grant too much power to their government now seem to me clearly to be (1) the control of the press and (2) the control of the liberty of the citizens through the secret police. The latter is the most abhorrent of the two." (Diary, October 23, 1944)

Although the question of freedom in Russia and freedom in nations surrounding her seemed steadily more significant to Stimson in the months that followed, he continued to believe that Mr. Roosevelt was wholly correct in trying to handle the postwar settlement on the basis of Big Three agreement. There seemed to him no doubt that such agreement was the essential prerequisite to true stability in the peace settlement, and he looked with favor on the President's method of direct bargaining. Hearing about Yalta from Stettinius, the new Secretary of State, Stimson was particularly pleased by "the increase in cordiality that has appeared between Stalin and the rest of us. This is lucky because we will need it. There are so many sources of friction between the three great nations now that there are liberated countries for them all to wiggle around in and rub up against each other." (Diary, March 13, 1945)

But in March and April, 1945, a series of episodes showed both Stalin's good humor and Russian "bad manners" in a striking light. None of these incidents was important in itself but messages arrived during each of them indicating "a spirit in Russia which bodes evil in the coming difficulties of the postwar scene." (Diary, March 17, 1945) First, the Russians showed suspicion and mistrust over Anglo-American negotiations for the surrender of the German forces in northern Italy. To Stimson it appeared that this as a strictly military surrender was a matter in which Russia had no more business than the United States would have had at Stalingrad, and President Roosevelt strongly agreed, but there was some disagreement in Anglo-American circles, Mr. Churchill particularly preferring to lean over backwards in correctness. The matter was finally settled on a compromise basis, but the tone and feeling on both sides were sharp. A similar sharpness developed in negotiations over prisoners, both Americans in the Russian lines and persons from Russian or Russian-occupied territory in American hands. Although there seemed to be little doubt that the ordinary Russian soldier and officer were friendly to liberated Americans, official obstructionism to American efforts to care for Americans was extremely irritating and finally led to a sharp telegram from the President to Stalin. At the same time the Russians indicated a keen interest in the "repatriation" of many men in American hands who showed no desire whatever to be handed over to Russian control, and the Americans were faced with the unpleasant alternative of offending a great ally or abandoning the great principle of political asylum.

In all these lesser matters Stimson was in favor of firmness. For a long time he had felt that the Americans tended to give way too easily on these smaller questions, leaving the Russians with the impression that they had only to be disagreeable to get what they wanted. Small-minded haggling was no part of Mr. Roosevelt's nature, and in the larger sense this was most fortunate, but it left lesser officials at a considerable disadvantage in trying to make co-operation mutual. This difficulty was by no means peculiar to dealings with the Russians, but there was a discernible tendency among the Russians to build their whole policy on the other fellow's good nature, and Stimson thought that toleration of such nonsense was foolish —he inclined to believe that Stalin was the sort of man with whom it was useful to speak bluntly.

Stimson, however, did not share the attitude of general impatience which came over the administration in the last weeks of President Roosevelt's life and in the early days of the Truman administration. Perhaps because he had not been closely connected with any of the negotiations with Russia, he did not feel the personal pique at unkept agreements and efforts to overreach which affected the thinking of so many who had dealings with the Soviets. Shortly after Mr. Roosevelt died it appeared that on two matters at least he had in his last weeks wholly lost sympathy with the Russians and had begun to follow a somewhat altered, 'firmer,' American policy. The failure of the Russians to carry out the Yalta provisions for a genuinely reconstructed Polish government and the aggressive attitude of the Yugoslavs toward Trieste had struck Mr. Roosevelt as wholly unjustified and deeply disquieting; he had outlined policies designed to make clear American disapproval of the Lublin Polish government and American opposition to any Yugoslav coup in Trieste. Both of these policies were inherited by Mr. Truman, and both soon came before his advisers. In a meeting on April 23 the question of Poland was discussed and the general sentiment was strongly in favor of vigorous protest against the Soviet failure to keep the Yalta agreement. Stimson's own reaction was different; although he admitted that he was not fully informed, he was very doubtful about the wisdom of too 'strong' a policy. "So I . . . told the President that I was very much troubled by it. . . . I said that in my opinion we ought to be very careful and see whether we couldn't get ironed out on the situation without getting into a head-on collision. . . . I . . . pointed out that I believed in firmness on the minor matters where we had been yielding in the past and have said so frequently, but I said that this [Polish problem] was too big a question to take chances on; and so it went on. . . ."

On the question of Trieste Stimson took a similar position. The core of his feeling here was that the Balkans and their troubles were beyond the sphere of proper United States action.[6] This had been the American position throughout the war, and he saw no reason for any present change, although he

[6] This view Stimson revised in 1947; by then the whole international situation had so changed that the Balkans were very much a United States problem; no longer able to limit their participation to traditional areas, the Americans had inherited a new responsibility from a weakened Great Britain.

relished as little as anyone else the proposal of Yugoslavian domination of Trieste. Fortunately it proved possible to take and hold Trieste without any important clash of arms.

Occurring as they did during the period of the San Francisco Conference, which was drawing up a charter for the permanent organization of the United Nations, such incidents as these were extremely unpleasant. To Stimson they seemed a further confirmation of his long-held belief that basic agreement among the major powers should be achieved *before* any new world organization was set up. Contemplating the embarrassment of the State Department as it faced the problem of excluding the Lublin government from San Francisco, together with the possibility that this exclusion might seriously damage Russo-American relations, he wrote in his diary: "Contrary to what I thought was the wise course, they have not settled the problems that lie between the United States and Russia and Great Britain and France, the main powers, by wise negotiations before this public meeting in San Francisco, but they have gone ahead and called this great public meeting of all the United Nations, and they have got public opinion all churned up over it and now they feel compelled to bull the thing through. Why, to me, it seems that they might make trouble between us and Russia in comparison with which the whole possibilities of the San Francisco meeting amount to nothing. . . . I have very grave anxiety as a result since then as to what will happen. I am very sorry for the President because he is new on his job and he has been brought into a situation which ought not to have been allowed to come in this way." (Diary, April 23, 1945)

And a further difficulty was that in those cases in which there *had* been prior negotiations, the American negotiator had not been sufficiently hard-boiled. "I think the meeting at Yalta was primarily responsible for it because it dealt a good deal in altruism and idealism instead of stark realities on which Russia is strong and now they have got tied up in this mess." And again: "Although at Yalta she [Russia] apparently agreed to a free and independent ballot for the ultimate choice of the representatives of Poland, yet I know very well from my experience with other nations that there are no nations[7] in the world except the U. S. and the U. K. which have a real idea of what an independent free ballot is." (Diary, April 23, 1945)

Stimson's own notion of the proper general policy was to reverse these two earlier tendencies: first, to aim at agreement between the major powers before placing any emphasis on the United Nations as a whole, and second, to negotiate carefully and in good temper, on facts and not theories, with the difficult Russians. "It seems to me that it is a time for me to use all the restraint I can on these other people who have been apparently getting a little more irritated. I have myself been in the various crises enough to feel the importance of firm dealing with the Russians but . . . what we want is to state our facts with perfectly cold-blooded firmness and not show any temper." (Diary, April 3, 1945)

This remained Stimson's attitude throughout the spring of 1945. But as the days passed, a new and important element entered into his thinking about Russia, and by midsummer it had become almost dominant, dwarfing lesser aspects of the problem.

---

[7] The phrase "no nations" was an evident exaggeration. Stimson had no intention of excluding the democracies of western Europe, for example, from his list of nations that understood the free ballot.

CHAPTER XXIII

The Atomic Bomb and the
Surrender of Japan

---

1. MAKING A BOMB

ON AUGUST 6, 1945, an atomic bomb was dropped by an American Army airplane on the Japanese city of Hiroshima. There was thus awfully announced to the world man's mastery of a force vastly more deadly, and potentially more beneficial too, than any other in human history. In the months that followed, as Americans considered in mingled pride and fear the extraordinary achievement of the free world's scientists in combination with American engineers and industry, there was much discussion of the Hiroshima attack. As one of those largely concerned in this decision, Stimson at length concluded that it would be useful "to record for all who may be interested my understanding of the events which led up to the attack." The paper which he published in February, 1947, in *Harper's Magazine*, contains a careful record of his personal connection with this issue to which only occasional comments need be added.

"It was in the fall of 1941 that the question of atomic energy was first brought directly to my attention. At that time President Roosevelt appointed a committee consisting of Vice President Wallace, General Marshall, Dr. Vannevar Bush, Dr. James B. Conant, and myself. The function of this committee was to advise the President on questions of policy relating to the study of nuclear fission which was then proceeding both in this country and in Great Britain. For nearly four years thereafter I was directly connected with all major decisions of policy on the development and use of atomic energy, and from

May 1, 1943, until my resignation as Secretary of War on September 21, 1945, I was directly responsible to the President for the administration of the entire undertaking; my chief advisers in this period were General Marshall, Dr. Bush, Dr. Conant, and Major General Leslie R. Groves, the officer in charge of the project. At the same time I was the President's senior adviser on the military employment of atomic energy.

"The policy adopted and steadily pursued by President Roosevelt and his advisers was a simple one. It was to spare no effort in securing the earliest possible successful development of an atomic weapon. The reasons for this policy were equally simple. The original experimental achievement of atomic fission had occurred in Germany in 1938, and it was known that the Germans had continued their experiments. In 1941 and 1942 they were believed to be ahead of us, and it was vital that they should not be the first to bring atomic weapons into the field of battle. Furthermore, if we should be the first to develop the weapon, we should have a great new instrument for shortening the war and minimizing destruction. At no time, from 1941 to 1945, did I ever hear it suggested by the President, or by any other responsible member of the government, that atomic energy should not be used in the war. All of us of course understood the terrible responsibility involved in our attempt to unlock the doors to such a devastating weapon; President Roosevelt particularly spoke to me many times of his own awareness of the catastrophic potentialities of our work. But we were at war, and the work must be done. I therefore emphasize that it was our common objective, throughout the war, to be the first to produce an atomic weapon and use it. The possible atomic weapon was considered to be a new and tremendously powerful explosive, as legitimate as any other of the deadly explosive weapons of modern war. The entire purpose was the production of a military weapon; on no other ground could the wartime expenditure of so much time and money have been justified. The exact circumstances in which that weapon might be used were unknown to any of us until the middle of 1945, and when that time came, as we shall presently see, the military use of atomic energy was connected with larger questions of national policy."

During these years, from 1941 to 1945, the atomic project occupied a gradually increasing proportion of Stimson's time. In addition to his duties in general supervision of the brilliant work of General Groves, he became chairman of a Combined Policy Committee, composed of British and American officials and responsible directly to the President and Prime Minister Churchill. The atomic undertaking was not solely American, although the managerial direction was exercised through American leaders working mainly with American resources. It was rather another and conspicuous example of co-operation between the United States and the British Commonwealth, in this instance represented by Great Britain and Canada, the latter being a critically important source of the necessary raw materials. In all these matters Stimson's direct agent was Bundy, who maintained constant contact with the work of General Groves and served as American secretary of the Combined Policy Committee.

A further responsibility faced by Stimson and his associates was that of securing the necessary appropriations from Congress. Until 1944 work on the atom was financed from funds elastically available from other appropriations, but as the expenditure increased, and the size of the gamble too, it was decided that direct appropriation would be necessary and that congressional leaders should be informed. Accordingly, in February, 1944, Stimson, Marshall, and Bush made their case before Speaker Rayburn and the two party leaders of the House of Representatives, Congressmen McCormack and Martin. With great courage and co-operation these leaders piloted the necessary appropriation through the House without public discussion. A meeting in June with Senators Barkley, White, Bridges, and Thomas of Oklahoma produced similar results in the Senate. Again in 1945 further large appropriations were obtained in the same manner. Although one or two members of Congress desired to investigate the enormous construction work in Tennessee and Washington, they were successfully held off, sometimes by their own colleagues and at least once by Stimson's direct refusal to permit such investigation. Similar difficulties were surmounted in arranging for Treasury handling of atomic funds and forestalling antitrust action against the Du Pont Company, whose executives must not be disturbed in their great labors for the construction of plants at Clinton and Hanford for a profit of one dollar.

"As time went on it became clear that the weapon would not be available in time for use in the European theater, and the war against Germany was successfully ended by the use of what are now called conventional means. But in the spring of 1945 it became evident that the climax of our prolonged atomic effort was at hand. By the nature of atomic chain reactions, it was impossible to state with certainty that we had succeeded until a bomb had actually exploded in a full-scale experiment; nevertheless it was considered exceedingly probable that we should by midsummer have successfully detonated the first atomic bomb. This was to be done at the Alamogordo Reservation in New Mexico. It was thus time for detailed consideration of our future plans. What had begun as a well-founded hope was now developing into a reality.

"On March 15, 1945, I had my last talk with President Roosevelt. My diary record of this conversation gives a fairly clear picture of the state of our thinking at that time. I have removed the name of the distinguished public servant who was fearful lest the Manhattan (atomic) project 'be a lemon'; it was an opinion common among those not fully informed.

" 'The President . . . had suggested that I come over to lunch today. . . . First I took up with him a memorandum which he sent to me from —— who had been alarmed at the rumors of extravagance in the Manhattan project. —— suggested that it might become disastrous and he suggested that we get a body of 'outside' scientists to pass upon the project because rumors are going around that Vannevar Bush and Jim Conant have sold the President a lemon on the subject and ought to be checked up on. It was rather a jittery and nervous memorandum and rather silly, and I was prepared for it and I gave the President a list of the scientists who were actually engaged on it to show the very high standing of them and it comprised four Nobel Prize men, and also how practically every physicist of standing was engaged with us in the project. Then I outlined to him the future of it and when it was likely to come off and told him how important it was to get ready. I went over with him the two schools of thought that exist in respect to the future control after the war of this project, in case it is successful, one of them being the secret close-in attempted control of the project by those who control it now, and the other being the international control based upon freedom both of science and of access. I told him that those things must be settled before the first projectile is used and that he must be ready with a statement to come out to the people on it just as soon as that is done. He agreed to that. . . .'

"This conversation covered the three aspects of the question which were then uppermost in our minds. First, it was always necessary to suppress a lingering doubt that any such titanic undertaking could be successful. Second, we must consider the implications of success in terms of its long-range postwar effect. Third, we must face the problem that would be presented at the time of our first use of the weapon, for with that first use there must be some public statement."

In order to insure careful consideration of the extraordinary problems now presented, Stimson set up in April a committee "charged with the function of advising the President on the various questions raised by our apparently imminent success in developing an atomic weapon." This committee, known as the Interim Committee,[1] held discussions which "ranged over the whole field of atomic energy, in its political, military, and scientific aspects. . . . The committee's work included the drafting of the statements which were published immediately after the first bombs were dropped, the drafting of a bill for the domestic control of atomic energy, and recommendations looking toward the international control of atomic energy."

[1] "I was its chairman, but the principal labor of guiding its extended deliberations fell to George L. Harrison, who acted as chairman in my absence. . . . Its members were the following, in addition to Mr. Harrison and myself:

"James F. Byrnes (then a private citizen) as personal representative of the President.

"Ralph A. Bard, Under Secretary of the Navy.

"William L. Clayton, Assistant Secretary of State.

"Dr. Vannevar Bush, Director, Office of Scientific Research and Development, and president of the Carnegie Institution of Washington.

"Dr. Karl T. Compton, Chief of the Office of Field Service in the Office of Scientific Research and Development, and president of the Massachusetts Institute of Technology.

"Dr. James B. Conant, Chairman of the National Defense Research Committee, and president of Harvard University."

But the first and greatest problem was the decision on the use of the bomb—should it be used against the Japanese, and if so, in what manner?

The Interim Committee, on June 1, recommended that the bomb should be used against Japan, without specific warning, as soon as possible, and against such a target as to make clear its devastating strength. Any other course, in the opinion of the committee, involved serious danger to the major objective of obtaining a prompt surrender from the Japanese. An advisory panel of distinguished atomic physicists reported that "We can propose no technical demonstration likely to bring an end to the war; we see no acceptable alternative to direct military use."

"The committee's function was, of course, entirely advisory. The ultimate responsibility for the recommendation to the President rested upon me, and I have no desire to veil it. The conclusions of the committee were similar to my own, although I reached mine independently. I felt that to extract a genuine surrender from the Emperor and his military advisers, there must be administered a tremendous shock which would carry convincing proof of our power to destroy the Empire. Such an effective shock would save many times the number of lives, both American and Japanese, that it would cost.

"The facts upon which my reasoning was based and steps taken to carry it out now follow." The argument which follows represents the opinion held not only by Stimson but by all his senior military advisers. General Marshall particularly was emphatic in his insistence on the shock value of the new weapon.

2.   THE ACHIEVEMENT OF SURRENDER

"The principal political, social, and military objective of the United States in the summer of 1945 was the prompt and complete surrender of Japan. Only the complete destruction of her military power could open the way to lasting peace.

"Japan, in July, 1945, had been seriously weakened by our increasingly violent attacks. It was known to us that she had gone so far as to make tentative proposals to the Soviet

Government, hoping to use the Russians as mediators in a negotiated peace. These vague proposals contemplated the retention by Japan of important conquered areas and were therefore not considered seriously. There was as yet no indication of any weakening in the Japanese determination to fight rather than accept unconditional surrender. If she should persist in her fight to the end, she had still a great military force.

"In the middle of July, 1945, the intelligence section of the War Department General Staff estimated Japanese military strength as follows: in the home islands, slightly under 2,000,-000; in Korea, Manchuria, China proper, and Formosa, slightly over 2,000,000; in French Indo-China, Thailand, and Burma, over 200,000; in the East Indies area, including the Philippines, over 500,000; in the by-passed Pacific islands, over 100,000. The total strength of the Japanese Army was estimated at about 5,000,000 men. These estimates later proved to be in very close agreement with official Japanese figures.

"The Japanese Army was in much better condition than the Japanese Navy and Air Force. The Navy had practically ceased to exist except as a harrying force against an invasion fleet. The Air Force had been reduced mainly to reliance upon Kamikaze, or suicide, attacks. These latter, however, had already inflicted serious damage on our seagoing forces, and their possible effectiveness in a last ditch fight was a matter of real concern to our naval leaders.

"As we understood it in July, there was a very strong possibility that the Japanese Government might determine upon resistance to the end, in all the areas of the Far East under its control. In such an event the Allies would be faced with the enormous task of destroying an armed force of five million men and five thousand suicide aircraft, belonging to a race which had already amply demonstrated its ability to fight literally to the death.

"The strategic plans of our armed forces for the defeat of Japan, as they stood in July, had been prepared without reliance upon the atomic bomb, which had not yet been tested in New Mexico. We were planning an intensified sea and air blockade, and greatly intensified strategic air bombing, through the summer and early fall, to be followed on November 1 by an invasion of the southern island of Kyushu. This would be followed in turn by an invasion of the main island of Honshu in the spring of 1946. The total U. S. military and naval force involved in this grand design was of the order of 5,000,000 men; if all those indirectly concerned are included, it was larger still."

(These plans did not bear any significant impress from Stimson, who was never directly concerned in the handling of Pacific strategy. In his view, however, they were wholly sound; he had been throughout 1944 and early 1945 an opponent of the contrary plan for a preliminary invasion of China, holding in the Pacific to the same general theory of the straight and heavy blow, with no diversions, which he had advocated for the European war.)

"We estimated that if we should be forced to carry this plan to its conclusion, the major fighting would not end until the latter part of 1946, at the earliest. I was informed that such operations might be expected to cost over a million casualties, to American forces alone. Additional large losses might be expected among our allies and, of course, if our campaign were successful and if we could judge by previous experience, enemy casualties would be much larger than our own.

"It was already clear in July that even before the invasion we should be able to inflict enormously severe damage on the Japanese homeland by the combined application of 'conventional' sea and air power. The critical question was whether this kind of action would induce surrender. It therefore became necessary to consider very carefully the probable state of mind of the enemy, and to assess with accuracy the line of conduct which might end his will to resist.

"With these considerations in mind, I wrote a memorandum for the President, on July 2, which I believe fairly represents the thinking of the American Government as it finally took shape in action. This memorandum was prepared after discussion and general agreement with Joseph C. Grew, Acting Secretary of State, and Secretary of the Navy Forrestal, and when I discussed it with the President, he expressed his general approval."

This memorandum was originally prompted not by the problem of atomic energy but by the American desire to achieve a Japanese surrender without invading the home islands. The distinction is an important one, and Stimson thought it worth noting that the germ of the memorandum, from which the Potsdam ultimatum later developed, was in a meeting at the White House on June 18 at which final plans for the invasion of Japan were approved. The inclusion of civilian advisers at this meeting was a return to the procedure which Franklin Roosevelt had abandoned in 1942, and the presence of Stimson and McCloy, combined with President Truman's insistent desire to be sure that there was no alternative to invasion, was the beginning of the political actions which so greatly assisted in obtaining surrender.

"July 2, 1945

"Memorandum for the President.

PROPOSED PROGRAM FOR JAPAN

"1. The plans of operation up to and including the first landing have been authorized and the preparations for the operation are now actually going on. This situation was accepted by all members of your conference on Monday, June 18.

"2. There is reason to believe that the operation for the occupation of Japan following the landing may be a very long, costly, and arduous struggle on our part. The terrain, much of which I have visited several times, has left the impression on my memory of being one which would be susceptible to a last ditch defense such as has been made on Iwo Jima and Okinawa and which of course is very much larger than either of those two areas. According to my recollection it will be much more unfavorable with regard to tank maneuvering than either the Philippines or Germany.

"3. If we once land on one of the main islands and begin a forceful occupation of Japan, we shall probably have cast the die of last ditch resistance. The Japanese are highly patriotic and certainly susceptible to calls for fanatical resistance to repel an invasion. Once started in actual invasion, we shall in my opinion have to go through with an even more bitter finish fight than in Germany. We shall incur the losses incident to such a war and we shall have to leave the Japanese islands even more thoroughly destroyed than was the case with Ger- many. This would be due both to the difference in the Jap- anese and German personal character and the differences in the size and character of the terrain through which the opera- tions will take place.

"4. A question then comes: Is there any alternative to such a forceful occupation of Japan which will secure for us the equivalent of an unconditional surrender of her forces and a permanent destruction of her power again to strike an aggres- sive blow at the 'peace of the Pacific'? I am inclined to think that there is enough such chance to make it well worth while our giving them a warning of what is to come and definite opportunity to capitulate. As above suggested, it should be tried before the actual forceful occupation of the homeland islands is begun and furthermore the warning should be given in ample time to permit a national reaction to set in.

"We have the following enormously favorable factors on our side—factors much weightier than those we had against Germany:

"Japan has no allies.

"Her navy is nearly destroyed and she is vulnerable to a surface and underwater blockade which can deprive her of sufficient food and supplies for her population.

"She is terribly vulnerable to our concentrated air attack upon her crowded cities, industrial and food resources.

"She has against her not only the Anglo-American forces but the rising forces of China and the ominous threat of Russia.

"We have inexhaustible and untouched industrial re- sources to bring to bear against her diminishing potential.

"We have great moral superiority through being the victim of her first sneak attack.

"The problem is to translate these advantages into prompt and economical achievement of our objectives. I believe Japan *is* susceptible to reason in such a crisis to a much greater extent than is indicated by our current press and other current com- ment. Japan is not a nation composed wholly of mad fanatics of an entirely different mentality from ours. On the contrary, she has within the past century shown herself to possess extremely intelligent people, capable in an unprecedentedly short time of adopting not only the complicated technique of Occidental civilization but to a substantial extent their culture and their political and social ideas. Her advance in all these respects during the short period of sixty or seventy years has been one of the most astounding feats of national progress in history—a leap from the isolated feudalism of centuries into the position of one of six or seven great powers of the world. She has not only built up powerful armies and navies. She has maintained an honest and effective national finance and respected position in many of the sciences in which we pride ourselves. Prior to the forcible seizure of power over her government by the fanatical military group in 1931, she had for ten years lived a reasonably responsible and respectable international life.

"My own opinion is in her favor on the two points involved in this question:

"a. I think the Japanese nation has the mental intelligence and versatile capacity in such a crisis to recognize the folly of a fight to the finish and to accept the proffer of what will amount to an unconditional surrender; and

"b. I think she has within her population enough liberal leaders (although now submerged by the terrorists) to be depended upon for her reconstruction as a responsible member of the family of nations. I think she is better in this last respect than Germany was. Her liberals yielded only at the point of the pistol and, so far as I am aware, their liberal attitude has not been personally subverted in the way which was so general in Germany.

"On the other hand, I think that the attempt to exterminate her armies and her population by gunfire or other means will tend to produce a fusion of race solidity and antipathy which has no analogy in the case of Germany. We have a national interest in creating, if possible, a condition wherein the Japanese nation may live as a peaceful and useful member of the future Pacific community.

"5. It is therefore my conclusion that a carefully timed

warning be given to Japan by the chief representatives of the United States, Great Britain, China, and, if then a belligerent, Russia, by calling upon Japan to surrender and permit the occupation of her country in order to insure its complete demilitarization for the sake of the future peace.

"This warning should contain the following elements:

"The varied and overwhelming character of the force we are about to bring to bear on the islands.

"The inevitability and completeness of the destruction which the full application of this force will entail.

"The determination of the Allies to destroy permanently all authority and influence of those who have deceived and misled the country into embarking on world conquest.

"The determination of the Allies to limit Japanese sovereignty to her main islands and to render them powerless to mount and support another war.

"The disavowal of any attempt to extirpate the Japanese as a race or to destroy them as a nation.

"A statement of our readiness, once her economy is purged of its militaristic influence, to permit the Japanese to maintain such industries, particularly of a light consumer character, as offer no threat of aggression against their neighbors, but which can produce a sustaining economy, and provide a reasonable standard of living. The statement should indicate our willingness, for this purpose, to give Japan trade access to external raw materials, but not longer any control over the sources of supply outside her main islands. It should also indicate our willingness, in accordance with our now established foreign trade policy, in due course to enter into mutually advantageous trade relations with her.

"The withdrawal from their country as soon as the above objectives of the Allies are accomplished, and as soon as there has been established a peacefully inclined government, of a character representative of the masses of the Japanese people. I personally think that if in saying this we should add that we do not exclude a constitutional monarchy under her present dynasty, it would substantially add to the chances of acceptance.

"6. Success of course will depend on the potency of the

warning which we give her. She has an extremely sensitive national pride, and, as we are now seeing every day, when actually locked with the enemy will fight to the very death. For that reason the warning must be tendered before the actual invasion has occurred and while the impending destruction, though clear beyond peradventure, has not yet reduced her to fanatical despair. If Russia is a part of the threat, the Russian attack, if actual, must not have progressed too far. Our own bombing should be confined to military objectives as far as possible."

HENRY L. STIMSON
Secretary of War.

Stimson's *Harper's* account went on:

"It is important to emphasize the double character of the suggested warning. It was designed to promise destruction if Japan resisted, and hope, if she surrendered.

"It will be noted that the atomic bomb is not mentioned in this memorandum. On grounds of secrecy the bomb was never mentioned except when absolutely necessary, and furthermore, it had not yet been tested. It was of course well forward in our minds, as the memorandum was written and discussed, that the bomb would be the best possible sanction if our warning were rejected.

"The adoption of the policy outlined in the memorandum of July 2 was a decision of high politics; once it was accepted by the President, the position of the atomic bomb in our planning became quite clear. I find that I stated in my diary, as early as June 19, that 'the last chance warning . . . must be given before an actual landing of the ground forces in Japan, and fortunately the plans provide for enough time to bring in the sanctions to our warning in the shape of heavy ordinary bombing attack and an attack of S-1.' S-1 was a code name for the atomic bomb.

"There was much discussion in Washington about the timing of the warning to Japan. The controlling factor in the end was the date already set for the Potsdam meeting of the Big Three. It was President Truman's decision that such a warning should be solemnly issued by the U. S. and the U. K. from this meeting, with the concurrence of the head of the Chinese Government, so that it would be plain that *all* of Japan's principal enemies were in entire unity. This was done, in the Potsdam ultimatum of July 26, which very closely followed the above memorandum of July 2, with the exception that it made no mention of the Japanese Emperor.

"On July 28 the Premier of Japan, Suzuki, rejected the Potsdam ultimatum by announcing that it was 'unworthy of public notice.' In the face of this rejection we could only proceed to demonstrate that the ultimatum had meant exactly what it said when it stated that if the Japanese continued the war, 'the full application of our military power, backed by our resolve, will mean the inevitable and complete destruction of the Japanese armed forces and just as inevitably the utter devastation of the Japanese homeland.'

"For such a purpose the atomic bomb was an eminently suitable weapon. The New Mexico test occurred while we were at Potsdam, on July 16. It was immediately clear that the power of the bomb measured up to our highest estimates. We had developed a weapon of such a revolutionary character that its use against the enemy might well be expected to produce exactly the kind of shock on the Japanese ruling oligarchy which we desired, strengthening the position of those who wished peace, and weakening that of the military party.

"Because of the importance of the atomic mission against Japan, the detailed plans were brought to me by the military staff for approval. With President Truman's warm support I struck off the list of suggested targets the city of Kyoto. Although it was a target of considerable military importance, it had been the ancient capital of Japan and was a shrine of Japanese art and culture. We determined that it should be spared. I approved four other targets including the cities of Hiroshima and Nagasaki.

"Hiroshima was bombed on August 6, and Nagasaki on August 9. These two cities were active working parts of the Japanese war effort. One was an army center; the other was naval and industrial. Hiroshima was the headquarters of the Japanese Army defending southern Japan and was a major military storage and assembly point. Nagasaki was a major seaport and it contained several large industrial plants of great wartime importance. We believed that our attacks had struck cities which must certainly be important to the Japanese military leaders, both Army and Navy, and we waited for a result. We waited one day.

"Many accounts have been written about the Japanese surrender. After a prolonged Japanese Cabinet session in which the deadlock was broken by the Emperor himself, the offer to surrender was made on August 10. It was based on the Potsdam terms, with a reservation concerning the sovereignty of the Emperor."

This Japanese reservation precipitated a final discussion in Washington. For months there had been disagreement at high levels over the proper policy toward the Emperor. Some maintained that the Emperor must go, along with all the other trappings of Japanese militarism. Others urged that the war could be ended much more cheaply by openly revising the formula of "unconditional surrender" to assure the Japanese that there was no intention of removing the Emperor if it should be the desire of the Japanese people that he remain as a constitutional monarch. This latter view had been urged with particular force and skill by Joseph C. Grew, the Under Secretary of State, a man with profound insight into the Japanese character. For their pains Grew and those who agreed with him were roundly abused as appeasers.

Stimson wholly agreed with Grew's general argument, as the July 2 memorandum shows. He had hoped that a specific assurance on the Emperor might be included in the Potsdam ultimatum. Unfortunately during the war years high American officials had made some fairly blunt and unpleasant remarks about the Emperor, and it did not seem wise to Mr. Truman and Secretary of State Byrnes that the Government should reverse its field too sharply; too many people were likely to cry shame. Now, in August, the Americans were face to face with the issue they had dodged in previous months. The Japanese were ready to surrender, but, even after seeing in dreadful reality the fulfillment of Potsdam's threats, they required some assurance that the Potsdam Declaration "does not comprise any demand which prejudices the prerogatives of His Majesty as a Sovereign Ruler."

August 10 was hectic in Washington. Radio reports from Japan announced the surrender offer before official notification reached Washington by way of Switzerland. At nine o'clock Stimson was called to the White House where the President was holding a conference on the surrender terms. All those present seemed eager to make the most of this great opportunity to end the war, but there was some doubt as to the propriety of accepting the Japanese condition.

"The President then asked me what my opinion was and I told him that I thought that even if the question hadn't been raised by the Japanese we would have to continue the Emperor ourselves under our command and supervision in order to get into surrender the many scattered armies of the Japanese who would own no other authority and that something like this use of the Emperor must be made in order to save us from a score of bloody Iwo Jimas and Okinawas all over China and the New Netherlands. He was the only source of authority in Japan under the Japanese theory of the State." (Diary, August 10, 1945)

The meeting at the White House soon adjourned to await the official surrender terms. Meanwhile Secretary Byrnes drafted a reply to which Stimson gave his prompt approval. In a later meeting this masterful paper was accepted by the President; it avoided any direct acceptance of the Japanese condition, but accomplished the desired purpose of reassuring the Japanese.

The *Harper's* article continued:

"While the Allied reply made no promises other than those already given, it implicitly recognized the Emperor's position by prescribing that his power must be subject to the orders of the Allied supreme commander. These terms were accepted on August 14 by the Japanese, and the instrument of surrender was formally signed on September 2, in Tokyo Bay. Our great objective was thus achieved, and all the evidence I have seen indicates that the controlling factor in the final Japanese decision to accept our terms of surrender was the atomic bomb."

After the *Harper's* article was published, Stimson found

that some of his friends retained certain doubts about the atomic decision, believing that it was based on an incorrect appreciation of the Japanese attitude. They asked whether the use of the bomb might not have been avoided if the American Government had been fully aware in the spring and early summer of the strength of the Japanese will to surrender.

This question, in Stimson's view, was based on a double misunderstanding—first, of the meaning of war, and second, of the basic purpose of the American Government during this period.

The true question, as he saw it, was not whether surrender could have been achieved without the use of the bomb but whether a different diplomatic and military course would have led to an earlier surrender. Here the question of intelligence became significant. Interviews after the war indicated clearly that a large element of the Japanese Cabinet was ready in the spring to accept substantially the same terms as those finally agreed on. Information of this general attitude was available to the American Government, but as Stimson's own paper of July 2 clearly shows, it was certainly not the view of American leaders that the Japanese already considered themselves beaten. It is possible, in the light of the final surrender, that a clearer and earlier exposition of American willingness to retain the Emperor would have produced an earlier ending to the war; this course was earnestly advocated by Grew and his immediate associates during May, 1945. But in the view of Stimson and his military advisers, it was always necessary to bear in mind that at least some of Japan's leaders would seize on any conciliatory offer as an indication of weakness. For this reason they did not support Grew in urging an immediate statement on the Emperor in May. The battle for Okinawa was proceeding slowly and with heavy losses, and they feared lest Japanese militarists argue that such a statement was the first proof of that American fatigue which they had been predicting since 1941. It seemed possible to Stimson, in 1947, that these fears had been based on a misreading of the situation.

Yet he did not believe that any intelligence reports, short of a direct report that the Japanese were fully ready to surrender, would have changed the basic American attitude. No such report was made, and none could have been made, for it was emphatically not the fact that Japan had decided on surrender before August 6; forces in the Japanese government for and against surrender continued in balance until the tenth of August. There were reports of a weakening will to resist and of "feelers" for peace terms. But such reports merely stimulated the American leaders in their desire to press home on *all* Japanese leaders the hopelessness of their cause; this was the nature of warmaking. In war, as in a boxing match, it is seldom sound for the stronger combatant to moderate his blows whenever his opponent shows signs of weakening. To Stimson, at least, the only road to early victory was to exert maximum force with maximum speed. It was not the American responsibility to throw in the sponge for the Japanese; that was one thing they must do for themselves. Only on the question of the Emperor did Stimson take, in 1945, a conciliatory view; only on this question did he later believe that history might find that the United States, by its delay in stating its position, had prolonged the war.

The second error made by critics after the war, in Stimson's view, was their assumption that American policy was, or should have been, controlled or at least influenced by a desire to avoid the use of the atomic bomb. In Stimson's view this would have been as irresponsible as the contrary course of guiding policy by a desire to insure the use of the bomb. Stimson believed, both at the time and later, that the dominant fact of 1945 was war, and that therefore, necessarily, the dominant objective was victory. If victory could be speeded by using the bomb, it should be used; if victory must be delayed in order to use the bomb, it should *not* be used. So far as he knew, this general view was fully shared by the President and all his associates. The bomb was thus not treated as a separate subject, except to determine whether it should be used at all; once that decision had been made, the timing and method of the use of the bomb were wholly subordinated to the objective of victory; no effort was made, and none was seriously considered, to achieve surrender merely in order not to have to use the bomb. Surrender was a goal sufficient in itself, wholly transcending the use or nonuse of the bomb. And as it turned out, the use of the bomb, in accelerating the surrender, saved many more lives than it cost.

In concluding his *Harper's* article, Stimson considered briefly the question whether the atomic bombs had caused more damage than they prevented.

"The two atomic bombs which we had dropped were the only ones we had ready, and our rate of production at the time was very small. Had the war continued until the projected invasion on November 1, additional fire raids of B-29's would have been more destructive of life and property than the very limited number of atomic raids which we could have executed in the same period. But the atomic bomb was more than a weapon of terrible destruction; it was a psychological weapon. In March, 1945, our Air Forces had launched the first great incendiary raid on the Tokyo area. In this raid more damage was done and more casualties were inflicted than was the case at Hiroshima. Hundreds of bombers took part and hundreds of tons of incendiaries were dropped. Similar successive raids burned out a great part of the urban area of Japan, but the Japanese fought on. On August 6 one B-29 dropped a single atomic bomb on Hiroshima. Three days later a second bomb was dropped on Nagasaki and the war was over. So far as the Japanese could know, our ability to execute atomic attacks, if necessary by many planes at a time, was unlimited. As Dr. Karl Compton has said, 'it was not one atomic bomb, or two, which brought surrender; it was the experience of what an atomic bomb will actually do to a community, *plus the dread of many more*, that was effective.'[2]

"The bomb thus served exactly the purpose we intended. The peace party was able to take the path of surrender, and the whole weight of the Emperor's prestige was exerted in favor of peace. When the Emperor ordered surrender, and the small but dangerous group of fanatics who opposed him were brought under control, the Japanese became so subdued that the great undertaking of occupation and disarmament was completed with unprecedented ease."

[2] K. T. Compton, "The Atomic Bomb and the Surrender of Japan," *Atlantic Monthly,* January, 1947.

And then, in a "personal summary," Stimson reviewed the whole question as he had seen it in 1945.

"Two great nations were approaching contact in a fight to a finish which would begin on November 1, 1945. Our enemy, Japan, commanded forces of somewhat over 5,000,000 armed men. Men of these armies had already inflicted upon us, in our break-through of the outer perimeter of their defenses, over 300,000 battle casualties. Enemy armies still unbeaten had the strength to cost us a million more. *As long as the Japanese Government refused to surrender*, we should be forced to take and hold the ground, and smash the Japanese ground armies, by close-in fighting of the same desperate and costly kind that we had faced in the Pacific islands for nearly four years.

"In the light of the formidable problem which thus confronted us, I felt that every possible step should be taken to compel a surrender of the homelands, and a withdrawal of all Japanese troops from the Asiatic mainland and from other positions, before we had commenced an invasion. We held two cards to assist us in such an effort. One was the traditional veneration in which the Japanese Emperor was held by his subjects and the power which was thus vested in him over his loyal troops. It was for this reason that I suggested in my memorandum of July 2 that his dynasty should be continued. The second card was the use of the atomic bomb in the manner best calculated to persuade that Emperor and the counselors about him to submit to our demand for what was essentially unconditional surrender, placing his immense power over his people and his troops subject to our orders.

"In order to end the war in the shortest possible time and to avoid the enormous losses of human life which otherwise confronted us, I felt that we must use the Emperor as our instrument to command and compel his people to cease fighting and subject themselves to our authority through him, and that to accomplish this we must give him and his controlling advisers a compelling reason to accede to our demands. This reason furthermore must be of such a nature that his people could understand his decision. The bomb seemed to me to furnish a unique instrument for that purpose.

"My chief purpose was to end the war in victory with the

least possible cost in the lives of the men in the armies which I had helped to raise. In the light of the alternatives which, on a fair estimate, were open to us I believe that no man, in our position and subject to our responsibilities, holding in his hands a weapon of such possibilities for accomplishing this purpose and saving those lives, could have failed to use it and afterwards looked his countrymen in the face."

He might have added here a still more personal comment. In March he visited an Air Forces redistribution center in Florida. There he met and talked with men on their way to the Pacific after completing a term of duty in Europe. The impression he received was profound. These men were weary in a way that no one merely reading reports could readily understand. They would go to the Pacific, and they would fight well again, but after this meeting Stimson realized more clearly than ever that the primary obligation of any man responsible for and to these Americans was to end the war as quickly as possible. To discard or fail to use effectively any weapon that might spare them further sacrifice would be irresponsibility so flagrant as to deserve condign punishment. Paraphrasing Shakespeare (but with life and not death as his end), Stimson could have said, as he felt, that "He hates them who would upon the rack of this tough war stretch them out longer."

And yet to use the atomic bomb against cities populated mainly by civilians was to assume another and scarcely less terrible responsibility. For thirty years Stimson had been a champion of international law and morality. As soldier and Cabinet officer he had repeatedly argued that war itself must be restrained within the bounds of humanity. As recently as June 1 he had sternly questioned his Air Forces leader, wanting to know whether the apparently indiscriminate bombings of Tokyo were absolutely necessary. Perhaps, as he later said, he was misled by the constant talk of "precision bombing," but he had believed that even air power could be limited in its use by the old concept of "legitimate military targets." Now in the conflagration bombings by massed B-29's he was permitting a kind of total war he had always hated, and in recommending the use of the atomic bomb he was implicitly confessing that there could be no significant limits to the horror of modern war. The decision was not difficult, in 1945, for peace with victory was a prize that outweighed the payment demanded. But Stimson could not dodge the meaning of his action. The following were the last two paragraphs of his article:

"As I read over what I have written, I am aware that much of it, in this year of peace, may have a harsh and unfeeling sound. It would perhaps be possible to say the same things and say them more gently. But I do not think it would be wise. As I look back over the five years of my service as Secretary of War, I see too many stern and heart-rending decisions to be willing to pretend that war is anything else than what it is. The face of war is the face of death; death is an inevitable part of every order that a wartime leader gives. The decision to use the atomic bomb was a decision that brought death to over a hundred thousand Japanese. No explanation can change that fact and I do not wish to gloss it over. But this deliberate, premeditated destruction was our least abhorrent choice. The destruction of Hiroshima and Nagasaki put an end to the Japanese war. It stopped the fire raids, and the strangling blockade; it ended the ghastly specter of a clash of great land armies.

"In this last great action of the Second World War we were given final proof that war is death. War in the twentieth century has grown steadily more barbarous, more destructive, more debased in all its aspects. Now, with the release of atomic energy, man's ability to destroy himself is very nearly complete. The bombs dropped on Hiroshima and Nagasaki ended a war. They also made it wholly clear that we must never have another war. This is the lesson men and leaders everywhere must learn, and I believe that when they learn it they will find a way to lasting peace. There is no other choice."

CHAPTER XXIV

The Bomb and Peace with Russia

THE first reaction of the American people to the advent of atomic energy was a great feeling of pride and satisfaction in a colossal wartime achievement. The bomb which exploded over Hiroshima made it clear that the victory was at hand. But this reaction was quickly succeeded by others relating to the disquieting future. As Stimson put it on August 9:

"Great events have happened. The world is changed and it is time for sober thought. It is natural that we should take satisfaction in the achievement of our science, our industry, and our Army in creating the atomic bomb, but any satisfaction we may feel must be overshadowed by deeper emotions.

"The result of the bomb is so terrific that the responsibility of its possession and its use must weigh heavily on our minds and on our hearts. We believe that its use will save the lives of American soldiers and bring more quickly to an end the horror of this war which the Japanese leaders deliberately started. Therefore, the bomb is being used.

"No American can contemplate what Mr. Churchill has referred to as 'this terrible means of maintaining the rule of law in the world' without a determination that after this war is over this great force shall be used for the welfare and not the destruction of mankind."

This statement was the public expression of thoughts which had been for many months heavily on the minds of those familiar with the atomic project. When Stimson went to the White House on April 25, 1945, to discuss the atomic bomb with a President from whom the matter had hitherto been kept secret, he took with him a memorandum which dealt not so much with the military use of the bomb as with its long-range political meaning.

MEMORANDUM DISCUSSED WITH THE PRESIDENT

April 25, 1945

"1. Within four months we shall in all probability have completed the most terrible weapon ever known in human history, one bomb of which could destroy a whole city.

"2. Although we have shared its development with the U. K., physically the U. S. is at present in the position of controlling the resources with which to construct and use it and no other nation could reach this position for some years.

"3. Nevertheless it is practically certain that we could not remain in this position indefinitely.

"a. Various segments of its discovery and production are widely known among many scientists in many countries, although few scientists are now acquainted with the whole process which we have developed.

"b. Although its construction under present methods requires great scientific and industrial effort and raw materials, which are temporarily mainly within the possession and knowledge of U. S. and U. K., it is extremely probable that much easier and cheaper methods of production will be discovered by scientists in the future, together with the use of materials of much wider distribution. As a result, it is extremely probable that the future will make it possible to be constructed by smaller nations or even groups, or at least by a large nation in a much shorter time.

"4. As a result, it is indicated that the future may see a time when such a weapon may be constructed in secret and used suddenly and effectively with devastating power by a willful nation or group against an unsuspecting nation or group of much greater size and material power. With its aid even a very powerful unsuspecting nation might be conquered within a very few days by a very much smaller one. . . .

"5. The world in its present state of moral advancement

compared with its technical development would be eventually at the mercy of such a weapon. In other words, modern civilization might be completely destroyed.

"6. To approach any world peace organization of any pattern now likely to be considered, without an appreciation by the leaders of our country of the power of this new weapon, would seem to be unrealistic. No system of control heretofore considered would be adequate to control this menace. Both inside any particular country and between the nations of the world, the control of this weapon will undoubtedly be a matter of the greatest difficulty and would involve such thoroughgoing rights of inspection and internal controls as we have never heretofore contemplated.

"7. Furthermore, in the light of our present position with reference to this weapon, the question of sharing it with other nations and, if so shared, upon what terms, becomes a primary question of our foreign relations. Also our leadership in the war and in the development of this weapon has placed a certain moral responsibility upon us which we cannot shirk without very serious responsibility for any disaster to civilization which it would further.

"8. On the other hand, if the problem of the proper use of this weapon can be solved, we would have the opportunity to bring the world into a pattern in which the peace of the world and our civilization can be saved. . . ."

And it was already apparent that the critical questions in American policy toward atomic energy would be directly connected with Soviet Russia. Whatever might be the complications of domestic atomic policy, and whatever difficulties might arise in negotiations with noncommunist Allied nations, it seemed reasonable to believe that the overwhelming menace of uncontrolled atomic power would in these areas compel satisfactory agreement and effective controls. But in the case of Russia matters were wholly different. There was no assurance that the Russians would hasten to agree on controls, nor could any agreement including Russia be regarded with any great confidence unless it contained such far-reaching rights of inspection as to counterbalance (and perhaps, in Russian eyes, to undermine) the protective and fearsome secrecy of a police state.

Even the immediate tactical discussion about the bomb involved the Russians. Much of the policy of the United States toward Russia, from Teheran to Potsdam, was dominated by the eagerness of the Americans to secure a firm Russian commitment to enter the Pacific war. And at Potsdam there were Americans who thought still in terms of securing Russian help in the Pacific war. Stimson himself had always hoped that the Russians would come into the Japanese war, but he had had no part in the negotiations by which Franklin Roosevelt tried to insure this result, and in June, 1945, he was disturbed to find that a part of the Russian price was a Soviet lease of Port Arthur and Soviet participation with the Chinese in the control of the Manchurian railways. This agreement was accompanied by a Russian promise to leave the Chinese in full control of Manchuria, but in the light of the Polish situation Russian promises of this character no longer seemed reliable. Such an agreement was perhaps better than nothing, but it would be an irony indeed if a new Manchurian crisis should one day develop because of arrangements made during a war whose origins were in that very area.

The news from Alamogordo, arriving at Potsdam on July 16, made it clear to the Americans that further diplomatic efforts to bring the Russians into the Pacific war were largely pointless. The bomb as a merely probable weapon had seemed a weak reed on which to rely, but the bomb as a colossal reality was very different. The Russians may well have been disturbed to find that President Truman was rather losing his interest in knowing the exact date on which they would come into the war.

The Russians at Potsdam were not acting in a manner calculated to increase the confidence of the Americans or the British in their future intentions. Stalin expressed a vigorous and disturbing interest in securing bases in the Mediterranean and other areas wholly outside the sphere of normal Russian national interest, while Russian insistence on *de facto* control of Central Europe hardly squared with the principles of the Atlantic Charter to which the Russians had so firmly announced their adherence in early 1942. These extravagant demands were backed by the Red Army, which was daily increasing in its relative strength in Europe, as the Americans began their redeployment for the Pacific attack. Naturally, therefore, news of the atomic bomb was received in Potsdam with great and unconcealed satisfaction by Anglo-American leaders. At first blush it appeared to give democratic diplomacy a badly needed "equalizer."

Stimson personally was deeply disturbed, at Potsdam, by his first direct observation of the Russian police state in action. The courtesy and hospitality of the Russians was unfailing, but there was evident nonetheless, palpable and omnipresent, the atmosphere of dictatorial repression. Nothing in his previous life matched this experience, and it was not particularly heartening to know that the Soviet machine for the time being was operating to insure the comfort and safety of the Allied visitors. Partly at firsthand and partly through the reports of Army officers who had observed the Russians closely during the first months of the occupation, Stimson now saw clearly the massive brutality of the Soviet system and the total suppression of freedom inflicted by the Russian leaders first on their own people and then on those whose lands they occupied. The words "police state" acquired for him a direct and terrible meaning. What manner of men were these with whom to build a peace in the atomic age?

For the problem of lasting peace remained the central question. Any "equalizing" value of the atomic bomb could only be of short-range and limited value, however natural it might be for democratic leaders to be cheered and heartened by the knowledge of their present possession of this final arbiter of force. As Stimson well knew, this advantage was temporary.

But could atomic energy be controlled, he asked himself, if one of the partners in control was a state dictatorially and repressively governed by a single inscrutable character? Could there be *any* settlement of lasting value with the Soviet Russia of Stalin? With these questions and others crowding his mind, he wrote in Potsdam for the President a paper headed, "Reflections on the Basic Problems Which Confront

Us." It was a tentative and, as he later thought, an incomplete piece of work, presenting only one side of a many-sided question. But it was all right as far as it went.

The central concern of this paper was the Russian police state, and only secondly the atomic bomb. Stimson's first main point was that the present state of Russia, if continued without change, would very possibly in the end produce a war.

"1. With each international conference that passes and, in fact, with each month that passes between conferences, it becomes clearer that the great basic problem of the future is the stability of the relations of the Western democracies with Russia.

"2. With each such time that passes it also becomes clear that that problem arises out of the fundamental differences between a nation of free thought, free speech, free elections, in fact, a really free people, [and] a nation which is not basically free but which is systematically controlled from above by secret police and in which free speech is not permitted.

"3. It also becomes clear that no permanently safe international relations can be established between two such fundamentally different national systems. With the best of efforts we cannot understand each other. Furthermore, in an autocratically controlled system, policy cannot be permanent. It is tied up with the life of one man. Even if a measure of mental accord is established with one head the resulting agreement is liable to be succeeded by an entirely different policy coming from a different successor.

"4. Daily we find our best efforts for co-ordination and sympathetic understanding with Russia thwarted by the suspicion which basically and necessarily must exist in any controlled organization of men.

"5. Thus every effort we make at permanent organization of such a world composed of two such radically different systems is subject to frustration by misunderstandings arising out of mutual suspicion.

"6. The great problem ahead is how to deal with this basic difference which exists as a flaw in our desired accord. I believe we must not accept the present situation as permanent for the result will then almost inevitably be a new war and the destruction of our civilization."

It was easier to state the problem and insist that it be solved than to suggest any course likely to be effective. Stimson found some hope in the brave words of the Soviet Constitution of 1936. They were an indication that Stalin knew at least what freedom *ought* to mean. But they did not suggest any clear answer to the questions he then posed. "(a) When can we take any steps without doing more harm than good? (b) By what means can we proceed? (1) by private diplomatic discussion of the reasons for our distrust? (2) by encouraging open public discussions? (3) by setting conditions for any concessions which Russia may ask in respect to territorial concessions, loans, bases, or any other concessions?

"How far these conditions can extend is a serious problem. At the start it may be possible to effect only some amelioration of the local results of Russia's secret police state."

All these aspects of the Russian problem paled in meaning before the question of Russia and atomic energy. And in the last paragraph of his Potsdam reflections Stimson came to a gloomy conclusion.

"7. The foregoing has a vital bearing upon the control of the vast and revolutionary discovery of X [atomic energy] which is now confronting us. Upon the successful control of that energy depends the future successful development or destruction of the modern civilized world. The committee appointed by the War Department which has been considering that control has pointed this out in no uncertain terms and has called for an international organization for that purpose. After careful reflection I am of the belief that *no* world organization containing as one of its dominant members a nation whose people are not possessed of free speech, but whose governmental action is controlled by the autocratic machinery of a secret political police, can give effective control of this new agency with its devastating possibilities.

"I therefore believe that before we share our new discovery with Russia we should consider carefully whether we can do so safely under any system of control until Russia puts into effective action the proposed constitution which I have mentioned. If this is a necessary condition, we must go slowly in any disclosures or agreeing to any Russian participation whatsoever and constantly explore the question how our head-start in X and the Russian desire to participate can be used to bring us nearer to the removal of the basic difficulties which I have emphasized."

Returning from Potsdam Stimson found himself nearing the limits of his strength, and after two weeks made crowded by the atomic attacks and their announcement, followed by the surrender negotiations, he retreated from Washington for three weeks of rest. In the quiet of the Adirondacks he thought again about the atom and Russia. Twice McCloy came from Washington to talk with him, and at the other end of the secret telephone were Harrison and Bundy; the War Department civilian staff was thinking long and painful thoughts about the atomic triumph.

Stimson was worried. Granting all that could be said about the wickedness of Russia, was it not perhaps true that the atom itself, not the Russians, was the central problem? Could civilization survive with atomic energy uncontrolled? And was it practical to hope that the atomic "secret"—so fragile and short-lived—could be used to win concessions from the Russian leaders as to their cherished, if frightful, police state? A long talk with Ambassador Harriman persuaded Stimson that such a hope was unfounded; the Russians, said Harriman, would regard any American effort to bargain for freedom in Russia as a plainly hostile move. Might it not then be better to reverse the process, to meet Russian suspicion with American candor, to discuss the bomb directly with them and try to reach agreement on control? Might not trust beget trust; as Russian confidence was earned, might not the repressive—and aggressive—tendencies of Stalinism be abated? As he pondered these questions—and above all as he pondered a world of atomic competition—Stimson modified his earlier opinion and on September 11 he sent to the President a memorandum urging immediate and direct negotiations with the Russians looking toward a "covenant" for the control of the atom. With its covering letter, the memorandum is self-explanatory.

September 11, 1945

Dear Mr. President:

In handing you today my memorandum about our relations with Russia in respect to the atomic bomb, I am not unmindful of the fact that when in Potsdam I talked with you about the question whether we could be safe in sharing the atomic bomb with Russia while she was still a police state and before she put into effect provisions assuring personal rights of liberty to the individual citizen.

I still recognize the difficulty and am still convinced of the ultimate importance of a change in Russian attitude toward individual liberty but I have come to the conclusion that it would not be possible to use our possession of the atomic bomb as a direct lever to produce the change. I have become convinced that any demand by us for an internal change in Russia as a condition of sharing in the atomic weapon would be so resented that it would make the objective we have in view less probable.

I believe that the change in attitude toward the individual in Russia will come slowly and gradually and I am satisfied that we should not delay our approach to Russia in the matter of the atomic bomb until that process has been completed. My reasons are set forth in the memorandum I am handing you today. Furthermore, I believe that this long process of change in Russia is more likely to be expedited by the closer relationship in the matter of the atomic bomb which I suggest and the trust and confidence that I believe would be inspired by the method of approach which I have outlined.

Faithfully yours,
HENRY L. STIMSON
Secretary of War.

The President,
The White House.

MEMORANDUM FOR THE PRESIDENT

11 September 1945

Subject: Proposed Action for Control of Atomic Bombs.
"The advent of the atomic bomb has stimulated great mili-

tary and probably even greater political interest throughout the civilized world. In a world atmosphere already extremely sensitive to power, the introduction of this weapon has profoundly affected political considerations in all sections of the globe.

"In many quarters it has been interpreted as a substantial offset to the growth of Russian influence on the continent. We can be certain that the Soviet Government has sensed this tendency and the temptation will be strong for the Soviet political and military leaders to acquire this weapon in the shortest possible time. Britain in effect already has the status of a partner with us in the development of this weapon. Accordingly, unless the Soviets are voluntarily invited into the partnership upon a basis of co-operation and trust, we are going to maintain the Anglo-Saxon bloc over against the Soviet in the possession of this weapon. Such a condition will almost certainly stimulate feverish activity on the part of the Soviet toward the development of this bomb in what will in effect be a secret armament race of a rather desperate character. There is evidence to indicate that such activity may have already commenced.

"If we feel, as I assume we must, that civilization demands that some day we shall arrive at a satisfactory international arrangement respecting the control of this new force, the question then is how long we can afford to enjoy our momentary superiority in the hope of achieving our immediate peace council objectives.

"Whether Russia gets control of the necessary secrets of production in a minimum of say four years or a maximum of twenty years is not nearly as important to the world and civilization as to make sure that when they do get it they are willing and co-operative partners among the peace-loving nations of the world. It is true if we approach them now, as I would propose, we may be gambling on their good faith and risk their getting into production of bombs a little sooner than they would otherwise.

"To put the matter concisely, I consider the problem of our satisfactory relations with Russia as not merely connected with but as virtually dominated by the problem of the atomic bomb. Except for the problem of the control of that bomb, those relations, while vitally important, might not be immediately pressing. The establishment of relations of mutual confidence between her and us could afford to await the slow progress of time. But with the discovery of the bomb, they became immediately emergent. *Those relations may be perhaps irretrievably embittered by the way in which we approach the solution of the bomb with Russia. For if we fail to approach them now and merely continue to negotiate with them, having this weapon rather ostentatiously on our hip, their suspicions and their distrust of our purposes and motives will increase.*[1] It will inspire them to greater efforts in an all-out effort to solve the problem. If the solution is achieved in that spirit, it is much less likely that we will ever get the kind of covenant we may desperately need in the future. This risk is, I believe, greater than the other, inasmuch as our objective must be to get the best kind of international bargain we can—one that has some chance of being kept and saving civilization not for five or for twenty years, but forever.

"The chief lesson I have learned in a long life is that the only way you can make a man trustworthy is to trust him; and the surest way to make him untrustworthy is to distrust him and show your distrust.

"If the atomic bomb were merely another though more devastating military weapon to be assimilated into our pattern of international relations, it would be one thing. We could then follow the old custom of secrecy and nationalistic military superiority relying on international caution to prescribe the future use of the weapon as we did with gas. But I think the bomb instead constitutes merely a first step in a new control by man over the forces of nature too revolutionary and dangerous to fit into the old concepts. I think it really caps the climax of the race between man's growing technical power for destructiveness and his psychological power of self-control and group control—his moral power. If so, our method of approach to the Russians is a question of the most vital importance in the evolution of human progress.

"Since the crux of the problem is Russia, any contemplated action leading to the control of this weapon should be

---

[1] Italics added. Stimson later considered those sentences and one later passage to be the heart of the memorandum.

primarily directed *to* Russia. It is my judgment that the Soviet would be more apt to respond sincerely to a direct and forthright approach made by the United States on this subject than would be the case if the approach were made as a part of a general international scheme, or if the approach were made after a succession of express or implied threats or near threats in our peace negotiations.

"My idea of an approach to the Soviets would be a direct proposal after discussion with the British that we would be prepared in effect to enter an arrangement with the Russians, the general purpose of which would be to control and limit the use of the atomic bomb as an instrument of war and so far as possible to direct and encourage the development of atomic power for peaceful and humanitarian purposes. Such an approach might more specifically lead to the proposal that we would stop work on the further improvement in, or manufacture of, the bomb as a military weapon, provided the Russians and the British would agree to do likewise. It might also provide that we would be willing to impound what bombs we now have in the United States provided the Russians and the British would agree with us that in no event will they or we use a bomb as an instrument of war unless all three Governments agree to that use. We might also consider including in the arrangement a covenant with the U. K. and the Soviets providing for the exchange of benefits of future developments whereby atomic energy may be applied on a mutually satisfactory basis for commercial or humanitarian purposes.

"I would make such an approach just as soon as our immediate political considerations make it appropriate.

"*I emphasize perhaps beyond all other considerations the importance of taking this action with Russia as a proposal of the United States—backed by Great Britain but peculiarly the proposal of the United States. Action of any international group of nations, including many small nations who have not demonstrated their potential power or responsibility in this war would not, in my opinion, be taken seriously by the Soviets.*[2] The loose debates which would surround such proposal, if put before a conference of nations, would provoke

[2] Italics added; this was the most important point of all.

but scant favor from the Soviet. As I say, I think this is the most important point in the program.

"After the nations which have won this war have agreed to it, there will be ample time to introduce France and China into the covenants and finally to incorporate the agreement into the scheme of the United Nations. The use of this bomb has been accepted by the world as the result of the initiative and productive capacity of the United States, and I think this factor is a most potent lever toward having our proposals accepted by the Soviets, whereas I am most skeptical of obtaining any tangible results by way of any international debate. I urge this method as the most realistic means of accomplishing this vitally important step in the history of the world.

"HENRY L. STIMSON
"Secretary of War."

These opinions, which he urgently expressed again to the President and the Cabinet on the day of his retirement, were the ones with which Stimson left office. As an expression of his views in 1947, they were seriously incomplete. A major point of his September memorandum was that the best way to make a man trustworthy was to trust him. This point he publicly re-emphasized in his last press conference. But what if the man whose trust you sought was a cynical "realist" who did not choose to be your friend? What if Stalin and his lieutenants were in this final and essential test of purpose no different from Hitler? What if the police state were no transitional revolutionary device but a fixed and inevitable accompaniment of nationalistic aggression? Would trust and candor by themselves break down or even modify the menace to the world in such a case?

These questions and others like them acquired for Stimson new and pregnant meaning in the two years that followed his presentation of the September memorandum. The behavior of the Russians during this period filled him with astonishment and regret. Like many other Americans, he had met and talked with Stalin during the years of effective wartime alliance (at Potsdam in July, 1945). Like other Americans, he had received Stalin's cordial acquiescence in his general statement that Russia and the United States were natural friends and allies. But in the two years after Potsdam Russian policy everywhere was based on broken pledges, and the United States replaced Nazi Germany as the target of Communist abuse. Russian hostility to the Western democracies was not in the main a reaction to antecedent Western wickedness. It was the Russians who ended the wartime friendship.

Soviet threats against Greece and Turkey, Soviet aggression in Iran, and the maneuvers of Russian-dominated Communists everywhere raised deep and serious questions about the basic intentions of the Kremlin. It was a daring and imaginative democrat indeed who could ignore in 1947 the mountain of evidence supporting the hypothesis that Stalin and his associates were committed to a policy of expansion and dictatorial repression. In so far as it insufficiently emphasized this aspect of the Russian problem, Stimson's September memorandum was dangerously one-sided.

Yet that memorandum was not designed to present a complete policy, but only to urge a certain tactical procedure. Presented at a time when some Americans were eager for their country to browbeat the Russians with the atomic bomb "held rather ostentatiously on our hip," it was designed to present an alternative line, aiming at a great effort to persuade the Russians that, in a choice between two worlds and one, they could find more profit in the latter. Stimson had no desire to criticize the course actually followed by the United States between September and December, 1945, but he did not believe that this course represented precisely the policy and method he had in mind in presenting his September memorandum. This was not by any means the result of a purely American decision; the Russians continued to make it extremely difficult for any American negotiator to conduct the sort of bed-rock discussion of fundamental problems which Stimson was advocating. The good faith and honorable intentions of those charged with American policy in this period seemed to Stimson unquestionable. If he had a difference with them, it was in method and emphasis, and not in basic purpose. Nor could he claim with any certainty that his own policy would have been more successful. If there had been an immediate and direct effort, in September, 1945, to reach agreement with Russia on the control of atomic energy, would it have been successful? Stimson could not say. Much would have depended on the manner in which the attempt was made; there would have been required a clear understanding, detailed and definitive, of what was meant by the "covenant" Stimson proposed; such a covenant would surely have involved more than the mutual assurances that had been so quickly violated by the Russians after Yalta and Potsdam. In talking with the Russians about the atom it would have been necessary to "talk turkey." If these points were not clearly stated in the September memorandum, it was because at that time it was Stimson's primary object to turn the thoughts of his colleagues back to the great principle of direct negotiation on basic issues which had been so long pursued by Franklin Roosevelt, and upon which Stimson's whole experience in forty years of public service had led him to rely. If the Americans and the Russians could reach real agreement, face to face, on atomic energy, then the world could breathe more easily and turn back with renewed optimism to lesser questions. In 1947 Stimson was inclined to think the chances of a successful direct approach in 1945 had been smaller than he thought at the time; but the existence of any chance at all would have justified the attempt, so great was the objective at stake.

And even two years later he still believed that there was every reason to keep open wide the door to Russian-American agreement. The detailed plan for international control of atomic energy developed and advocated by the American Government he thoroughly approved. Yet he could not believe that in the United Nations Commission, in an atmosphere of charge and countercharge, with a dozen nations free to comment and amend, there was available to the United States the best means of winning Russian adherence to those proposals. The way to agreement was still in direct action.

But in 1947 he was no longer able to believe that American policy could be based solely on a desire for agreement with

Russia, and writing in the summer of 1947[3] he saw the proper line of policy as a sort of synthesis of his two memoranda of 1945. He dismissed as "naïve and dangerous" any refusal "to recognize the strong probability that one of our great and powerful neighbor nations is at present controlled by men who are convinced that the very course of history is set against democracy and freedom, as we understand those words."

He continued with an explanation of his unhappy conclusions: "We have been very patient with the Soviet Government, and very hopeful of its good intentions. I have been among those who shared in these hopes and counseled this patience. The magnificent and loyal war effort of the Russian people, and the great successful efforts at friendliness made during the war by President Roosevelt, gave us good reason for hope. I have believed—and I still believe—that we must show good faith in all our dealings with the Russians, and that only by so doing can we leave the door open for Russian good faith toward us. I cannot too strongly express my regret that since the early spring of 1945—even before the death of Mr. Roosevelt—the Soviet Government has steadily pursued an obstructive and unfriendly course. It has been our hope that the Russians would choose to be our friends; it was and is our conviction that such a choice would be to their advantage. But, for the time being, at least, those who determine Russian policy have chosen otherwise, and their choice has been slavishly followed by Communists everywhere.

"No sensible American can now ignore this fact, and those who now choose to travel in company with American Communists are very clearly either knaves or fools. This is a judgment which I make reluctantly, but there is no help for it. I have often said that the surest way to make a man trustworthy is to trust him. But I must add that this does not always apply to a man who is determined to make you his dupe. Before we can make friends with the Russians, their leaders will have to be convinced that they have nothing to gain, and everything to lose, by acting on the assumption

[3] "The Challenge to Americans," *Foreign Affairs*, October, 1947.

that our society is dying and that our principles are outworn. Americans who think they can make common cause with present-day communism are living in a world that does not exist."

But Stimson was not willing to accept the argument of extreme anti-Russians that only force would stop communism. "An equal and opposite error is made by those who argue that Americans by strong-arm methods, perhaps even by a 'preventive war,' can and should rid the world of the Communist menace. I cannot believe that this view is widely held. For it is worse than nonsense; it results from a hopeless misunderstanding of the geographical and military situation, and a cynical incomprehension of what the people of the world will tolerate from *any* nation. Worst of all, this theory indicates a totally wrong assessment of the basic attitudes and motives of the American people. Even if it were true that the United States now had the opportunity to establish forceful hegemony throughout the world, we could not possibly take that opportunity without deserting our true inheritance. Americans as conquerors would be tragically miscast."

He preferred a middle course. "In dealing with the Russians, both uncritical trust and unmitigated belligerence are impossible. There is a middle course. We do not yet know surely in what proportion unreasonable fears and twisted hopes are at the root of the perverted policy now followed by the Kremlin. Assuming both to be involved, we must disarm the fears and disappoint the hopes. We must no longer let the tide of Soviet expansion cheaply roll into the empty places left by war, and yet we must make it perfectly clear that we are not ourselves expansionist. Our task is to help threatened peoples to help themselves. . . .

"Soviet intransigence is based in very large part on the hope and belief that all noncommunist systems are doomed. Soviet policy aims to help them die. We must hope that time and the success of freedom and democracy in the Western world will convince both the Soviet leaders and the Russian people now behind them that our system is here to stay. This may not be possible; dictators do not easily change their hearts, and the modern armaments they possess may make it hard for their people to force such a change. Rather than be persuaded of their error, the Soviet leaders might in desperation resort to war, and against that possibility we have to guard by maintaining our present military advantages. We must never forget that while peace is a joint responsibility, the decision for war can be made by a single power; our military strength must be maintained as a standing discouragement to aggression.

"I do not, however, expect the Russians to make war. I do not share the gloomy fear of some that we are now engaged in the preliminaries of an inevitable conflict. Even the most repressive dictatorship is not perfectly unassailable from within, and the most frenzied fanaticism is never unopposed. Whatever the ideological bases of Soviet policy, it seems clear that some at least of the leaders of Russia are men who have a marked respect for facts. We must make it wholly evident that a nonaggressive Russia will have nothing to fear from us. We must make it clear, too, that the Western noncommunist world is going to survive in growing economic and political stability. If we can do this, then slowly—but perhaps less slowly than we now believe—the Russian leaders may either change their minds or lose their jobs."

In such a policy atomic control must wait for a change of attitude in Russia. Stimson continued to believe that "the riven atom uncontrolled can only be a growing menace to us all," and that "upon us, as the people who first harnessed and made use of this force, there rests a grave and continuing responsibility for leadership, turning it toward life, not death." He was further convinced that "lasting peace and freedom cannot be achieved until the world finds a way toward the necessary government of the whole." But he was forced to the conclusion also that these goals were dependent on Russian agreement. "We cannot have world government or atomic control by wishing for them, and we cannot have them, in any meaningful sense, without Russia. If in response to our best effort there comes no answer but an everlasting 'NO,' then we must go to work in other fields to change the frame of mind that caused that answer. We cannot ignore it."

But the core of this statement, published on Stimson's

eightieth birthday, was not his opinion of Russia, though that was what the press mainly noted. His central argument was directed once again, in hope and challenge, to the American people. Drawing on his unhappy knowledge of past failures as well as his experience of success, he summarized his understanding of the central issues of American foreign policy. And he found the final question to be "one of will and understanding." The following excerpts may stand as a better summary of his position than any restatement would be.

"Americans must now understand that the United States has become, for better or worse, a wholly committed member of the world community. This has not happened by conscious choice; but it is a plain fact, and our only choice is whether or not to face it. For more than a generation the increasing interrelation of American life with the life of the world has outpaced our thinking and our policy; our refusal to catch up with reality during these years was the major source of our considerable share of the responsibility for the catastrophe of World War II.

"It is the first condition of effective foreign policy that this nation put away forever any thought that America can again be an island to herself. No private program and no public policy, in any sector of our national life, can now escape from the compelling fact that if it is not framed with reference to the world, it is framed with perfect futility. This would be true if there were no such thing as nuclear fission, and if all the land eastward from Poland to the Pacific were under water. Atomic energy and Soviet Russia are merely the two most conspicuous present demonstrations of what we have at stake in world affairs. The attitude of isolationism—political or economic—must die; in all its many forms the vain hope that we can live alone must be abandoned.

"As a corollary to this first great principle, it follows that we shall be wholly wrong if we attempt to set a maximum or margin to our activity as members of the world. The only question we can safely ask today is whether in any of our actions on the world stage we are doing enough. In American policy toward the world there is no place for grudging or limited participation, and any attempt to cut our losses by setting bounds to our policy can only turn us backward onto the deadly road toward self-defeating isolation.

"Our stake in the peace and freedom of the world is not a limited liability. Time after time in other years we have tried to solve our foreign problems with halfway measures, acting under the illusion that we could be partly in the world and partly irresponsible. Time after time our Presidents and Secretaries of State have been restrained, by their own fears or by public opinion, from effective action. It should by now be wholly clear that only failure, and its follower, war, can result from such efforts at a cheap solution.

"We have fresh before us the contrary example of our magnificent success in wartime, when we have not stopped to count the cost. I have served as Secretary of State in a time of frightened isolationism, and as Secretary of War in a time of brave and generous action. I know the withering effect of limited commitments, and I know the regenerative power of full action. I know, too, that America can afford it—as who does not know it, in the face of our record in the last seven years? . . .

"The essential question is one which we should have to answer if there were not a Communist alive. Can we make freedom and prosperity real in the present world? If we can, communism is no threat. If not, with or without communism, our own civilization would ultimately fail.

"The immediate and pressing challenge to our belief in freedom and prosperity is in western Europe. Here are people who have traditionally shared our faith in human dignity. These are the nations by whose citizens our land was settled and in whose tradition our civilization is rooted. They are threatened by communism—but only because of the dark shadows cast by the hopelessness, hunger, and fear that have been the aftermath of the Nazi war. Communism or no communism, menace or no menace, it is our simple duty as neighbors to take a generous part in helping these great peoples to help themselves.

"The reconstruction of western Europe is a task from which Americans can decide to stand apart only if they wish to desert every principle by which they claim to live. And, as a decision of policy, it would be the most tragic mistake in our history. We must take part in this work; we must take our full part; we must be sure that we do enough.

"I must add that I believe we should act quickly. The penalty of delay in reconstruction is to increase the size of the job and to multiply difficulties. We require a prompt and large-scale program. The Government must lead the way, but we who are private citizens must support that leadership as men in all parties supported help to our allies in 1941. The sooner we act, the surer our success—and the less it will cost us. . . .

"As we take part in the rebuilding of Europe, we must remember that we are building world peace, not an American peace. Freedom demands tolerance, and many Americans have much to learn about the variety of forms which free societies may take. There are Europeans, just as there are Americans, who do not believe in freedom, but they are in a minority, and . . . we shall not be able to separate the sheep from the goats merely by asking whether they believe in our particular economic and political system. Our co-operation with the free men of Europe must be founded on the basic principles of human dignity, and not on any theory that their way to freedom must be exactly the same as ours. We cannot ask that Europe be rebuilt in the American image. If we join in the task of reconstruction with courage, confidence, and good will, we shall learn—and teach—a lot. But we must start with a willingness to understand.

"The reconstruction of western Europe is the immediate task. With it we have, of course, a job at home. We must maintain freedom and prosperity here. This is a demanding task in itself, and its success or failure will largely determine all our other efforts. If it is true that our prosperity depends on that of the world, it is true also that the whole world's economic future hangs on our success at home. We must go forward to new levels of peacetime production, and to do this we must all of us avoid the pitfalls of laziness, fear, and irresponsibility. Neither real profits nor real wages can be permanently sustained—and still less increased—by anything but rising production.

"But I see no reason for any man to face the American future with any other feeling than one of confident hope. However grave our problems, and however difficult their solution, I do not believe that this country is ready to acknowledge that failure is foreordained. It is our task to disprove and render laughable that utterly insulting theory. Our future does not depend on the tattered forecasts of Karl Marx. It depends on us. . . .

"We need not suppose that the task we face is easy, or that all our undertakings will be quickly successful. The construction of a stable peace is a longer, more complex, and greater task than the relatively simple work of warmaking. But the nature of the challenge is the same. The issue before us today is at least as significant as the one which we finally faced in 1941. By a long series of mistakes and failures, dating back over a span of more than twenty years, we had in 1941 let it become too late to save ourselves by peaceful methods; in the end we had to fight. This is not true today. If we act now, with vigor and understanding, with steadiness and without fear, we can peacefully safeguard our freedom. It is only if we turn our backs, in mistaken complacence or mistrusting timidity, that war may again become inevitable.

"How soon this nation will fully understand the size and nature of its present mission, I do not dare to say. But I venture to assert that in very large degree the future of mankind depends on the answer to this question. And I am confident that if the issues are clearly presented, the American people will give the right answer. Surely there is here a fair and tempting challenge to all Americans, and especially to the nation's leaders, in and out of office."

CHAPTER XXV

The Last Month

WHEN Franklin Roosevelt died and Harry Truman succeeded him, Stimson like other members of the Cabinet submitted his resignation to the new President. Mr. Truman promptly and earnestly assured his Secretary of War that he was wanted not just temporarily but as long as he could stay, and Stimson and the War Department continued to receive from the White House the firm and understanding support to which they had become accustomed in the previous five years.

But already, in April, 1945, Stimson knew that he was in a race. Humanly, he wanted to stay at his job until victory was achieved. Just as humanly, he was beginning to tire. He was now nearly seventy-eight, and the accumulated strain of five years in Washington had begun to affect his heart. More and more he was forced to limit his effort, concentrating after April mainly on the policy questions presented by the atomic bomb. His personal staff and General Marshall combined to save him work wherever possible, but neither they nor he himself could desire that he should remain beyond the time when he could usefully serve.

The European war ended in May. In July Stimson went to Potsdam. On August 6 the first atomic bomb was dropped. The Japanese war seemed almost over. But on August 8 Stimson prepared to face retirement; his doctors had told him that he needed a complete rest and he went again to the White House to suggest his resignation. Mr. Truman told him to take his rest at once for a month if necessary, and then to report back for duty if he could. The war was almost over, he said, and he wanted Stimson with him at its end. Then on August

10 the surrender message came through. Stimson went away for a rest, but it was already clear that he was resting for the final ordeal of winding up his affairs in office, and not for further active service. On his return he formally requested that his resignation be accepted, and President Truman and he fixed September 21 as a suitable date. It would be his seventy-eighth birthday.

1. JUDGMENT ON THE ARMY

Between the tenth of August and the twenty-first of September Stimson was mainly occupied with two subjects: the future of the atomic bomb, which has been discussed in the last chapter, and the recognition by appropriate awards of his associates in the War Department. It was a time for casting up the balance and weighing the achievement of men who had served the Army in the war. Naturally too it was a time for looking over the achievement of the Army as a whole.

The Army of the United States in World War II was a triumphant compound of many elements—troops, commanders, staff, and high command. All of them, of course, were sustained and equipped by the unflagging spirit and the unparalleled productive strength of their countrymen at home, but as his mind turned back over five years of service it was not the weapons or the supplies that Stimson mainly pondered—it was the men. He would not admit that anything they had shown themselves to be had surprised him, but he was proud to say that they had measured fully up to his highest expectations.

The troops had been mobilized as if from nowhere, until in five crowded years a skeleton force of a quarter-million men became a fully armed and battle-trained victorious host of over eight million. This was America in arms—not four men in a hundred had been professional soldiers before. And the Army had been America's finest, losing nothing in comparison with its three great predecessors of the Revolution, the Civil War, and World War I.

The spirit and quality of these troops defied description, for as the war was unexampled in complexity, so the activities and accomplishments of American soldiers were of unnumbered variety. Yet everywhere that Stimson saw them certain things remained constant. They were young in heart and innocent, though they might have laughed with soldiers' oaths to hear themselves so called. They were technically skillful and self-confident. They were good in attack, brilliant in pursuit, and best of all, surprised, angry, and magnificent in defense. They hated the whole ghastly business of war, and sometimes they were sorry for themselves, yet they paid out their strength to the limit in a war which they imperfectly understood. On his visits abroad, a civilian from home, Stimson learned from every man he met that they were the most homesick troops in the world, and he knew how they felt, for twenty-five years before, with all the advantage in spirit of a volunteer catching up with twenty years of military hopes, he had felt exactly the same way.

For if there was one conviction deeper than another in the hearts of these soldiers, it was the belief behind each soldier's uniform that he was an individual to whom life offered special values. Thoughtless or thoughtful, ignorant or profoundly aware, schooled to the discipline of war and its terror or let off easily with work far from the enemy and free from danger, these men were individuals, and they knew it.

And the Army knew it, too. When first sergeants groaned about paper work and critics jeered at the administrative overhead of the Army, did they remember how much this burden was the product of the Army's recognition of the soldier as a unique man and a citizen? Allotments and insurance, point scores and specialties, mail service and the Red Cross, courts-martial, and inspectors general, chaplains and psychiatrists, all were the Army's instruments for wrestling with its colossal problem—to build and maintain a fighting machine composed of individuals.

In this task, of course, the most important tool was leadership. It was one of the regrets of Stimson's service as Secretary of War that he did not see more of the junior officers of the Army, the men from second lieutenant to colonel who led the troops in the field. Their record spoke for itself, and having served one war earlier in this echelon, Stimson knew well the magnitude of their accomplishment. These leaders, targets for the hasty abuse of all who disliked military authority, had successfully faced the great and challenging task of commanding men whom they could and should know as individuals.

The men whom Stimson was able to meet personally were mainly at a higher rank, starting with commanders of divisions and corps. This was the critical level of professional competence. Here it was required that the Army find men in considerable numbers equipped to handle arms and services in effective combination. More than that, it was necessary that these men be able to operate under constantly changing higher commanders—and, in the case of corps commanders, with constantly shifting subordinate formations—for it was a major element of the high commander's strength that he should be able to regroup his forces rapidly in accordance with a changing situation. This required a uniformly first-rate set of commanders. And such commanders were found. Stimson knew well how stern and trying had been the continuing problem of command at these middle levels in previous wars. No part of the Army's achievement in World War II impressed him more than its success in producing fighting major generals. On the leadership and professional skill of these men, of whom few received the public attention they deserved, rested much of the achievement of still higher commanders.

Yet the high command in the field well deserved such subordinates, and Stimson fully shared the nation's pride in Mac-Arthur, Eisenhower, Devers, Bradley, Hodges, Patton, Clark, Krueger, Patch, Eichelberger, Simpson, and Stilwell. All of them he knew; he might have written for each one a personal citation of assessment and honor. But the important thing about these men was not their quality as individuals but rather that the Army met its greatest test with such a group of leaders. As individuals they needed no praise from Stimson. As a group they were proud proof that the American Army could produce field leaders of the highest caliber.

Supporting the field forces were supply commanders overseas and at home. The accomplishments of these men were of particular interest to Stimson. A Secretary of War could only watch in delighted admiration while General Patton set his tanks to run around in France "like bedbugs in a Georgetown kitchen." The problems of supply he could see more directly, for many of them came right back to him and to his immediate subordinates. From General Somervell downward, the supply officers of the Army seemed to him the worthy teammates of the field command; it was they who translated the prodigious economic strength of America into a new way of war which combined mobility with matériel so effectively that field campaigns were regularly and decisively won without troop superiority.

At all echelons was the staff. The staff work of the American Army came of age in World War II. What brilliant individuals had done in earlier wars was done this time by thousands of officers trained in the maturing tradition of Leavenworth. Nearly half a century before, Stimson had heard about staff work when it was only a bright idea in the minds of a few farsighted men led by Elihu Root. In World War I he had himself taken staff training at a time when many senior officers were still skeptical. The Army of his last five years in office had mastered the concept. Stimson felt safe in leaving the record of staff officers to the commanders; rare was the general who had been successful without superior staff work.

His own thoughts turned particularly to the staff in Washington. On the day before he retired he called three hundred of them together in order that he might pay his personal tribute to their work. Their vision, their insistence on teamwork, their ability to merge the individual interests of all arms and services in the great over-all mission of furnishing maximum fighting power to the front—these talents, applied with superior devotion to duty, in the face of the natural eagerness of the soldier for field assignment, had combined to produce staff work far better than that of the German and Japanese high commands.

And then there was his own civilian staff. Stimson himself wrote the citation for awards of the Distinguished Service Medal to Patterson, McCloy, Lovett, and Bundy. Their services to the Army and the nation were clear without further comment from him; so was the accomplishment of other close associates—Dorr, Harrison, Martyn, and Bowles. But again it was as a group that he thought these men important. These were men who put the job ahead of themselves and the common interest ahead of special pleading. What they had meant to Stimson himself he could not trust himself to put on paper. Whatever he had been able to do he had done with their devoted help.

Yet he knew that they joined with him in the firm conviction that the work of the Army in the war was essentially a record of the quality of the American Army officer. On September 20 he called to his office his civilian staff and a dozen of the senior War Department general officers, and he spoke informally in tribute to them all; his remarks to the soldiers were remembered and later reported by McCloy in a form that Stimson was proud to take as his own:

"Through these years I have heavily depended upon my civilian staff, but they and I know that it is to the work, thought, and devotion to duty you men have displayed that we owe the victory. You have lived up to the exacting standards of personal integrity and constant application which I first came to know and appreciate when I was formerly Secretary of War. You and those whom you represent have shown yourselves brave but not brutal, self-confident but not arrogant, and above all, you have prepared, guided, and wielded the mighty power of this great country to another victory without the loss of our liberties or the usurpation of any power."[1]

Though his own training and fighting had been as a ground soldier, the Army for which Stimson was Secretary was an Army which included the Air Forces, and he did not forget it. Had he been minded to take part in the pointless discussion as to who won the war, he could have argued as heartily for the fliers as for any single group. It seemed wiser to say simply that the Air Forces performed with magnificent courage and skill, under the imaginative and forceful direction of a splendid group of officers. Their commanding general, Henry H. Arnold, was a man for whom Stimson felt a special regard. He had shown vision combined with loyalty, force combined with tact, and a comprehension of the larger issues of strategy which gave his word great weight in the

[1] John J. McCloy, "In Defense of the Army Mind," *Harper's Magazine*, April, 1947.

councils of the War Department, and in the Joint and Combined Chiefs of Staff. In 1947 the Air Forces, full grown and eager for autonomy, separated from the Army. Stimson believed that under Lovett and Arnold this strapping young giant had learned well to fly alone.

2. THE CHIEF OF STAFF

The civilians might bow to the soldiers, and the soldiers to the civilians, the commanders might give honor to their troops, and the nation might give rousing greeting to returning generals, but to Stimson the greatness of the American Army of World War II was the projection of the greatness of George C. Marshall, and in the last weeks of his service he did what he could to make this opinion clear.

Marshall's professional skill was written in history. "His mind has guided the grand strategy of our campaigns. . . . It was his mind and character that carried through the trans-Channel campaign against Germany. . . . Similarly his views have controlled the Pacific campaign although there he has been most modest and careful in recognizing the role of the Navy. His views guided Mr. Roosevelt throughout.

"The construction of the American Army has been entirely the fruit of his initiative and supervision. Likewise its training. As a result we have had an army unparalleled in our history with a high command of supreme and uniform excellence. . . . With this Army we have won a most difficult dual war with practically no serious setbacks `and astonishingly 'according to plan.' The estimate of our forces required has been adequate and yet not excessive. For instance, Marshall estimated against the larger estimates of others [including Stimson] that eighty-nine American divisions would suffice. On the successful close of the war, all but two of these divisions had been committed to action in the field. His timetables of the successive operations have been accurate and the close of the war has been ultimately achieved far sooner than most of us had anticipated.

"Show me any war in history which has produced a general

with such a surprisingly perfect record as his in this greatest and most difficult war of all history."[2]

But mere professional skill would hardly have won General Marshall his outstanding position. He had in addition shown the greatest of force in advocacy, combined with a continual insistence on unity.

"From the very beginning, he insisted on unity between the services and among our allies. He realized that only by this means could our combined resources be employed to the fullest advantage against the enemy. To achieve wholehearted co-operation, he was always willing to sacrifice his own personal prestige. To him agreement was more important than any consideration of where the credit belonged. His firm belief that unity could be preserved in the face of divergent opinions was a decisive factor in planning throughout the war."

And the whole had been founded on the rock of character.

"General Marshall's leadership takes its authority directly from his great strength of character. I have never known a man who seemed so surely to breathe the democratic American spirit. He is a soldier, and yet he has a profound distaste for anything that savors of militarism. He believes that every able-bodied citizen has a personal responsibility for the nation's security and should be prepared to assume that responsibility whenever an emergency arises. But he is opposed to a large standing Army as un-American.

"His trust in his commanders is almost legendary. During the critical period of the Ardennes break-through no messages went from the War Department to General Eisenhower which would require his personal decision and reply. This is standard practice with General Marshall. When one of his commanders is in a tight spot, he does everything possible to back him up. But he leaves the man free to accomplish his purpose unhampered.

"He is likewise the most generous of men, keeping himself in the background so that his subordinates may receive all credit for duties well done.

"His courtesy and consideration for his associates, of whatever rank, are remarked by all who know him. His devotion

[2] Letter to President Truman, September 18, 1945.

to the nation he serves is a vital quality which infuses everything he does. During the course of a long lifetime, much of it spent in positions of public trust, I have had considerable experience with men in Government. General Marshall has given me a new gauge of what such service should be. The destiny of America at the most critical time of its national existence has been in the hands of a great and good citizen. Let no man forget it."[3]

What it meant to Stimson personally to serve with such a man he had tried to express before a small gathering of War Department leaders on VE-day.

"I want to acknowledge my great personal debt to you, sir, in common with the whole country. No one who is thinking of himself can rise to true heights. You have never thought of yourself. Seldom can a man put aside such a thing as being the commanding general of the greatest field army in our history. This decision was made by you for wholly unselfish reasons. But you have made your position as Chief of Staff a greater one. I have never seen a task of such magnitude performed by man.

"It is rare in late life to make new friends; at my age it is a slow process but there is no one for whom I have such deep respect and I think greater affection.

"I have seen a great many soldiers in my lifetime and you, sir, are the finest soldier I have ever known."

3. THE COMMANDER IN CHIEF

One other name must be remembered in the Army's roll of honor for superb achievement in World War II. Stimson could not pretend to give a final judgment on the total labor of Franklin D. Roosevelt, but he was wholly certain that the Army had never had a finer Commander in Chief. In the turbulence of the war years there were many incidents on which Stimson and his President disagreed; the significant ones have been recorded in previous chapters. But throughout that period Stimson never wavered in his admiration for Mr. Roosevelt's great qualities, and his affection for the man who

[3] Press conference, September 19, 1945.

carried his burdens with such buoyant courage constantly increased. Against the great human leadership of the President minor differences and difficulties became insignificant, and Stimson, who did not hesitate to disagree with the President, never concealed his contempt for those who had allowed years of disagreement to ripen into general bitterness. Speaking at a Harvard commencement on June 11, 1942, he went out of his way to speak of Mr. Roosevelt to an audience which he suspected might contain a number of full-blown Roosevelt-haters.

"I think it is appropriate that here at the home of his Alma Mater I should say a word as to the leadership of that Harvard man who is the Commander in Chief of this great Army. It has been my privilege to observe him in time of conference and of crisis and of incessant strain and burden, of which he has cheerfully borne by far the heaviest share. His clarity of foresight and his unfailing grasp of the essential strategic factors of a world-wide struggle, you have all been able to follow. But only those who have been his lieutenants in the struggle can know the close personal attention with which he has vitalized every important decision. And only they can fully appreciate the courage and determination he has shown in time of threatened disaster, or the loyalty and consideration by which he has won the support of all of his war associates. Out of these characteristics comes the leadership which will achieve the final victory."

This opinion was reinforced during the next three years, and as he wrote for his diary on April 15, 1945, a summary of his feelings about Mr. Roosevelt, Stimson found that in the retrospect of nearly five years, "the importance of his leadership and the strong sides of his character loom up into their rightful proportions. He has never been a good administrator and the consequence of this has made service under him as a Cabinet officer difficult and often harassing for he has allowed himself to become surrounded by a good many men of small caliber who were constantly making irritating and usually selfish emergencies. But his vision over the broad reaches of events during the crises of the war has always been vigorous and quick and clear and guided by a very strong faith in the future of our country and of freedom, democracy, and humanitarianism throughout the world. Furthermore, on matters of military grand strategy, he has nearly always been sound and he has followed substantially throughout with great fidelity the views of his military and naval advisers. In the Army on no important occasion has he ever intervened with personal or political desires in the appointment of commanders. He has always been guided in this respect by the views of the Staff and myself. The Staff has recommended to him many thousands of general officers and he has accepted their selections practically without exception. I can only remember one or two where he has insisted upon appointments according to his own views and those were of minor importance. In these last respects I think he had been without exception the best war President the United States has ever had. . . . On the whole he has been a superb war President—far more so than any other President of our history. His role has not at all been merely a negative one. He has pushed for decisions of sound strategy and carried them through against strong opposition from Churchill, for example, and others. The most notable instance was where he accepted the views of our Staff in regard to the final blow at Germany across the Channel. . . . That was a great decision."

To Stimson personally the President's kindness and courtesy were unfailing. The two men had always been friendly, but Stimson knew that on his side at least the years of crisis and war had produced a feeling that far exceeded anything based merely on the official relations of a Cabinet officer to his chief. It might be irritating that Mr. Roosevelt was so good a talker that his Secretary of War was proud when he could claim to have been given 40 per cent of the time of their meetings for his own pearls of wisdom—but the President's talk was almost always heart-warming. And in dozens of little ways, with messages and personal notes, and Cabinet badinage, the two men, so different in many ways, showed each other their mutual respect and affection.

On the whole, Stimson was content to stand, in his judgment of President Roosevelt, on a letter written just after his death:

April 16, 1945

My dear Mrs. Roosevelt:

The sudden breaking off of the official ties which I have enjoyed with your husband and with you is a very great shock and grief to me. In the midst of it I find it very difficult to adequately express the affection and honor which I have held for you both. I have never received from any chief, under whom I have served, more consideration and kindness than I did from him, even when he was laboring under the terrific strain of a great war and in spite of the fact that I was a new-comer in his Cabinet and a member of another party. He thus made natural and easy relations which might otherwise have been difficult. Out of these his characteristics grew the very real and deep affection which I came to have for him.

He was an ideal war Commander in Chief. His vision of the broad problems of the strategy of the war was sound and accurate, and his relations to his military advisers and com-manders were admirably correct. In the execution of their duties he gave them freedom, backed them up, and held them responsible. In all these particulars he seems to me to have been our greatest war President. And his courage and cheer-iness in times of great emergency won for him the loyalty and affection of all who served under him.

Lastly and most important, his vision and interpretations of the mission of our country to help establish a rule of freedom and justice in this world raised a standard which put the United States in the unique position of world leadership which she now holds. Such facts must constitute priceless memories to you now in your sad bereavement. You may well hold your head high to have been his worthy helpmate at such a time and in such a task.

With very deep respect and affection, I am

Very sincerely yours,
HENRY L. STIMSON

4. THE END

With such memories of the men with whom he had served, Stimson prepared to leave Washington. Twice before he had

left Cabinet office, each time convinced that he would not return. This was the third strike, and he was surely out now. But
where before he had left with defeated administrations, to be
sure with few regrets and no bitterness, now he was leaving at
the triumphant climax of five years which had been "the high
point of my experience, not only because of the heavy responsibility of guiding the nation's military establishment, but because of the opportunity they offered me to serve the nation
in a great war. I shall always be grateful to Mr. Roosevelt for
giving me that opportunity."[4]

On the twenty-first of September he went as usual to
the War Department. There were still one or two letters to be
signed and a few appointments to be kept. In the middle of
the morning the members of his civilian staff came in to give
him a silver tray in token of farewell. A little later he had a
last talk with General Marshall. At twelve-thirty he went to
lunch as usual in the General Officers' Mess and was there
greeted by an enormous birthday cake—the Army had always
remembered his birthdays. After lunch he went to keep an
appointment at the White House and found that the President
had sent for him to present him with the Distinguished Service Medal—"as Secretary of War from the beginning of the
actual mobilization of the Army to the final victory over
Japan, Henry Lewis Stimson gave the United States of America a measure of distinguished service exceptional in the history of the nation. . . ."

Then he attended his last Cabinet meeting.

"Immediately after the Cabinet meeting I said good-by to
the President and to the Cabinet and hurried away to the Pentagon Building where I picked up Mabel and Colonel Kyle
[his aide] who were waiting for me there and went to the
Washington Airport. There to my surprise was a huge meeting of apparently all the general officers in Washington, lined
up in two rows, together with my immediate personal civilian
staff. It was a very impressive sight and a complete surprise
to me. These men had been standing there for an hour because
the time of my departure was supposed to have been at three
o'clock, and the Cabinet meeting had lasted so long that I did

4 Press conference, September 19, 1945.

not get there until four o'clock. The nineteen-gun salute was given as Mabel and I reached the two lines of generals and the band played 'Happy Birthday' and 'Auld Lang Syne.' Then after waving a general good-by and salute to the whole lines that we passed, I shook hands with Marshall and the top commanders at the end of the line and with my own civilian staff, and Mabel and I entered the plane together and took off for home."

AFTERWORD

THIS book has recorded forty years spent largely in public life; from this record others may draw their own conclusions, but it seems not unreasonable that I should myself set down in a few words my own summing up.

Since 1906 the problems of our national life have expanded in scope and difficulties beyond anything we ever dreamed of in those early times. It is a far cry from the problems of a young district attorney to the awesome questions of the atomic age.

Yet I do not wish that the clock could be turned back. Neither a man nor a nation can live in the past. We can go only once along a given path of time and we can only face in one direction, forward.

No one can dispute the progress made by the man of today from the prehistoric man—mentally, morally, and spiritually. No one can dispute the humanitarian progress made more recently, since those times before the age of steam and electricity, when man's growth was limited by sheer starvation, and the law of Malthus was an immediate reality.

It is true that the record of my own activity inevitably includes my conviction that in the last forty years the peoples and nations of the world have made many terrible mistakes; it is a sad thing that more than half of such a book as this should have to be devoted to the problem of warmaking. Yet even so, it is well also to reflect how much worse the state of mankind would be if the victorious peoples in each of the two world wars had not been willing to undergo the sacrifices which were the price of victory. I have always believed that the long view of man's history will show that his destiny on earth is progress toward the good life, even though that progress is based on sacrifices and sufferings which taken by themselves seem to constitute a hideous mélange of evils.

This is an act of faith. We must not let ourselves be engulfed in the passing waves which obscure the current of progress. The sinfulness and weakness of man are evident to anyone who lives in the active world. But men are also good and great, kind and wise. Honor begets honor; trust begets trust; faith begets faith; and hope is the mainspring of life. I have lived with the reality of war, and I have praised soldiers; but the hope of honorable faithful peace is a greater thing and I have lived with that, too. That a man must live with both together is inherent in the nature of our present stormy stage of human progress, but it has also many times been the nature of progress in the past, and it is not reason for despair.

I think the record of this book also shows my deep conviction that the people of the world and particularly our own American people are strong and sound in heart. We have been late in meeting danger, but not too late. We have been wrong but not basically wicked. And today with that strength and soundness of heart we can meet and master the future.

Those who read this book will mostly be younger than I, men of the generations who must bear the active part in the work ahead. Let them learn from our adventures what they can. Let them charge us with our failures and do better in their turn. But let them not turn aside from what they have to do, nor think that criticism excuses inaction. Let them have hope, and virtue, and let them believe in mankind and its future, for there is good as well as evil, and the man who tries to work for the good, believing in its eventual victory, while he may suffer setback and even disaster, will never know defeat. The only deadly sin I know is cynicism.

HENRY L. STIMSON

A NOTE OF EXPLANATION AND ACKNOWLEDGMENT

SINCE this book is rather unusual in its form, some explanation of the method of its construction may be of value to careful readers and students.

Although it is written in the third person, the book has no other aim than to present the record of Mr. Stimson's public life as he himself sees it. It is an attempt to substitute a joint effort for the singlehanded autobiography he might have undertaken if he were a little younger. It follows that we have made no effort at an external assessment, and in the writing I have sought not to intrude any views of my own, but rather to present Mr. Stimson's actions as he himself understands them. Thus objective praise and blame are equally absent; and for the latter, I fear, another student altogether will be necessary.

The major sources of the book are two: Mr. Stimson himself and his records. If I have held the laboring oar, Mr. Stimson has held the tiller rope, and the judgments and opinions expressed are always his. We have however tried to make a clear distinction between his views as they were during any given period and his present opinions, and wherever memory or desire has conflicted with the written record, we have followed the record.

The most important written record of Mr. Stimson's public life is his diary. It begins in 1910, but until 1930 it was not kept from day to day; entries were made only as time and inclination permitted. The first passages are a short undated description of the Saratoga Convention of 1910 and a long account of the period May, 1911 to March, 1913, written in the spring of the latter year. The diary continues with sporadic entries between 1915 and 1926. There is a separate manuscript volume containing entries made by Lieutenant Colonel Stimson overseas in 1918. The Nicaraguan episode and the Philippine year are both covered by separate volumes of almost daily notes and comment. But the first eighteen months of Mr. Stimson's term as Secretary of State have unfortunately no diary, though a short summary of this period was written in August, 1930.

It is in September, 1930 that the daily diary begins. In that month Mr. Stimson acquired a dictaphone which he kept at his home in Washington, and the diary contains an entry for very nearly every day in which he held public office from that time forward, whether he was in Washington or traveling abroad. In most cases these entries were made the same day or early the following morning. Very occasionally a period of two or three days passed before the entry could be dictated. The average daily entry is two or three typewritten pages in length, but on important occasions there are as many as ten. The diary for the last thirty months of the State Department years fills eleven bound volumes; that of the period 1940 to 1945 fills twenty. There are three volumes of occasional entries covering the period 1933 to 1940.

For the periods it fully covers, the diary is the basic document; it shows what was really in Mr. Stimson's mind at any given time as no files or correspondence can do. In studying the work of a modern public servant, whose signature must appear on thousands of documents each year, it is often important to know what he merely approved and what was a part of his own personal activity. The diary serves as an invaluable check on this point. It also contains expressions of opinion which did not find their way into any official documents or public statements.

The diary has been liberally quoted, and wherever the date of an entry is of any significance, it is given. Omissions are indicated by the usual dots; in most cases the omissions are merely for brevity; in a few, they involve comments or expressions which Mr. Stimson does not now wish to publish, either because he no longer agrees with himself or because they might cause unnecessary pain to men who were his associates and are his friends. One or two alterations have been made in order to clarify confusing entries, and these are noted with the usual brackets. And since the diary was typed from a dictaphone record, we have felt free to make occasional changes in punctuation and spelling. But in general, the diary text is astonishingly clean and clear, and the changes we have made are no more than elementary copyreading. We have made no effort to edit away the informal and conversational style of the usual entry.

Supplementing the diary, and serving as a substitute in those periods which are not covered by a daily record, are Mr. Stimson's papers—reports, speeches, books, memoranda, and correspondence. These have been extensively studied but I cannot claim to have "exhausted the material"; lawyers do not throw things away, and only the intelligent and sympathetic help of Miss Elizabeth Neary, Mr. Stimson's personal secretary, has made it possible for me to find my way in reasonable order through his papers. These materials too have been freely quoted in the text, and the source given wherever it seemed relevant.

In addition to the personal records, I have of course made extensive use of published materials dealing with events in which Mr. Stimson had a part. No bibliography is given, since these volumes usually have been consulted only to give me a working familiarity with matters with which Mr. Stimson was already intimately acquainted. But where these books, magazines, and newspapers are quoted, due acknowledgment is made, and we are indebted to all the publishers who have permitted quotation, both of other writings and of Mr. Stimson's own published work.

An even more important source of help has been the advice and comment of many of Mr. Stimson's intimate associates and colleagues. These men have had the kindness to read parts of the manuscript, and to their comments we owe many a correction and addition. Since most of them are men whose work is praised by Mr. Stimson in the text, I will not embarrass them by listing their names; it is fair to note, however, that almost without exception they have asked to have their own work minimized.

We owe a particular debt to the Department of the Army, whose officers have read and cleared Part III as free from violations of military security. We are still more in the debt of Dr. Rudolph A. Winnacker, without whose generous help this part of the book could hardly have been written at all. Dr. Winnacker's basic historical studies of the work of the Office of the Secretary of War broke the back of the job of getting a connected record of Mr. Stimson's activities between 1940 and 1945. His rounded study of the whole wartime work of the War Department's civilian leaders will contain much about Mr. Stimson which lack of space has forced us to omit, and a great deal more of the work of associates, which has not come within the scope of this book.

The making of a book involves many problems with which neither Mr. Stimson nor I was familiar when we began to work, and we have been greatly assisted by the sympathetic counsel of Mr. Stimson's old friend, associate, and neighbor Arthur W. Page. We have also had the constant co-operation of Mr. Cass Canfield and the experienced staff of Harper and Brothers. And there are many others who will note that in one place or another the book has taken a shape that marks our effort to follow their advice.

The final and fundamental source of the book, however, is Mr. Stimson himself. I have spent most of the last eighteen months as his guest, and daily we have met to work together. At first we simply talked for hours on end. Later, as I began to work with the written records, each point of interest was referred to Mr. Stimson, and all questions of meaning and emphasis were worked out together. The outline of each chapter was the product of joint consideration, and every section of the book, in its several drafts, has been read by Mr. Stimson and revised to meet his criticisms. From our discussions have come many observations and recollections which I have quoted, but in order to set off these remembered comments from passages found in contemporary written records, I have in these cases used the single and not the double quotation mark.

In every important sense, then, this is Mr. Stimson's book. It is his experience and his reflections which have informed its every page. In the nature of things, the responsibility for errors of fact and deficiencies of style is mine, but even in these areas his close attention to detail and his mastery of clear English have prevented many mistakes.

I must take this opportunity of expressing my indebtedness to the Senior Fellows of the Society of Fellows of Harvard University, who encouraged me to undertake this work under my appointment as a Junior Fellow. I have a special obligation also to Mr. John Finley, the Master of Eliot House, for his kindness in giving me "a room of one's own" when I have been in Cambridge. To be a Junior Fellow and a member of Eliot House is to enjoy an opportunity for undisturbed work and enlightening company which is not, in these postwar days, the general lot of students.

But of course my principal personal indebtedness is to Mr. and Mrs. Stimson, whose kindness and generosity, added to the intrinsic and absorbing interest of the task, have made this year and a half a landmark in my life.

McGeorge Bundy

BRIEF CHRONOLOGY OF
WORLD WAR II

This brief chronological listing of outstanding events is included as a guide for those readers who may be interested in checking Mr. Stimson's war service against the progress of the war at any given time. The listing makes no pretense of completeness and aims rather to reconstruct something of the headline atmosphere of those years.

1939	September	1	Germany invades Poland
		3	France and Great Britain declare war on Germany
	November	4	United States modifies Neutrality Act to permit cash-and-carry trade with belligerents
		30	Russia invades Finland
1940	March	12	Russo-Finnish war ends
	April	9	Germany invades Denmark and Norway
	May	10	Germany invades Holland, Belgium, and Luxembourg
		11	Winston Churchill becomes Prime Minister of the United Kingdom
		14–16	Germans break through French lines at Sedan
		28	Belgian King surrenders
		29	Retreat from Dunkirk begins
	June	10	Italy declares war on France and Great Britain
		14	Paris falls to Germans
		17	Petain asks for an armistice
		22	France surrenders
		24	Opening of Republican Convention which nominates Wendell Willkie for President
	September	3	Destroyer Deal announced
		15	British shoot down 175 German planes in Battle of Britain
		16	Selective Service Act of 1940 is signed
		27	Japan, Germany, and Italy sign Tri-Partite Pact aimed at United States
	October	28	Italy invades Greece
	November	5	Franklin Roosevelt re-elected President
	December	14	British victory over Italians in Egypt
1941	March	11	Lend-Lease Act signed
	April	3	Axis forces defeat British in North Africa

1941	April	6	Germany attacks Yugoslavia and joins in war on Greece
		18	Yugoslavian Army surrenders
		27	Athens falls
		29	British withdraw from Greece
	May	20	Germans execute air-borne invasion of Crete
		27	German battleship *Bismarck* sunk
	June	1	Crete conquered
		22	Germany attacks Russia
	July	7	United States troops land in Iceland
		24	Japan occupies southern Indo-China
		26	United States freezes Japanese assets
	August	9–12	Atlantic Charter meeting
		12	House extends Selective Service, 203–202
	September	11	President announces shoot-on-sight order to Atlantic naval forces
	October	19	Moscow in state of siege
	November	17	Neutrality Act amended to permit American merchant ships to carry arms to Allies
		19	Second British offensive in Libya begins
		26	Secretary Hull restates American position to Japanese emissaries
		27	War and Navy Departments send warnings of imminent war to Pacific commanders
	December	7	Japan attacks Pearl Harbor, declaring war on United States and Great Britain
		8	United States and Great Britain declare war on Japan
		11	Germany and Italy declare war on the United States and United States recognizes state of war with these countries
		11	Japanese land in the Philippines
		22	Winston Churchill arrives in Washington for first allied war council
1942	January	2	Japanese enter Manila
		2	"Declaration by United Nations" signed at White House
	February	15	Singapore falls
	March	6	Batavia, Java, falls
		17	General MacArthur arrives in Australia
	April	8	Second Axis offensive begins in Libya
		9	Bataan falls
		18	Carrier-based Army bombers raid Tokyo
	May	6	General Wainwright surrenders on Corregidor
		6–8	Battle of the Coral Sea
		8	Germans begin second Russian campaign
		30	First British 1000-bomber raid on Germany

1942	June	4–7	Battle of Midway
		18	Winston Churchill arrives in Washington for second allied war council
		21	Tobruk falls to Axis; Rommel enters Egypt
	July	1	Germans capture Sevastopol
	August	7	Marines land at Guadalcanal
		9	Battle of Savo Island
		17	First independent United States bombing attack in Europe
		18	Canadians and British raid Dieppe
	November	4	British victory at Alamein in Egypt
		7	Anglo-American forces land in North Africa
		12–15	Battle of Guadalcanal
		21	Russians begin great counteroffensive in Caucasus
	December	24	Darlan assassinated
1943	January	24	President Roosevelt and Prime Minister Churchill announce ten-day meeting of third allied war council at Casablanca—the "unconditional surrender" meeting
		31	Battle of Stalingrad ends in surrender of German Sixth Army
	February	14	Americans suffer setback at Kasserine Pass
	March	1–3	Battle of the Bismarck Sea
		29	British break through the Mareth line in Tunisia
	May	11	Prime Minister Churchill in Washington for fourth allied war council
		11	Americans land on Attu
		12	North African campaign concluded in great allied victory
	June	30	Americans land on Rendova
	July	10	Anglo-American forces land in Sicily
		25	Mussolini falls
	August	15	Allies land at Kiska and find no Japanese
		17	Prime Minister Churchill and President Roosevelt meet in Quebec for fifth allied war council
		17	Sicilian campaign completed
		17	Eighth Air Force anniversary raid on Schweinfurt and Regensburg
	September	3	Allies invade Italy
		8	Italy surrenders
		9	Amphibious landing at Salerno, Italy
		16	Americans take Lae in New Guinea
	October	1	Naples falls
		19	Moscow Conference of Foreign Secretaries begins
	November	1	Marines land at Bougainville
		6	Red Army retakes Kiev

1943	November	21	Americans land on Tarawa and Makin in the Gilbert Islands
		22	President Roosevelt, Prime Minister Churchill, and Generalissimo Chiang-kai-shek meet at Cairo
		28	President Roosevelt, Prime Minister Churchill, and Marshal Stalin meet at Teheran
	December	15	Americans land at Arawe in New Britain
		21	Stilwell begins second Burma campaign
		29	Russians break through west of Kiev, entering Poland
1944	January	11	Pre-invasion strategic air offensive from Britain begins
		22	Allies land at Nettuno-Anzio beachhead south of Rome
		31	Americans land in Marshall Islands
	March	28	Allies admit failure at Cassino in Italy
	April	10	Russians recapture Odessa
		22	Americans land at Hollandia in Dutch New Guinea
	May	10	Russians recapture Sevastopol
		11	Allies renew Italian offensive
		17	Myitkyina airstrip captured
	June	4	Rome liberated
		6	Anglo-American forces land in Normandy
		15	Americans land in Saipan, in the Mariana Islands
		25	Cherbourg liberated
	July	3	Russians take Minsk
		9	British take Caen
		20	Hitler survives attempted assassination and coup d'état
		21	Americans land on Guam
		25	American offensive begins at Avranches, Normandy
	August	2	Russians reach the Baltic Sea in Latvia
		3	Myitkyina falls
		15	Franco-American forces land in Southern France
		25	Paris liberated
	September	4	British free Brussels
		11	Americans free Luxembourg
		12	Americans enter Germany
		13	Prime Minister Churchill and President Roosevelt meet at Quebec for seventh allied war council
		15	Marines land at Peleliu
		17–28	Battle of Arnhem
	October	7	Dumbarton Oaks Conference ends
		20	Americans return to the Philippines
		20	Red Army enters East Prussia
		23–26	Battle of Leyte Gulf
		28	General Stilwell recalled

1944	November	7	Franklin Roosevelt re-elected President
		20	Americans enter Metz
		24	Tokyo bombed by B-29 bombers from Saipan
	December	3	Civil war in Greece
		16	German counteroffensive launched in the Ardennes
		27	Bastogne relieved
		31	Russian-sponsored Polish government set up in Lublin
1945	January	9	Americans land on Luzon
		17	Russians take Warsaw
	February	4–10	President Roosevelt, Generalissimo Stalin, and Prime Minister Churchill meet at Yalta in eighth war council
		19	Marines land on Iwo Jima
	March	7	At Remagen Americans capture bridgehead across Rhine
		21	British retake Mandalay
		27	Americans take Frankfurt
	April	1	Americans land at Okinawa
		1	Double envelopment of Ruhr completed
		9	Russians take Vienna
		11	Americans reach the Elbe
		12	Franklin D. Roosevelt dies
		17	Americans take Nuremberg
		22	Red Army fighting in Berlin
		25	Russian and American troops meet at Torgau, Germany
		25	San Francisco Conference opens
	May	1	Death of Adolf Hitler
		2	Berlin falls
		8	V–E day
	June	21	Okinawa taken
		26	United Nations Charter signed at San Francisco
	July	16	Atomic bomb exploded in New Mexico
		17	President Truman, Prime Minister Churchill and Generalissimo Stalin meet at Potsdam in final war council
		26	The Potsdam Ultimatum issued to Japan
		26	Clement Attlee becomes British Prime Minister
	August	6	Atomic bomb dropped on Hiroshima
		8	Russia declares war on Japan
		9	Atomic bomb dropped on Nagasaki
		10	Japan sues for peace
		14	Japan accepts Allied terms
		15	V–J day
	September	2	Japanese surrender signed on U.S.S. Missouri in Tokyo Bay

INDEX